# Cycles in American Politics

# Cycles in American Politics

how political, economic and cultural trends have shaped the nation.

*Michael A Alexander*

iUniverse, Inc.
New York   Lincoln   Shanghai

Cycles in American Politics
how political, economic and cultural trends have shaped the nation.

iUniverse, Inc.

For information address:
iUniverse, Inc.
2021 Pine Lake Road, Suite 100
Lincoln, NE 68512
www.iuniverse.com

ISBN: 0-595-32721-4

Printed in the United States of America

# *Contents*

# List of Figures

# List of Tables

# Chapter One

# Introduction

This book is about socioeconomic cycles and what they have to say about today's political landscape. I developed an interest in cycles in the course of my stock market research. Over the past four years I have learned of a number of cycles, first in the stock market, then in the economy. Later I learned of other, related cycles in social and political history. All these cycles seem to be related to each other. By combining several cycles together one can obtain insights that are unavailable from consideration of only a single cycle. Initially I employed these cycles to gain insight into economic developments to guide investment strategy. In this book I will explore applications to politics.

My objective is to see if my cycle ideas can be extended into the realm of politics. If these ideas are correct, I predict that an opportunity will arise over the next 15 years to solve a number of long-standing national problems. Against this possibility I have outlined some possible approaches that might be taken to deal with these problems. I have also identified some nonsolutions that might be proposed (and be rejected) over the next decade or so. I will begin by describing all the relevant cycles beginning with a recap of the findings in my three previous books.

## *The Stock Cycle and the Kondratiev cycle (K-cycle)*

My first book, *Stock Cycles*, introduced the concept of secular stock market trends: lengthy periods in which stock returns were unusually good or bad. Economists use the term "secular" to refer to economic trends that are longer than an ordinary business cycle. Secular trends do not refer to up-and-down trends in stocks that last for a few years, what are typically called (ordinary) bull or bear markets. A secular bull market is a period when stocks trend upwards for a decade or more. The most recent secular bull market was the great 1982-2000 advance. A secular bear market is a lengthy period in which stocks don't make any progress in real terms. The most recent complete secular bear market was the 1966-1982 period. We are currently in a secular bear market that began in 2000. The combination of a secular bull market and a secular bear market is the Stock Cycle. The term is capitalized to distinguish it from shorter stock cycles composed of ordinary bull and bear markets. Detailed methods for characterizing secular stock market trends are presented in *Stock Cycles*. Historical secular bull and bear markets appear in Table 1.1.

The Stock Cycle is tied to a longer economic cycle called the Kondratiev cycle or simply K-cycle. Two adjacent Stock Cycles make up one K-cycle. The K-cycle can also be described as a cycle of monetary factors such as debt, interest rates, and price inflation. A period of generally rising prices, debt or interest rates is called the Kondratiev upwave. The upwave ends with a price/interest rate maximum called the Kondratiev peak. The Kondratiev peak is followed by a deflationary period with falling interest rates called the downwave, which ends at the Kondratiev trough. The combination of an upwave and downwave comprises one Kondratiev cycle. Historical Kondratiev waves are also shown in Table 1.1. The detailed development of these ideas is given in my second book, *The Kondratiev Cycle*.

The Stock Cycle and K-cycle are aligned. Because two secular trends are found in a Stock Cycle, and two Stock Cycles fall into one K-cycle, there are four secular trends in a K-cycle, each of which defines one quarter of the Kondratiev cycle. These quarter-cycles are given seasonal names: (Kondratiev) spring, summer, fall and winter. Spring is the secular bull market during the upwave while summer is the upwave secular bear market. Similarly, fall is the secular bull market during the downwave and winter is the downwave secular bear market. Currently we are in Kondratiev winter.

Table 1.1 The Kondratiev cycle characterized in four ways

| Secular Trends | Price waves | Innovation-based | War Cycle |
|---|---|---|---|
| 2000-      (winter - bear) <br> 1982-2000 (fall - bull) | 1981-      (down) | -- | -- |
| 1966-1982 (summer - bear) <br> 1949-1966 (spring - bull) | 1946-1981 (up) | 1944-1973 | Fall of USSR (1991) |
| 1929-1949 (winter - bear) <br> 1921-1929 (fall - bull) | 1920-1946 (down) | -- | -- |
| 1906-1921 (summer - bear) <br> 1896-1896 (spring - bull) | 1896-1920 (up) | 1889-1917 | WW I (1918) |
| 1881-1896 (winter - bear) <br> 1861-1881 (fall - bull) | 1864-1896 (down) | -- | -- |
| 1853-1861 (summer - bear) <br> 1843-1853 (spring - bull) | 1843-1864 (up) | 1837-1861 | Civil War (1865) |
| 1835-1843 (winter - bear) <br> 1815-1835 (fall - bull) | 1814-1843 (down) | -- | -- |
| 1802-1815 (summer - bear) <br> -- | 1789-1814 (up) | 1787-1806 | War of 1812 (1814) |
| -- | 1774-1789 (down) | -- | -- |
| -- | 1736-1774 (up) | 1739-1768 | French & Ind War (1763) |
| | 1711-1736 (down) | -- | -- |
| -- | 1688-1711 (up) | 1705-1725 | Queen Anne's War (1714) |
| | 1650-1688 (down) | -- | -- |
| -- | 1621-1650 (up) | 1630-1665 | Thirty Years War (1648) |
| | 1598-1621 (down) | -- | -- |
| -- | 1583-1598 (up) | 1580-1598 | Armada War (1604) |
| | 1555-1583 (down) | -- | -- |

The Kondratiev cycle is often related to a cycle of innovation in which startlingly new economic activities called *basic innovations* appear once per cycle. So pervasive are the changes produced by these basic innovations that they can be said to create a whole new economy. One sort of basic innovation comes from technological developments leading to new products and industries. For example, the development of the automobile and electric power transformed the economy of Western nations in the early 20th century, creating what I call the mass-market economy. This economy followed an earlier "railroad-industrial economy" which was launched by the development of railroads and new industrial technologies such as low-cost steel making. This topic will be described in more detail in chapter five.

New technologies are not the only source of basic innovations. Development of new trade routes, new markets or new business strategies can serve as innovations too. For example, the discovery of the New World and the route to the Indies in the late 15th century transformed the economies of Spain and Portugal, leading to the national greatness of the Iberian nations in the 16th century.

The progress of this "new economy" can be measured by the growth of key industries of the new economy relative to overall economic growth. When the new industries are just starting out, their growth is relatively slow. Then, as they reach a critical size, they take off and show rapid growth. For a while these new industries grow faster than the overall economy and contribute disproportionately to overall economic growth, making them *leading sectors* in the process of economic development. Eventually the markets for the new enterprises become saturated, growth slows and no longer exceeds overall economic growth. The new economy industries no longer function as leading sectors. The new economy is said to have peaked when this happens.

A plot of the growth of a cluster of leading sectors is called an innovation wave. Figure 1.1 shows innovation waves that define successive new economies. The period between the mid-point of the rising part of the wave and the peak roughly correspond to Kondratiev upwaves. Thus, the spacing of these waves serves as a third measure of the cycle, complementary to that obtained from stocks or monetary data. Table 1.1 shows "innovation-based" Kondratiev upwaves obtained from consideration of these innovation waves.

Figure 1.1. Historical innovation waves

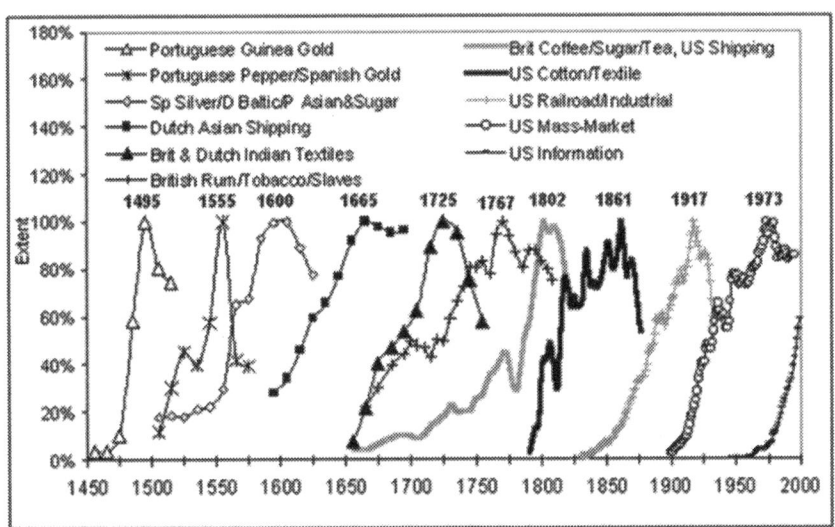

A fourth way to characterize the Kondratiev cycle is through the war cycle. The American political scientist Quincy Wright (1942) was the first to describe the phenomenon of regular cycles of war. Although wars themselves are scattered more or less randomly throughout history, the incidence of major wars between Great Powers is not. Table 1.1 provides the ending dates for specific Anglo-American wars as a way to date the war cycle. Peaks in war tend to occur at about the same time as Kondratiev peaks. Thus the spacing of these "peak wars" provides yet another definition of the Kondratiev cycle. This topic is described in more detail in chapter six.

Figure 1.2. Kondratiev cycle length by four measures over the years

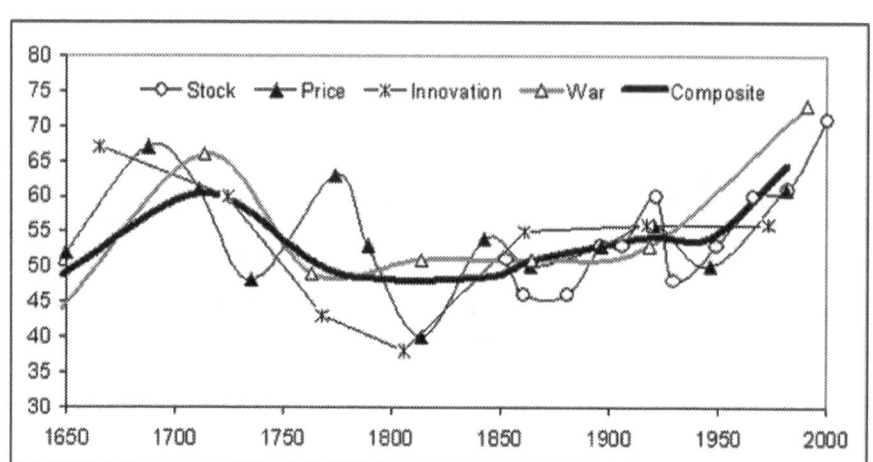

The four independent measures shown in Table 1.1 provide four definitions for the Kondratiev cycle: (1) a pair of Stock Cycles, (2) a pair of Kondratiev price/interest waves, (3) the spacing of adjacent innovation waves and (4) the frequency of major Great Power conflicts. They also provide assessments of the cycle length. Figure 1.2 shows plots of the cycle length obtained from each of these four measures over time. The overall average length of the cycle is 53 years. The two longest cycles are the most recent war-based cycle that ended in 1991 at 73 years and the most recent stock-based cycle that ended in 2000 at 71 years. This observation suggests the possibility that the cycle might be getting longer today, a possibility that was suggested by a detailed analysis of the innovation wave in *Stock Cycles*. But the cycle was also fairly long around 1700 so it might just be a random variation.

The K-cycle is also related to cycles in "social stress". Social stress is measured by a number of indicators. Class strife, as measured by the frequency of social unrest such as strikes, race riots, slave revolts, peasant uprisings and repressive laws, tends to rise and fall with a Kondratiev frequency. Alcohol production in the British Isles in the 18th and 19th centuries shows a Kondratiev pattern of rising and falling per capita consumption that parallels the cycle of unrest, with rising production during times of rising social unrest. A similar pattern in seen in crime rates during the 18th and first half of the 19th centuries. These can be combined to produce what I call the stress cycle. The stress cycle shows a close correspondence with a generational cycle called the saeculum. Before going further, some background on the saeculum will be necessary.

## *The generational cycle called the saeculum*

William Strauss and Neil Howe wrote a fascinating book called *Generations: the History of American's Future* that interprets U.S. history in terms of a repeating series of four basic types of generations. Each generation leaves its own stamp on events of the day, and in turn is shaped by the times. That is, generations shape history and history shapes generations. In their follow up work, *The Fourth Turning*, Strauss and Howe propose that history moves in long cycles, each four generations long, which they call the *saeculum*, after the ancient Etruscan cycle of similar length. Examples of how generations affect one's world view (and actions taken) abound. Thirty years ago it was assumed that people tended to be politically liberal when young and gradually grow more conservative as they age. This idea explained the facts at that time of liberal youth and conservative elders. Yet by the 1990's the situation had reversed, elders tended to be more liberal than young people. The 1980's sitcom *Family Ties* humorously underlined this developing trend with the young arch-conservative Alex Keaton and his liberal parents.

Today's young adults, what is called Generation X, have a collective outlook on life that is more conservative than Baby Boomers had at the same age. This conservative outlook is part of what Strauss and Howe call the *peer personality* of a generation. Generations with similar peer personalities will share beliefs and behavior patterns. For example, the Lost generation, born at the end of the nineteenth century, and Generation X have similar peer personalities, making both of them the same type of generation

The peer personality of a particular generation is shaped by the generation's historical location relative to a *social moment*. A social moment is an era, typically lasting about a decade, when people perceive that historical events are radically altering their social environment. Thus, a generation's peer personality (what makes it a particular kind of generation) depends on when they were born relative to particularly eventful periods in history. There are two types of social moments: *secular crises*, when society focuses on reordering the outer world of institutions and public behavior; and *spiritual awakenings*, when society focuses on changing the inner world of values and private behavior.

Table 1.2 lists Anglo-American secular crises and spiritual awakenings spanning the last 500 years. The last three secular crises are easily recognized as momentous times in American history. The social moments in Table 1.2 are spaced about 88 years apart on average. The secular crises are located approximately halfway between the spiritual awakenings and vice versa. This recurring pattern of alternating crises and Awakenings define an 88 year cycle which Strauss and Howe maintain reflects a repeating succession of four generations of 22 year length.

Table 1.2. Social moments in American history (from *Generations* p 87)

| Cycle | Spiritual Awakening | Secular Crisis |
|---|---|---|
| Pre-Colonial | Reformation (1517-1539) | Spanish Armada (1580-1588) |
| Colonial | Puritan Awakening (1621-1640) | Glorious Revolution (1675-1692) |
| Revolutionary | Great Awakening (1734-1743) | American Revolution (1773-1789) |
| Civil War | Transcendental Awakening (1822-1837) | Civil War (1857-1865) |
| Great Power | Missionary Awakening (1886-1903) | Depression & WWII (1932-1945) |
| Millennial | Boom Awakening (1967-1980) | -- |

Strauss and Howe (1997) also develop the concept of *turnings*, historical periods associated with generations that show common characteristics just as do generations. Two of these turnings contain the social moments and take their names from them. Hence, an Awakening turning contains the spiritual awakening social moment. It is "a passionate era of spiritual upheaval, when the civic order comes under attack from a new values regime". Similarly, a Crisis turning contains the secular crisis social moment. It is "a decisive era of secular upheaval, when the values regime propels the replacement of the old civic order with a new one".

Strauss and Howe introduce two turnings in-between the social moments. The Unraveling turning, sandwiched between the Awakening and the Crisis, is a "downcast era of strengthening individualism and weakening institutions, when the old civil order decays and a new values regime implants." (Strauss and Howe, 1997b). Finally, the High turning, located between the Crisis and Awakening, is "an upbeat era of strengthening institutions and weakening individualism, when a new civic order implants and the old values regime decays".

Table 1.3. List of historical turnings according to Strauss and Howe

| Turning (dates) | Type | Turning (dates) | Type |
|---|---|---|---|
| Retreat from France (1435-1459) | Unraveling | American Revolution (1773-1794) | Crisis |
| War of the Roses (1459-1487) | Crisis | Era of Good Feelings (1794-1822) | High |
| Tudor Renaissance (1487-1517) | High | Transcendental Awakening (1822-1844) | Awakening |
| Protestant Reformation (1517-1542) | Awakening | Mexican War & Sectionalism (1844-1860) | Unraveling |
| Intolerance & Martyrdom (1542-1569) | Unraveling | Civil War (1860-1865) | Crisis |
| Armada Crisis (1569-1594) | Crisis | Reconstruction & Gilded Age (1865-1886) | High |
| Merrie England (1594-1621) | High | 3rd Great Awakening (1886-1908) | Awakening |
| Puritan Awakening (1621-1649) | Awakening | WW I & Prohibition (1908-1929) | Unraveling |
| Reaction & Restoration (1649-1675) | Unraveling | Depression & WW II (1929-1946) | Crisis |
| Glorious Revolution (1675-1704) | Crisis | American High (1946-1964) | High |
| Augustan Age of Empire (1704-1727) | High | Boom Awakening (1964-1984) | Awakening |
| Great Awakening (1727-1746) | Awakening | Culture Wars (1984-) | Unraveling |
| French & Indian Wars (1746-1773) | Unraveling | | |

In *Generations*, Strauss and Howe characterized generation length as a *phase of life* equal in length to the span between birth and coming of age. Based on the spacing of social moments they use 22 years as the standard length for a generation (or turning). Table 1.3 shows the 25 turnings since the end of the Middle Ages, when Strauss and Howe claim the saeculum began. As of the 1997 publication of *The Fourth Turning* the Culture Wars Unraveling was still in progress. There have been 11 completed turnings spanning 211 years since the beginning of the American nation, giving an average turning length of 19.2 years for the American turnings, which is a bit short of the 22 year standard. Notice the very short length of the Civil War turning. Strauss and Howe hold that the Civil War turning was anomalous in that it failed to produce the proper kind of generation. That is, the 211 year period shown on the right side of Table 1.3 spans only 10 generations, with average length of just over 21 years, which *is* fairly close to the 22 year standard length and so consistent with their phase of life concept.

A relatively fixed generation length is a prerequisite for using the generational cycle to make predictions. We entered an Unraveling turning in 1984 (see Table 1.3). At some point this turning will end and a new one, a Crisis turning, will begin. Using the average generational length of 22 years, Strauss and Howe predicted a "crisis of 2020":

> *When will the crisis come?* The climatic event may not arrive exactly in the year 2020, but it won't arrive much sooner or later. A cycle is the length of four generations, or roughly eighty-eight years. If we plot a half-cycle ahead from the Boom

Awakening (and find the forty-fourth anniversaries of Woodstock and the Reagan Revolution), we project a crisis lasting from 2013 to 2024. If we plot a full cycle ahead from the last secular crisis (and find the eighty-eighth anniversaries of the FDR landslide and Pearl Harbor Day), we project a crisis lasting from 2020-2029. By either measure, the early 2020's appear fateful (Generations, p 381)

This excerpt shows an application of a fixed cycle length to predict the start of the next Crisis turning sometime in the second decade of the 21st century. Events following the terrorist attack on September 11, 2001 in some respects resemble what one might expect of a Crisis turning, although it is really too early to tell. If it is later determined that a Crisis turning did indeed begin in 2001, the prediction made in *Generations* (based on an assumption of a fixed 22 year generation/turning length) will have been more than a decade late.

The three most recent turnings at 18.7 years average length aren't really very consistent with a 22-year standard length. Indeed, of the nine completed turnings since 1822, only two were 22 years long and none were longer. Their average length, at exactly 18 years, suggests that the true length of recent turnings is not 22 years. These observations suggest that generational length since 1822 has been less than the 22-year length suggested by Strauss and Howe's phase-of-life model.

Compelling evidence against the interpretation of a generation or turning length as a phase of life emerged with Strauss and Howe's *The Fourth Turning*. This book extended the generational cycle earlier in time from what had been presented in *Generations*. It shows a group of ten contiguous turnings from 1435 to 1704, whose average length of 27 years is simply too long to be a phase of life. In *The Fourth Turning*, Strauss and Howe acknowledge that generation length has been trending downward over the centuries. They give 2005 as their prediction for the beginning of the next Crisis turning, only 76 years after the beginning of the last one. This tacit acknowledgement that generations may be as short as 19 years today, while once they were almost 50% longer provides the final evidence to conclude that generation length does not reflect a phase of life.

## *Relation of the saeculum to economic cycles*

In *The Kondratiev Cycle*, I proposed an alternate explanation for generational length that explains their ~27 year length in the 15ᵗʰ through 17ᵗʰ centuries and their 23-24 year length during the 18ᵗʰ century. From Medieval times to the late 17ᵗʰ century social moment turnings were aligned with Kondratiev upwaves. I hypothesized that alternating periods of rising and falling prices (the K-cycle) were caused of alternating periods of greater and lesser population pressure on the food supply, caused by a lagged effect of population growth on food availability. During good times people would tend to marry earlier and have more children, leading to more adults and greater pressure on food supplies (i.e. bad times) a generation later. The generation experiencing bad times would tend to marry later, reducing their own fertility, which would show up as a relatively smaller population of adults the generation after that. The result of this oscillating fertility would be alternating periods of low population pressure (falling prices, good times) and high population pressure (rising prices, bad times). The bad times are social moment turnings (Awakening and Crisis) and the good times are the turnings in between (High and Unraveling). These periods (turnings) would be a biological generation in length (ca. 27 years). Two biological generations would complete one cycle in prices (the K-cycle), which over the long run has averaged 53 years in length. Thus, the saeculum contains two K-cycles, making it about 106 years long. Indeed, the first 2½ saecula in Table 1.3 average 107.6 years long, quite close to the expected value.

Kondratiev upwaves, being times of inflation, are good times for debtors. In late Medieval and early modern times, the biggest debtors were monarchs who borrowed funds to make war. By the 17ᵗʰ century, a cycle of warfare had come to be aligned with the Kondratiev cycle. Warfare was substantially more intense during upwaves than downwaves. As nations developed more elaborate means to finance their wars, the fighting of wars, or more properly, the accumulation of debt to fight wars, began to have its own effect on prices and interest rates, which reinforced the K-cycle. Upwaves became times of increasing money supply leading to general inflation as well as times of rising food shortages and food prices. Similarly, downwaves were not only times of relative food abundance, but times of general deflation and economic depression. These financial effects ultimately reversed the relation between the K-cycle and the saeculum. While downwaves were a time of relative food abundance due to lower population pressures, the resulting low food prices did little good for the urban worker left unemployed by the bankruptcy of his employer. Thus, social moment turnings shifted from an upwave to a down-wave phenomenon around 1700. This shift in alignment between the K-cycle and the saeculum meant the two saecula between 1675 and 1860 spanned only 3.5 K-cycles instead of four, implying a one-eighth drop in saeculum length. Such a drop in length is manifested by the shift from ~27 year generations before 1700 to ~23 year generations for more than a century afterward.

I also suggested that there was sufficient room for nine 18-year generations between 1822 and 1984 (one for each turning) instead of the eight 20-year generations Strauss and Howe propose. That is, I doubted that a "Civil War anomaly" had occurred. This implies that a sudden drop in generation length occurred right around 1820. It also meant that the saeculum had become uncoupled from the K-cycle. Only after 1929 did the two cycles re-align, but with only one K-cycle per saeculum instead of two. The K-cycle lengthened from ~53 years to 72 years to accommodate the alignment. This means that since 1929, the K-cycle and saeculum have been the same cycle, both reflecting an underlying 18-year generation. I attributed the change in generation length to industrialization, but did not supply any mechanism for how industrialization had produced the change, nor why an 18-year generation length should emerge.

In my third book, *Retiring Rich*, I presented information about shorter economic cycles. One of these is a cycle in land value and construction activity called the Kuznets cycle. It is associated with periodic financial panics and severe depressions and shows an average length of 18 years, just as I hypothesized that modern turnings do. The first panic occurred in 1819, right when I proposed that 18-year generations appeared. Table 1.4 shows a list of economic cycles consisting of Kondratiev waves before 1819, Kuznets cycles between 1819 and 1917 (Hoyt, 1970), and the Stock Cycle after 1917. The average length of the first four Kondratiev waves is about 26 years, consistent the typical length of Kondratiev cycles of about 53 years. Turnings, at about 24 years, are longer over this period than they would be afterward. They track the Kondratiev waves fairly well.

The next six economic periods, which correspond to the Kuznets real-estate cycle, average 18 years in length. The secular stock trends which are used to track the economic cycle after 1929 are also 18 years long and they too agree very well with the Strauss and Howe turnings. In between 1822 and 1929, there should be six turnings and six generations if there was no Civil War anomaly. These six turnings/generations should average 18 years long, just as those after 1929 do. It just so happens that between the Panic of 1819 and the Crash of 1929 there were exactly six 18-year Kuznets cycles. A set of six turnings that align with these

Kuznets cycles can be drawn (and appear in Table 1.4). I propose that these alternate turnings reflect a saeculum in which there was no Civil War anomaly, turning length simply shifted from correspondence with Kondratiev waves to correspondence with Kuznets cycles. In the 1920's as the industrial economy grew to be completely dominant, the saeculum stopped following 18-year cycles in land value and started following 18-year cycles in the stock market.

Table 1.4. Alternate American turnings

| Turning | Economic[1] | Stress[2] |
|---------|-------------|-----------|
| First Great Awakening (1727-1746) | 1715-1738 | *1722-1742* |
| French & Indian Wars (1746-1773) | 1738-1770 | 1742-1761 |
| American Revolution (1773-1794) | 1770-1787 | *1761-1793* |
| Era of Good Feelings (1794-1822) | 1787-1819 | 1793-1817 |
| Transcendental Awakening (1822-1844) | 1819-1842 | *1817-1840* |
| Mexican War & Sectionalism (1844-1860) | 1842-1857 | 1840-1861 |
| Civil War & Reconstruction (1860-1877) | 1857-1877 | *1861-1903* |
| Gilded Age (1877-1896) | 1877-1896 | 1903-1908 |
| Third Great Awakening (1896-1917) | 1896-1917 | *1908-1919* |
| World War I & Prohibition (1917-1929) | 1917-1929 | 1919-1931 |
| Depression & World War II (1929-1946) | 1929-1949 | *1931-1946* |
| American High (1946-1964) | 1949-1966 | 1946-1960 |
| Fourth Great Awakening (1964-1984) | 1966-1982 | *1960-1981* |
| Culture Wars (1984-2001) | 1982-2000 | 1981-???? |

[1]Kondratiev cycle before 1819, Kuznets cycle 1819-1917, Stock Cycle after 1917
[2]Rising stress in italics

Both the Kuznets cycle and the Stock Cycle are described in terms of an 18-year yardstick. Using this yardstick, one can make the prediction that the secular bull market that began in 1982 should have ended around 2000, which it did. One can make a prediction, as I did in August 2000, that a new Crisis turning should begin around the time of this stock peak (Alexander, 2000b). A year later the terrorist attacks on the World Trade Center and Pentagon created a new fear about foreign policy just as the stock collapse and recession has created fears about the economy. Interest rates have plummeted to depths not seen in 40 years. It very much seems were are "living in interesting times" or that "the worm turned" shortly after 2000.

If this feeling persists, in time we will come to acknowledge that a new era began with the terrorist attack in 2001, just as in the 1930's people came to realize that everything changed with the stock market crash in 1929. Should this realization occur it will establish that the length of turnings today is 18 years, and thus strongly support the idea of an anomaly-free 19$^{th}$ century saeculum with 18-year turnings. That is, it should help confirm the alternate saeculum that I propose here. In this book, I will proceed on the assumption that the 18-year turning is correct.

Also shown in Table 1.4 is the stress cycle. The stress cycle aligns with the Strauss and Howe's saeculum before 1860 and after 1929. It also aligns with the economic cycles. After 1860, the stress cycle continues to align with the Kondratiev cycle while the Strauss and Howe saeculum deviates. This suggests that stress is a Kondratiev phenomenon, while the turnings ceased to be so after 1820. After 1929 stress continued to be a Kondratiev phenomenon, simply following the seasons rather than the waves. By this time the turnings had also become aligned with the Kondratiev seasons, but with an interesting twist. The Kondratiev season had become 18 years long, forcing the Kondratiev cycle to lengthen to 72 years. That is, the saeculum was not being driven by the Kondratiev cycle, but rather, the Kondratiev cycle was now being driven by the saeculum. Prior to the 19$^{th}$ century, it was the saeculum that changed length to accommodate a new relationship with the Kondratiev cycle, which continued on unchanged. During the 19$^{th}$ century the two cycles became uncoupled. The saeculum developed an 18-year periodicity, which eventually was transmitted to the Kondratiev cycle, lengthening it.

The main purpose for the introduction of generational dynamics is to establish two key concepts. One is that the fundamental unit of measure today in long cycles in finance, economics, politics and social trends is 18 years. The other is the interplay between my paradigm model for the post-1820 saeculum and my ideological dissatisfaction model for the political cycle (see chapter four). The first of these is useful for accurately determining the current position within the relevant cycles. This is required in order to use historical analogy to provide insight into what the future may hold. The cycles presented here have all changed their lengths to conform to this 18 year "ruler". This idea is contrary to views of most theorists of the various cycles. This is extremely important. If our current position within the cycles were self-evident, then any predictions made based on this assessment would be necessarily wrong because other observers, having the same information, would have already acted on it, changing the future and rendered the predictions worthless. The second concept forms part of my explanation for how the political cycle operates.

Each conclusion I present in this book is one of several that could be reached by considering one or another of the cycles I describe. There is a standard interpretation for each of the cycles I discuss which if employed by itself will lead to a different conclusion than the one I present. For example, in the section above I presented a slightly modified version of the Strauss and Howe saeculum in which we are currently within a Crisis turning, rather than still within the Unraveling turning. This is important, because in a Crisis, the unorthodox is the norm, and can be expected.

The strategy I have taken is to characterize every cycle for which I could find adequate data and then to look for alignment between them. As a result of this work I have concluded that cycles like the Kondratiev or the saeculum are incomplete reflections of an underlying fundamental cyclic socioeconomic process. Using this idea I have modified the various cycles to explicitly reflect this alignment for today. As a result, my version of the K-cycle is a non-standard one (I believe it is 72 years long instead of the standard ~53 year length) as is my saeculum (also 72 years instead of the standard 80-90 years). This allows me to make predictions that differ from those that would be obtained from consideration of only one of the standard cycles.

For example, the financial writer Harry Dent (1998) projected the continuation of the secular bull market to the 2007-2010 period, by which time the Dow would reach 23,000-35,000. Dent based this projection on a demographic argument, which closely agreed with a projection based on an economic version of the saeculum cycle. The combination of the two ideas made a compelling presentation of the case for a continued bull market until close to 2010, after which there would be a another great depression. The appearance of this depression agreed very well with the projected timing for a coming secular crisis made by Strauss and Howe in *Generations*. Dent's economic cycle associated with his demographics was based on the saeculum and shared its timing, namely an 80 year cycle length. The "long boom" concept of the futurist Roger Cass shows an example of the same approach as Dent's, except a different cycle is used. Cass employs a standard Kondratiev cycle to forecast a long boom powered by new internet technology that will last to 2020 or thereabouts (Schwartz and Leyden, 1997).

Dent's economic cycle does an excellent job of explaining economic developments over the past century or so, but it does not work before then. In contrast, the standard Kondratiev cycle does a rather poor job of explaining recent economic events, but works much better for those of the past. Neither model accounts for the severe bear market that began in 2000. The hybrid model I developed in which the Kondratiev cycle and saeculum are aligned along the lines implied by Dent, but with the 18 year generational timing instead of 20 years does call for the severe bear market at the time it has actually occurred.

Having presented a summary of my earlier cycle work, I can now begin my exposition of the political cycles. The first cycle to be examined involves domestic American politics. In the next chapter I present an overview of American political history as a series of cycles in ideology, thus establishing the basic case that a cycle exists.

# *Chapter Two*

## *Cycles in American politics*

The American historian Arthur Schlesinger Sr. (1888-1965) proposed a cyclical concept of American politics in which the political "spirit of the times", or *zeitgeist*, oscillated between "liberal" and "conservative" eras (Schlesinger, 1949). The concept of liberalism and conservatism is a slippery thing. I will use the following definitions. Conservatism supports maintaining traditional elements of society that support the present social order. Traditional arrangements are justified as natural and good, having stood the test of time. Liberalism does not assume that the traditional social order is necessarily the best or most natural order. Liberals advocate change to accommodate the greatest good for the greatest number. They believe that what is good is to be defined by individuals through their participation in democracy.

People achieve different life outcomes because of differences in talent, resources, opportunity, drive, situation and luck. Conservatism views the differences between people that produce differential outcomes as natural and justifiable. For example, it is considered natural that a hard-working software engineer with an IQ of 140 lives very comfortably, while a hard-working custodian with an IQ of 80 lives much less well. Conservatism accepts the differences between people's situations as being appropriate as long as they occurred by the action of "natural" forces such as family background, education and personal growth, talent, and effort, all mediated through free market competition, religious beliefs, customs, and traditional cultural institutions. Conservatism frowns on government interventions designed to produce an unnatural outcome.

Liberalism sees some features of the traditional order as being arbitrary social constructs, and not natural. Liberals advocate for intervention to correct outcomes that arise from such arbitrary factors. For example, modern liberals favor provision of a publicly-subsidized education to all with the intellect and drive to take advantage of it. In the absence of subsidized education, children whose parents could not afford schooling would be more likely to become poor adults than children whose parents can afford schooling. Liberalism sees the situation of being born poor as arbitrary and the consequence of a lifetime of poverty as not being a natural (i.e. acceptable) outcome. Liberals also support individual freedom to "pursue happiness" in a wider variety of ways than do conservatives.

Like other ideologies, conservatism and liberalism can intersect with self-interest. Those who have done well in society will tend to be more supportive of the present order and thus favor the conservative ideology. Those who have not done so well, but feel that they should have, will often be less supportive of the present order and be more inclined towards the liberal ideology. These are only tendencies of course; there are many crosscurrents and individual differences. Nevertheless, the winners in society are more likely to uphold the current order as justified and oppose change proposed by liberals.

Schlesinger had some notable success in predicting shifts between conservatism and liberalism in his political cycle. In 1924, he predicted that Coolidge-style conservatism would last until 1932. As we shall see, it lasted until 1931. In 1939, he predicted that the liberal mood would end in about 1947 (Schlesinger, 1986). The exact date was 1946. In 1949, he predicted a shift to liberalism in 1962 and a shift back to conservatism in 1978 (Schlesinger, 1949). The actual dates were 1961 and 1980 for these shifts.

Although he never formally proposed a model to explain the cycle, Schlesinger suspected that the dynamics of political organization itself was responsible for the timing. A successful political party or movement takes about

15 years to define its agenda, mobilize its resources, implement its policies as best it can, and obtain the inevitably less-than-hoped-for results (Goertzel, 2001). This movement proceeds through several fairly predictable stages: growth and vitality under a charismatic leader, a period of mature leadership, and then a gradual decline as supporters tire of the message. With decline, the baton of leadership passes to the opposition. The result would be alternating periods of ascendancy that should last about 15 years.

I attempted to track this cycle empirically by assembling a list of political events that I labeled as either liberal or conservative (see Appendix A). I then calculated a moving sum of conservative events divided by the sum of all events over the prior 15 years and plotted the result in Figure 2.1. The 15-year summation period was selected based on the political organizational dynamic explanation. This ratio presumably measures swings in the trends in political zeitgeist over time, with a rising "conservative ratio" implying a conservative era and a falling conservative ratio a liberal era.

Figure 2.1. Conservative political waves

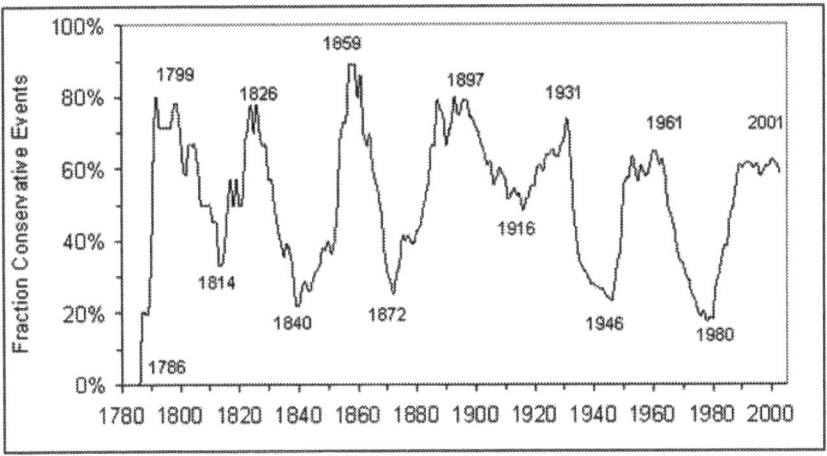

Note that the method I employ measures liberalism and conservatism independently of the political party that was in power when the event occurred. For example, Schlesinger's son Arthur Jr., who continued his father's studies, predicted a McGovern victory in 1972 because the country was in a liberal era at the time and Democrat McGovern was more liberal than Republican Nixon. Nixon won the election. However, note that 19 of the 21 events (90%) recorded in Appendix A for the Nixon administration were liberal. Thus, although Nixon was certainly more conservative than McGovern, his administration was more liberal than that of either President Eisenhower (38% liberal) or President Reagan (27% liberal), and thus reflected the liberal zeitgeist, despite the preferences of President Nixon himself. Thus, the type of era doesn't actually reflect what party is in power, but rather, what types of policies are pursued.

In order to gain a feeling for the nature of these political swings and how events are labeled as either liberal or conservative, a summary of American political history with respect to the cycles is outlined below. The cycle dates used are a consensus based on both the Schlesinger dates and Figure 2.1.

## Liberal era 1765-1787

This era began with the Stamp Act Congress and ended with the Constitutional Convention. It is roughly aligned with the 1770-1787 Kondratiev downwave and the associated period of social stress, and with a Crisis turning from 1773-1794. Crisis periods are filled with turmoil and significant change in the institutions of society. Successful Crisis turnings involve a change from the status quo and thus are inherently non-conservative. The Revolutionary Crisis certainly qualified as a successful Crisis that saw the American colonies liberated from colonial rule and a new republic founded. After a false start under the too-weak Articles of Confederation, a new government was formed under the much stronger Constitution of 1787, a document that, with amendments, continues in effect to this day.

## Conservative era 1787-1800

Authoritative leadership was required after the adoption of the Constitution, which was supplied by George Washington. The new government took over the Revolutionary debt from the states and thus required new revenues to repay them. After a proposed tariff was rejected, excise taxes on tobacco, liquor and similar goods were adopted. This tax provoked a violent reaction, the Whiskey Rebellion, which had to be put down by force in 1794. Relations with Great Britain were still strained and after proclaiming neutrality in 1793 (reneging on an earlier alliance with France), relations with France degraded as well. These worsening relations with European powers and suspicion about any designs they might have for North America led to the Adams administration's proposal for a standing army and national navy. Concern about foreign agents and internal insurrection led to repressive legislation like the Alien and Sedition Acts of 1798. These policies produced political divisions in the form of opposing parties: the Federalists, led by Alexander Hamilton, who supported the agenda of the Washington and Adams administrations, and the Democratic-Republicans led by Thomas Jefferson.

All these Federalist policy actions are basically conservative in nature, making the Federalists conservatives. Conservative policies are naturally part of the consolidation and institution-building typical of the post-Crisis period. Hence, the appearance of a conservative era after 1787 is to be expected. The lowered-stress and greater prosperity of the Kondratiev upwave is also consistent with a conservative era; there is little demand for change when things are going well. What is not expected based on the generational cycle or the Kondratiev cycle was the start of a new liberal era halfway through the High and the Kondratiev upwave.

## Liberal era 1800-1816

In the election of 1800, Jefferson's Democratic-Republicans mounted a successful campaign against President Adams and the Federalists. With no serious threats to the republic, Jefferson's hyper-libertarian program had real appeal. Jefferson's program was not an active one. He promised inaction rather than action, and in this respect it was actually quite conservative. But the inaction promised was radical: no army, no significant navy, bare-bones foreign policy, no borrowing, less government, lower taxes, opposition to the Alien and Sedition Acts and opposition to the moneyed elite—specifically central bankers and financiers. The decision of the Federal government to honor Revolutionary War debt at full value had made fortunes (at public expense) of pro-Federalist speculators who had bought up this debt at a fraction of its par value and then pressed Federalist leaders for just this policy. This sort of feeding at the public trough angered Jeffersonians.

Many of the Jeffersonian's favored policies strike one as conservative today rather than liberal. It is important to remember than in the late 1700's there was much less concentration of wealth amongst the electorate. The American electorate of the time consisted largely of small farmers and tradesmen. Those who did not own property, such as common laborers, could not vote. Low taxes and neutral relations with foreign powers were seen as beneficial to commerce and a good thing for all voters. The vast concentration of money power typical of industrialized society was still in the future—about the only important reservoir of financial wealth was government bonds. Federalist financial policies had created a class of wealthy men who had made their fortunes not through husbandry or commerce, but through paper manipulations. Resentment against such unearned riches fueled populist sentiment. When viewed in light of these realities, Jefferson's policies were friendlier to the (poor) common man than to the (rich) financial class and so do fit in with the modern understanding of the word liberal.

For example, tax increases were a conservative policy at this time because taxes were used primarily to repay government debt owed to wealthy bankers and speculators and to fund institutions protecting or enhancing the property values of the rich. Unlike today, ordinary people received little tangible benefit from government, and thus were quite unwilling to fund more government than was absolutely necessary. Conservatives generally favored expansion of government power; liberals opposed it.

For example, conservatives favored establishment of a central bank as a system for public finance. Through a central bank, the national government can mobilize the resources of the nation far more effectively. It was the superiority of British finance, anchored by the Bank of England, that gave her the victory over her larger and wealthier French rival in their frequent conflicts during the 18th century. British victories expanded the British Empire, which meant more opportunities for profitable commerce, which was a good thing in the eyes of the wealthy establishment. Thus, a central bank can be seen as a conservative institution in the early days of the nation. Similarly, expansion (and use) of the military, the chief instrument of national power, was also a conservative policy. Conservatives also favored public spending on internal improvements (roads, canals, harbors etc.) which would facilitate commerce.

Jefferson's platform in 1800 identified liberal positions on policy (anti-central bank, anti-tax, anti-military). Jefferson and the Democratic-Republicans also favored the expansion of political rights, particularly suffrage. Thus, for the early portion of the American nation's history, I have labeled positions in favor of a central bank, tariff, internal improvements, and military action as conservative. The opposing policies are liberal. Policies that increase individual political rights are liberal, those that restrict them are conservative.

Interestingly, once Jefferson was elected his policies were not as liberal as initially advertised. He authorized the Louisiana Purchase in 1801, expanding the national debt, despite the absence of a Constitutional provision for this. Two years later, he found a navy quite useful in the Tripolitan War. Jefferson did cut taxes, running a cumulative deficit of $17,000,000 compared to Adam's $600,000 surplus (Mitchell, 1998). Jefferson's choice of an embargo rather than war over the impressment issue, and Madison's refusal to recharter the First Bank of the United States in 1811 were consistent with liberal Democratic-Republican principles.

Jefferson's policies were generally popular and the Democratic-Republicans trounced the Federalist opposition in 1804 and 1808. Even a policy like the Louisiana Purchase, which was a clear expansion of national power and hence conservative in nature, did not play out politically as conservative. Territorial expansion provided land (the basis of most livelihoods) to a growing population. Politically it served as a welfare scheme by which wealth was extracted from the politically powerless indigenous population and sold at low cost to the American public. As such, national expansion was wildly popular.

The Democratic-Republicans faced a more vigorous challenge in the election of 1812, when early mismanagement of the War of 1812 made Madison vulnerable. This war underlined some of the deficiencies of the Jeffersonian small-government philosophy when faced with the reality of belligerent foreign nations. As a result, Democratic-Republican policies became more conservative.

## Conservative era 1816-1828

Following the successful conclusion of the war, the Democratic-Republicans won easily in 1816, the last election in which the Federalists fielded a candidate. The new Democratic-Republican president, James Monroe, presided over the only period of one-party rule in the US, what is called the "Era of Good Feelings", in which distinctly conservative policies were in favor. Already in Madison's second term, wartime exigencies had resulted in a change of heart about Jeffersonian philosophy. Financial difficulties in funding the war effort made Madison appreciative of the benefits of a central bank during wartime. The Second Bank of the United States was chartered for 20 years in 1816. Also, the loss of European trade during the war had resulted in government encouragement of domestic production of manufactured goods. After the end of the war, with trade resumed, these nascent industries faced ruination. A protective tariff was enacted, also in 1816. After the first large-scale war fought by the American republic, there no longer was a question about the need for armed forces, nor was neutrality a feasible policy. Later, President Monroe issued the Monroe Doctrine in which the United State warned against any encroachment by European powers into the Western hemisphere. Thus, by the election of Monroe most of the Jeffersonian principles expounded in 1800 had been abandoned by the Party of Jefferson. Monroe was even more fiscally conservative than Jefferson, running a cumulative deficit of $26 million compared to Jefferson's $41 million on an economy a third larger than Jefferson's (Mitchell, 1998).

One big debate during this time was over internal improvements; government-funded development projects such as roads and canals intended to spur economic development. These had been favored policy of Alexander Hamilton and were the domestic version of "big government" opposed by Jefferson. Henry Clay was a major proponent of government-sponsored economic development, as part of what he called the "American Plan" (which also included tariffs and central banking).

Another debate was slavery. At the time of the constitutional convention slavery was in decline. The cash crops most suitable for slave cultivation had become less profitable, due to declining prices (tobacco) or loss of British subsidies (rice and indigo). As a result slavery was dying out. Most observers in 1787 believed that the peculiar institution would disappear by itself. To accelerate this process a ban on the slave trade twenty years in the future was incorporated into the Constitution. Only seven years later, the development of the cotton gin, a device for separating cotton fibers from the seeds, made cotton a very profitable cash crop. The burgeoning textile industry in Britain created an enormous market for fibers. The combination of the two created explosive growth in cotton cultivation and in slavery. Thus, rather than die out, slavery became a growth industry.

Southern slaveowners now had a powerful incentive to keep slavery legal and to do this it was necessary that the number of slave states grow with the nation. Up to 1820, nine states had been added to the union, five slave and four free for a total of 22 states, evenly split between slave and free. As the population of the free states was considerably larger than that of the slave states, free states already outnumbered slave states in the House of Representatives. In 1819, Missouri asked Congress to join the union. The House passed the Tallmadge amendment, which forbid further importation of slaves into Missouri and called for the gradual emancipation of children born to slave parents already there. Southern states viewed the Tallmadge amendment as an ominous threat to sectional balance. Concerned by fast increase in northern population and political balance in the

House of Representatives, Southerners wished to maintain the Senate balanced between free and slave states.

Missouri was the first state entirely west of the Mississippi made from the Louisiana Territory and the Tallmadge amendment might set a precedent for the rest of the territory to be made free. Henry Clay played a key role in mediating a compromise in which Missouri was admitted as a slave state while Maine was admitted as a free state, keeping the balance at 12 to 12. Future slavery was prohibited north of the 36-30' line of latitude, the southern border of Missouri. The compromise was largely accepted by both sides, the South got Missouri and the North won the concession that it could forbid slavery in the remaining territories above the 36-30' line of latitude. The North held an advantage because Spanish territory in the southwest prevented significant Southern expansion westward. The issue of Southern expansion was to increasingly dominate politics over the next four decades.

The Democratic-Republicans under Madison and Monroe ended up adopting most of the Federalist policies of the last conservative era. Interestingly, the remnants of the Federalists had become strict constitutionalists and pacifists by 1816, essentially reversing the positions of the parties in 1800. It is this conversion of Democratic-Republicans into "neoFederalists", which was just about complete by 1816, that produced the shift from liberalism to conservatism. The entire 1800-1816 liberal era as well as parts of the conservative eras before and after fell into the High turning. One would expect the entire period to be one of conservatism. In a way, the Jeffersonian liberal era can be thought of as a political experiment that was part of a larger conservative period of nation building. Just as the new nation needed to provide for its security, it also needed to develop a mechanism for peaceful transfer of political power and to prevent dictatorship. The development of opposing political parties and the long-term shift in political power following the election of 1800 solved this problem.

The election of 1800 can also be considered as a spike in idealistic liberalism that gradually decayed back into Federalist conservatism when faced with the reality of governance. In this way, default conservatism simply settled back after the War of 1812 proved the liberal experiment was ineffective at dealing with the nation's problems. The next shift to liberalism would not be an experiment, but rather an actual change in political attitudes.

## Liberal era, the "Age of Jackson" 1828-1840

By the election of 1824, a split had arisen amongst the Democratic-Republicans, who were now known simply as Republicans. On one side there were those who believed the party had become too much like the Federalists of old and needed to return to their roots. This faction was led by Andrew Jackson and thought of themselves as true *Democratic*-Republicans. Later, they became known simply as Democrats to further stress their emphasis on democracy. The other "neoFederalist" faction was led by John Quincy Adams (the son of the Federalist John Adams) and Henry Clay. They came to call themselves National Republicans, and later, Whigs.

The election of 1824 saw a three-way race between Adams, Clay and Jackson. Jackson won a plurality of the popular and electoral vote, but no majority. The election then went to the House of Representatives in which Adams was given the victory because of a deal he had made with Clay. Clay's supporters threw their votes to Adams in exchange for Clay getting the Secretary of State position (traditionally the stepping stone to the Presidency).

By this time, the Awakening turning had begun and the economy was deep into the Kondratiev downwave. A new period of rising unrest was well underway and the electorate was ripe for change. Jacksonian Democrats took control of both houses of Congress in 1826, and Jackson was swept to power in a landslide in 1828, beginning a new liberal era.

The Jacksonians opposed high tariffs and central banking, both of which they believed served the interests of industrial and financial elites to the detriment of ordinary farmers. They favored expansion of the franchise to all white men, regardless of economic status. Like the earlier Jeffersonians, this concern for the common man and increased democracy is why the Jacksonians are considered liberal. Jacksonians were also enthusiastic about driving native Americans from their lands to make room for white settlement, views not congruent with modern concepts of liberalism. Consider that national expansion involved redistribution of wealth (land) for one group (Native Americans) to another (landless white Americans) through the intermediary services of land speculators. Land was the primary source of wealth and respectability and was in great demand from those who lacked it. National expansion created new public lands, which could be parceled up and sold to speculators, who would then sell it to settlers. Settlers often simply squatted on newly available lands and eventually gained rights to it. Through either mechanism national expansion served to grant wealth to poor

Americans. National expansion served as sort of a welfare program, which makes Jacksonian support of national expansion essentially a pro-welfare position consistent with modern liberalism. This interpretation completely ignores the impact on Native Americans, whose rights simply were not recognized.

Jackson's policy of forced eviction of Indians from their land was not uncontested. The most famous case involved Cherokee land in Georgia. The Cherokee were well aware of what had happened to the ancestral lands of other native Americans. In order to conform with European standards of nationhood, they had developed their own written language, established a tribal press, and built modern economic infrastructure such as roads, schools, and smithies. Most made their living as farmers or ranchers. They also adopted a written constitution, which established the laws under which they would live. This document proclaimed that the Cherokee nation had legal jurisdiction over its own territory.

Thus, when Georgia sought to confiscate their property the Cherokee applied to President Jackson for redress on the basis of their status as a sovereign nation. Jackson informed them that he would not interfere with the lawful prerogatives of the state of Georgia. Jackson, of course, favored the removal of the Cherokee (and other Indian nations). The next step was to appeal through the courts. In *Worcester v Georgia* Chief Justice John Marshall ruled that efforts by the state of Georgia to remove the Cherokee from their land were unconstitutional because state law did not apply to Indian nations. Jackson refused to enforce the courts finding and Georgia went ahead with the forced evacuation of the Cherokee population in what came to be called the Trail of Tears.

A philosophical basis for objection to Indian removal comes from consideration of the natural law theory of property. This concept holds that property belongs to the one who first settles the land and improves it in some way. This idea holds that property and property rights exists independently (and come before) the state. Conservatives often use natural law arguments to claim that government restrictions on the uses of private property are unjustified. Another view of property rights is that they derive from the state, by right of conquest. Private ownership is then represented by the state through a property deed that grants limited rights to the owner. The state reserves the right to levy taxes and enforce its own laws upon that property. This sort of "property is force" argument can be used by liberals to justify government regulation of private property. Indian removal is easily justified by liberal conceptions of property, but not conservative natural law concepts. In actual practice, conservatives generally supported Indian removal, believing that natural law applied only to white men.

Nevertheless, this philosophical argument can also be used to support the labeling of Indian removal policy as liberal.

Like any sort of government handouts, land redistribution created its own group of special interests (land speculators) who benefited from this policy. The fortunes of this group swung with the Kuznets cycle in land value and real estate activity. Each political era between the war of 1812 and the Civil War experienced its own boom in land speculation and subsequent crash. The post-war boom after the War of 1812 terminated with the Panic of 1819. The depressionary period afterward set the stage for a change in political order during the 1820's. The Jacksonian boom was terminated by the Panic of 1837 and the subsequent depression provided an opportunity for change. Similarly the 1850's boom was terminated by the panic of 1857, which was followed by yet another change in political order. To a certain extent the antebellum political cycles reflected a cycle of rent-seeking politics by different factions. Economists use the term "rent seeking" to refer to an attempt to obtain an outcome different from what normal market operation would provide by use of political means. Land distribution by the national government was one form of rent seeking. Another was tax policy.

Protective tariffs are an obvious example of rent seeking on the behalf of manufacturers, who were largely represented by the conservative National Republicans or Whig party. Jacksonian Democrats opposed high tariffs as regressive taxes levied to benefit special interests. Thus, the protective tariff, established in 1816, was raised in 1824 and 1828 under conservative rule and reduced in 1832 and 1833 under Jackson. Democrats also opposed large public expenditures for internal improvements because they saw them as rent-seeking for commercial (Whig) interests. Internal improvements of the sort favored by Jackson (stealing Indian land for sale to whites) cost the taxpayers nothing; it generated revenues instead.

Monetary policy was another issue of contention. Jacksonian Democrats were opposed to "money power" in the guise of the Second Bank of the United States, which they believed was responsible for the Panic of 1819 and the subsequent hard times. Jackson fought his famous "war" against the Second Bank of the United States and succeeded in shutting it down in 1836, when its 20-year authorization expired.

Jacksonian Democrats also favored increased democracy, which was reflected in revisions to state constitutions at this time that expanded suffrage to all white men, regardless of property ownership. On the other hand, Democrats were also pro-slavery. Upholding slavery was a conservative position not really in keeping with Jeffersonian ideas of democracy. The reason for this mix of conservative and liberal ideologies within the same party can be found in geography.

The physical size of the United States meant that the economies of different regions of the country were very different. The southern United States had always been particularly suitable to labor-intensive cash crops that thrive in a semitropical climate such as cotton. Cotton cultivation was a leading sector of the American economy early in the 19<sup>th</sup> century and a primary driver of national prosperity. It generated most of the foreign exchange required for trade and so indirectly provided the bulk of national government revenues through the tariff. Further north the climate was more suitable for less labor-intensive grain farming and animal husbandry. The soil and climate of New England had never been very suitable for profitable agriculture and this region had early on become a center of commerce and industry.

Slavery formed the basis of the Southern cotton economy, so Southerners were generally in favor of the institution. The New England economy rested increasingly on manufacturing as the nineteenth century progressed, and so they benefited from (and favored) a protective tariff. Farmers and traders generally were opposed to tariffs, while Northerners typically were neutral or opposed to slavery. Thus, the country could be roughly divided into three groups: pro-tariff, slavery-neutral New Englanders, anti-tariff, slavery-neutral Westerners, and anti-tariff, pro-slavery Southerners. As the anti-tariff party, the Democrats natural base was in the South and West. Of the two regions, the South was the more influential, so the Democrats were a Southern-leaning, pro-slavery party from their beginning. It is only natural that the abolition movement gained its strongest adherents in New England, the area of the nation least favorably inclined to South-friendly policies. Thus, just as the mostly liberal Jacksonian Democrats had a conservative streak as far as slavery was concerned, the mostly conservative Whigs had a (developing) liberal streak with respect to the same issue.

The slavery issue remained relatively quiescent over the 1828-1840 period, only two states joined the union, one slave and one free, so the balance established in 1820 was preserved. The balance would not be preserved forever, most of the territory acquired from the Louisiana purchase lay above the 36-30' line and so would someday become free states. As time went on this day grew closer and the issue of slavery became paramount.

### Conservative era 1840-1860

The age of Jackson continued until the election in 1840, in which a Whig victory ushered in a new conservative era. The Whigs had nominated the old war hero William Henry Harrison, through whom party leaders Henry Clay and Daniel Webster planned to rule. They had nominated Virginian John Tyler for Vice President, hoping for support from southern states'-righters who could not stomach Jacksonian policies. Their slogan, "Tippecanoe and Tyler too", implied flag-waving nationalism plus a dash of southern sectionalism. The campaign was successful, but Harrison died after a month in office and the lesser-known Tyler was suddenly president, the first time a Vice President had been elevated to the Presidency.

Monetary issues continued to be a major object of contention. Following the demise of the Second Bank and Panic of 1837, Democrats established the National Treasury in 1840 as a means for the government to control its own funds directly. Following the Whig electoral victory in 1840, Congress abolished the National Treasury in an effort to force the establishment of a new central bank. Congressional Whigs made two attempts to re-establish a central bank, both of which were vetoed by President Tyler as unconstitutional. In retaliation, the Whigs expelled Tyler from their party, and all but one of his Cabinet resigned in protest. A new National Treasury was eventually re-established by President Polk in 1846.

This era saw its rent-seeking politics with passage of the Graduation Act in 1854, which put long-unsold public lands on sale at 10% of the normal price, producing a speculative boom that ended with the Panic of 1857. Tariffs remained a hot issue. When President Tyler vetoed a Whig tariff bill in 1841, the first impeachment resolution against a President was introduced in the House of Representatives. The resolution failed.

The big issue of this era (and what makes it conservative) was slavery. For fifteen years after the Missouri Compromise no new states were admitted into the union. The next state admitted was Arkansas as a slave state in 1836, closely followed by Michigan as a free state in 1837. Although the balance was still intact in 1840, a simple glance at a map showed that trouble was coming. East of the Mississippi there were two territories not yet states: Wisconsin (free) and Florida (slave). Admission of these would not affect the balance. But, southern states extended further to the west than did the northern ones. By 1840, the southern territories immediately west of the Mississippi had all been admitted as slave states (Louisiana, Arkansas and Missouri). Neither of the corresponding northern territories (Iowa and Minnesota) had become states. In time, these territories would become free states, tipping the balance of power in favor of the anti-slavery forces.

A key objective for the South would then be to increase the number of slave states by aggressively pushing westward. The conservative steak within the Democratic party with respect to slavery waxed as Southern fear of imbalance grew. Increasingly, the Democrats became absorbed by the task of preserving the balance of power, becoming essentially conservatives. The Whigs remained basically conservative neo-Federalists, although they too started to fracture along slavery lines.

West of Louisiana was Texas, which had been part of New Spain and then Mexico after independence in 1821. The Mexican authorities encouraged settlement of Texas and many Americans moved there. In 1835, Mexican president Santa Anna abolished the Mexican constitution and Texas refused to submit to his authority. Santa Anna attempted to subdue them by force. He failed and Texas gained independence in 1836. After gaining independence Texans voted overwhelming in favor of annexation by the United States and applied for annexation in 1837. The Van Buren administration rejected their application, giving questions about the constitutionality of annexation and possible war with Mexico as reasons. Another, probably more important reason, was political; anti-slavery sentiment produced opposition within the US for annexation and Van Buren (a New York Democrat personally opposed to slavery) did not wish to inflame public opinion against his party at this time. The application was withdrawn in 1838, when a new administration opposed to annexation came to power in Texas.

The United States became alarmed over the friendly policy of Great Britain toward Texas in 1843. The British were interested in commercial relations with Texas. They were opposed to annexation, wishing to prevent further westward expansion of the United States. President Tyler (a slaveowner) proposed annexation, citing concern about Texas becoming a British satellite. The Whig-controlled U.S. Senate rejected Tyler's annexation treaty in 1844. Annexation became an issue in the presidential election of 1844 with Democrat Polk in favor (Texas added another slave state) and Whig Clay opposed. Polk won a narrow victory and Texas became a slave state in 1845. Florida became a slave state in the same year. Iowa and Wisconsin became free states in 1846 and 1848, respectively, maintaining the balance between slave and free states.

Acquiring Texas preserved the balance, but did not solve the problem. Eventually northern expansion would tip the sectional balance in favor of free states. Polk had run an unabashedly expansionist campaign in 1844, calling for annexation of Oregon. While in office he fought a popular war of conquest against Mexico and obtained additional southern territory for the United States. In 1846 and again in 1847, the free-majority House of Representatives passed the Wilmot proviso, a proposition that the Mexican territory be set aside as slave-free. Both times it was killed by the slave-majority Senate, theoretically maintaining the possibility of additional slave states being added to the union within the terms of the Missouri Compromise.

During the next Whig administration, California (one of the territories obtained from Mexico) petitioned Congress to join the Union. Mexico had abolished slavery in 1829 and so California would enter as a free state, which would upset the balance. The compromise of 1850 allowed the admission of California as a free state and the organization of New Mexico and Utah territories without mention of slavery. Their status would be determined by the territories themselves when they were ready to be admitted as states (a formula called popular sovereignty).

The South had placed itself in subject political status to the North and could expect that no further slave state would be admitted to the union. In exchange, the South demanded that the North use its power of majority to guarantee the legal and constitutional protections to slavery and to vigorously enforce a new fugitive slave law that required citizens to assist in the recovery of fugitive slaves. The North by and large did not enforce the national fugitive slave law; most northern states adopted local procedures that effectively nullified the federal statutes. Thus, the South came to feel swindled by the North in the Compromise of 1850.

Under the next Democratic administration there was an attempt to restore the balance disrupted by the Compromise of 1850. Spain had been approached about possibly selling Cuba to the United States during the Polk administration. Slavery existed in Cuba and such a territory would become a slave state. Spain declined to sell and the matter was dropped. A second attempt to try to buy Cuba from Spain was made during the Pierce administration. With the balance upset by the admission of California and the failure of Northern states to live up to the Compromise of 1850, this second attempt carried greater urgency. At the beginning of 1854, Secretary of State William Marcy directed the Ministers to Spain, France and Great Britain to meet in conference to decide if it was feasible to persuade Spain to sell Cuba to the United States. The ministers met at Ostend, Belgium during the summer. In October, they issued their findings in a document called the Ostend Manifesto. The manifesto proposed to threaten Spain with the invasion of Cuba if Spain remained obdurate on selling the island. The publication of the manifesto produced a storm of protest as the anti-slavery press accused the Democrats of trying to extend slavery by conquest. Marcy had not authorized publication of the Manifesto; the plan had been pursued without administration approval. It was immediately withdrawn and the Minister to Spain forced to resign.

Also during the Pierce administration, the issue of expansion west of Missouri was broached. By 1854 the organization of the country west of Iowa and Missouri was long overdue. According to the Missouri Compromise, this territory should become free states because it was north of the 36-30' line. Proslavery Congressmen did not want a free territory (Kansas) west of Missouri because they feared this would prevent any significant expansion of slave states and make permanent the imbalance caused by the admission of California four years earlier. Four attempts to organize a single territory for this area had already been defeated in Congress, largely because of Southern opposition to the Missouri Compromise. Eventually a bill was drafted that was acceptable to the South. This bill created two territories, Kansas and Nebraska, and called for the question of slave status to be settled by popular sovereignty. It explicitly overturned the Missouri Compromise.

Floods of settlers, some pro-slave, but most pro-free, streamed into Kansas. Each side was determined to dominate the elections that were to decide the issue. An election was held in November 1854 to select a territorial legislature. Large numbers of pro-slave Missourians crossed the border into Kansas and voted in this election, giving victory to the slavery cause. The new state legislature enacted laws that incorporated the Missouri slave code. Anti-slave forces were outraged and set up their own Free State legislature. Democratic president Pierce recognized the proslavery legislature only. A Congressional committee sent to investigate the elections ruled in favor of the Free State legislature. The controversy exploded into violence that eventually claimed 55 lives, in what has come to be known as "bleeding Kansas".

Finally, in the 1857 Dred Scott decision, the Supreme Court declared that the Missouri Compromise was unconstitutional; slavery could not be forbidden in any of the territories. This ruling created the possibility of slavery being extended far outside the boundaries of the South. From the point of view of

Southerners, such extension was necessary else their property could be stolen from them by legislative fiat. Northerners were adamantly opposed to the extension of slavery. Northern settlers of the West largely wished these territories to remain completely white, partly out of antipathy towards blacks and partly because they did not wish to compete with slave labor. There was also a fear that were slavery extended outside of where it had traditionally been practiced, it might come to be extended to poor whites as well as blacks.

Southerners became increasingly defensive as this conservative era drew to a close, fearing an assault upon their way of life was coming. Northerners became increasingly intolerant of the Southern position and also grew irrationally fearful of a Southern conspiracy to spread slavery everywhere, even into northern states where it had never been or had been abolished long ago. The stress caused by the culture war over slavery resulted in political turmoil as third parties appeared which addressed issues ignored by the focus upon slavery by the major parties.

The Free Soil party supported exclusively white settlement of the West with free land for settlers. They opposed extension of slavery beyond where it was. Free Soilers were a major player in the election of 1848, drawing off Democratic strength and handing the victory to the Whigs. The "Know Nothing" party was really more of a secret society of men opposed to immigration, particularly by Catholics. They were also supporters of temperance, one of the reform movements (like abolition) that came out of the Transcendental Awakening turning (1822-44). This party did not field candidates of their own; instead they threw their votes to individual candidates of any party whose views accorded with their own.

Besides the third parties, the Whig party increasingly split into "conscience Whigs" who were opposed to slavery and southern "cotton Whigs" who were not. After the Kansas-Nebraska Act the Whig party effectively disappeared, with the cotton Whigs moving into the Democrats. A group of northern Whigs took over the Know-Nothings, molding it into an anti-sectionalism, anti-Democratic nationalist party. A new party, the Republicans, arose in 1854, incorporating Free Soilers, abolitionists and some conscience Whigs. For the 1856 election the Know-Nothing/Whig nationalists merged into the Republicans and another major party had arisen to replace the Whigs.

It was only a matter of time before a catastrophe would break out. In the election of 1856 the Republicans ran John C. Frémont under the slogan Free Men, Free Soil and Frémont. The South threatened secession if Frémont won. The Democrats ran James Buchanan, billed as an experienced old hand who would lead the nation through this time of crisis. Buchanan won the election but failed spectacularly at leadership. The election of 1860 saw the Democrats fall apart when Northern and Southern Democrats split at the convention, nominating two candidates. By this time the South almost welcomed secession and were unwilling to compromise even with members of their own party. With the Democrats fatally weakened, Republican Abraham Lincoln won handily.

## Liberal era 1860-1872

Immediately after the election of Lincoln, South Carolina called a convention to consider the issue of secession and on December 20, 1860, voted to leave the union. Most observers at the time expected a compromise would be reached and the union would be preserved. Senator Crittenden of Kentucky proposed a series of constitutional amendments that amounted to a permanent constitutional guarantee of the rights of slaveholders that could be neither repealed nor amended. This Crittenden compromise was introduced into Congress two days before South Caroline seceded. It was killed by Republicans in Congress in mid-January 1861, by which time three more states had seceded. No further efforts to avert crisis were made and hostilities began with the shelling of Fort Sumter in April.

Most Northerners were neither racial egalitarians nor civil libertarians. Opponents of the extension of slavery (the official Republican position in the 1860 election) wanted slave-free and exclusively white territories—they had no problem with slavery as long as it was restricted to those states where it already existed. Thus, the Northern objectives in 1861 were reunion with the maintenance of slavery.

The Southern war strategy was to hold on until the North tired of war and signed an armistice acknowledging Southern independence and preserving slavery for all time. The North believed that their superior numbers and wealth would soon give them the victory and so didn't really have a war strategy. But the North did not quickly triumph; the war dragged on. As time went on Northern opinion changed in favor of the Radical Republican (abolitionist) argument that slavery was the fundamental basis of Southern power and that the decisive defeat of that power would require emancipation of the slaves. Thus, the war goal of the North and the Republican party shifted from reunion with slavery to the Radical Republican position of reunion with emancipation. The war took on the dimensions of a moral crusade and not just a political struggle.

This shift is what made this era liberal despite a government led by a party largely derived from the conservative Whigs. The Republican platform of 1860 contained traditional pro-business Whig policies: protective tariffs and internal improvements (specifically a transcontinental railroad). There were some liberal proposals such as land grants to settlers that had come from the Republican's Free Soil roots, but mostly what made the post-1860 era liberal was the shift towards emancipation and the adoption of liberal policies during the war and Reconstruction. Thus the 1860's not only saw the Whiggish Railway Act that gave land to railroads and increases in the tariff, but also the fiscally-liberal Legal Tender Act that helped finance the Civil War. At the close of the war, the 13th amendment abolishing slavery was passed and the Freedman's Bureau, which provided aid and protection to newly freed slaves, was created.

Immediately after the war, while Congress was not in session, President Johnson adopted a plan for reconstruction that he believed to be consistent with what Lincoln had intended. The Johnson plan called for state governments to be reconstituted under the laws existing at the time of secession provided they voided secession, abolished slavery, repudiated their war debt and ratified the 13th amendment. There was no requirement for black suffrage. Construction of a post-emancipation society was to be left to these new state governments, which remained under the control of Confederate officials. Eager to establish dominance over the freed slaves, these governments passed the "Black Codes", repressive laws restricting the rights of freedmen. Blacks and Republican officials who stood up for freedmen rights were often killed by terrorist "nightriders".

Once back in session, Congressional Republicans attempted to deal with the nightrider problem by increasing the power of the Freedmen's Bureau, giving it the power to try in military court people accused of depriving blacks of civil rights. This bill was passed over President Johnson's veto. They passed the Civil Rights Law of 1866, which made former slaves citizens of the United States and defined the rights possessed by citizens. It explicitly countermanded many of the Black Codes and was also passed over presidential veto. This law overrode the suffrage conditions under which the new state governments had been established, making them invalid. Not only that, but any valid new elections would have to involve voting by freedmen. A Fourteenth amendment to the Constitution was passed that put into fundamental law the provisions of the Civil Rights Law.

In 1867, Congress passed a Reconstruction law, which formally voided reconstruction that had occurred under President Johnson. The former Confederacy was divided into five military districts. All male citizens over twenty-one years of age, white and black, were to be registered as voters, except those disfranchised under the proposed Fourteenth amendment for participation in the war. No disfranchised person was eligible for any office. New state constitutions were to be drafted, each subject to approval by Congress. The States were to remain as provisional until the 14th Amendment was ratified.

Under Reconstruction rules Republican governments were elected in a number of former Confederate states on the strength of black voters, who were protected by Federal troops. Other states were able to comply with the terms of Reconstruction and still elect racist white "redeemer" governments. Redeemer governments were elected in Tennessee in 1869, Georgia, North Carolina and Virginia in 1870, and Texas in 1873. These governments were careful not to overtly violate the civil rights of former slaves (lest the army remove them from power), although they looked the other way when private terrorist groups did so.

The feat of social engineering attempted by Reconstruction is remarkable in its boldness. Northern liberals were attempting to take a population of slaves and their former masters and forge them into a civil democratic society in just a few years. Building a colorblind democratic society was not going to be possible as was shown by the election of racist redeemer governments in those states with a well-organized white majority. In states with a larger black population, it was possible to elect biracial Republican governments and even black congressmen as long as Federal troops were there to ensure participation by black voters

Reconstruction was partly idealistic and partly about the North punishing the South for inflicting the horrors of slavery and war upon the nation. As time passed, the Northern commitment towards Abolitionist ideals and the thirst for vengeance declined. Former Confederate officials, barred from office under Reconstruction, were granted amnesty in 1872 and rank-and-file Republicans became more concerned with the rampant corruption of the Grant administration and less interested in "nation building" in the South. The liberal thrust forged by the fire of war subsided and Republicans, tired of crusades, reverted to their natural pro-business conservatism.

It is important to appreciate the degree of change attempted during the Civil War liberal era. At the beginning of the era, the major area of disagreement between the liberal and conservative sides was over the expansion of slavery into the Western territories. By 1867, the liberal position had hardened into forced political equality of slave and master. This is an enormous movement when one considers the depth of racism fostered by the slave system. What ended up being achieved, emancipation of blacks on an unequal basis with respect to whites, was still a significant achievement.

The standard bearer for liberalism for the Civil War was the Republican party, which in large part had descended from the conservative Whigs and the Federalists before them. The Republicans of the Civil War era still favored traditional Whig/Federalist tenets such as a protective tariff and public projects. What made the era liberal was Radical Republican idealism. It was only a matter of time before the Radical fire dimmed and the natural conservatism of the Republicans took its place. And with no standard bearer on the Democratic side, conservatism was triumphant, as is shown by the extremely long duration for the next conservative era.

## Conservative era, the "Gilded Age" 1872-1901

By 1872 the zeitgeist had shifted. Reconstruction continued but it was clear that equality between the races wasn't going to happen. The war was over and a new era of economic boom times had begun. America was connected coast to coast by the first transcontinental railroad. Business was increasingly influential and the Grant administration was riddled with corruption, yet handily won in 1872 against token opposition by the short-lived Liberal Republican splinter party. The panic of 1873 threw the nation into depression and the economic turmoil saw the Democrats gain control of the House in the 1874 elections. With hard times and an egregiously corrupt outgoing administration, the Republicans quite rightly feared they would lose the next presidential election in 1876.

This election saw a very close race in which Democrat Samuel Tilden outpolled Republican Rutherford B. Hayes in the popular vote. The electoral vote issue was complicated by ambiguous results from three states. A Republican dominated electoral commission gave the victory to Hayes, but only after a concession had been reached in which Hayes agreed to end Reconstruction. Thus, pro-business conservative Republicans remained in power. But even if Tilden had won the result would have been conservative as both the Democratic and Republican platforms were very similar.

Both major parties were conservative during this entire era with corruption and personal politics issues dominating the political discussion. As with the 1840-1860 conservative era, liberal sentiment was relegated to minor parties. One of these was the Greenback Party, which was founded to promote currency expansion. Their constituents were primarily farmers of the West and South who faced bankruptcy by the collapse in farm prices after 1873 which left them unable to service debts contracted earlier when prices were higher.

Figure 2.2 shows a plot of the ten-year average of price inflation for a composite of agricultural prices. A peak in the plot reflects the end of a ten-year period when farm prices (and farm revenues) were rising particularly strongly. A trough reflects the end of a ten-year period when farm prices were falling at a high rate. The decades after the start of the War of 1812 and the Civil War were times of substantial price inflation for farmers. This high inflation is consistent with the Kondratiev peaks associated with these wars. These good times for farmers eventually ended and the average rate of price inflation fell, eventually falling below zero in 1823 and 1873. The fifty-year spacing between these dates reflects the fifty-year timing of the Kondratiev cycle. When the ten-year average price inflation falls below zero this means that farm revenues have fallen relative to what they had been over the previous decade and that debt contracted at the earlier times becomes harder and harder to pay back, leading to increased farmer bankruptcies and mortgage foreclosures.

Such periods could be expected to produce political opposition amongst farmers to the cause of their troubles: declining prices (rising value of money), suggesting an inadequate supply of money relative to demand. Farmers and other debtors during such times want to see an increase in money supply or bank loans. One might expect political parties to appear shortly after the development of hard times in 1823 and 1873 that attempted to address the problem of farm bankruptcies by expansion of money supply or increases in bank lending. Indeed, the very next year in both cases saw the appearance of a party that focused on protecting the common farmer from the scourge of deflation through monetary manipulations. In 1824, it was the Jacksonian Democrats, who fought "money power" in the guise of the Second Bank of the United States. In 1874 it was the Greenback party, who sought expansion of the amount of US paper currency or "greenbacks" in circulation. Greenbacks had been issued to help pay for the Civil War and rampant price inflation, particularly for farm prices, had been seen at this time. Greenbackers naturally associated the good times for farmers with the issuance of this currency and wanted more of the same.

Figure 2.2. Average ten-year farm price rise and the appearance of political parties

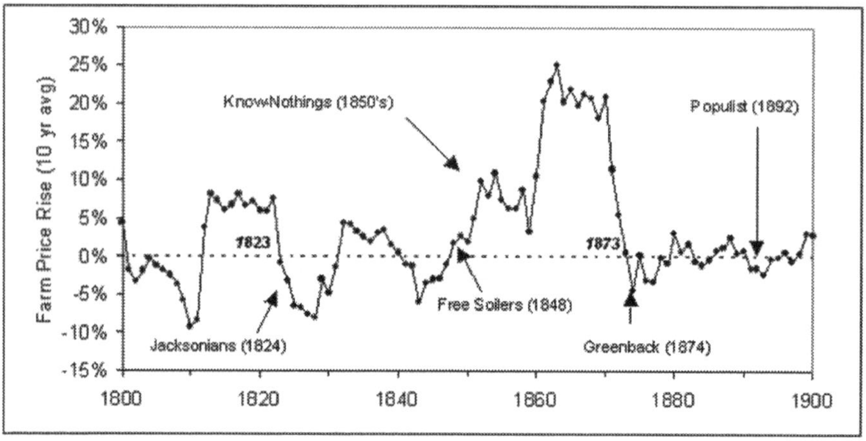

Thus, the Greenbackers were essentially reprising the role of the Jacksonian Democrats as defenders of the common man against the elite bankers. They sought to capture the Democratic party for their cause for the 1876 election but lost out to the more conservative Tilden forces. The failure of the Greenback party compared to the success of the Jacksonians reflected a number of issues. One was southern farmers were very much absorbed with the problem of race relations and Reconstruction and were not entirely focused on just their economic problems. Another was that nearly half of the country was not engaged in farming and did not benefit from rising farm prices. There simply wasn't a majority constituency for monetary expansion. Had there been, one of the major parties would have picked up the issue. In contrast, in the 1820's over 70% of the population was engaged in farming, and slavery had not yet become an important political issue. Thus, the Jacksonian Democrats were able to eventually win on this issue and launch a liberal era.

Figure 2.2 also shows the timing of the appearance of the Free Soilers in 1848. The appearance of this party did not coincide with a time of declining fortunes for farmers and according to the model being developed, should not have been concerned about monetary or banking issues. Indeed, the focus of the Free Soilers was on territorial expansion without expansion of slavery and free land for settlers, not money supply or central banking. Similarly, the Know Nothings, who arose shortly after the Free Soilers, were concerned with immigration and temperance, both social issues, and had no position on monetary issues.

The Greenback party, after a poor showing in 1876, widened its appeal by adopting a number of labor issues. Their 1878 platform contained labor demands on hours, government labor bureaus, contract prison labor, and immigration; but centered on the monetary issues. The party won nearly a million votes in the 1878 election. They elected 14 candidates to Congress in that year and made substantial gains in state legislatures.

Strong economic growth over 1879-80, accompanied by considerable inflation, dampened labor and agrarian discontent. In the 1880 election the party found its focus on the currency question had become obsolete and they polled only about 300,000 votes and elected 8 congressmen. The Greenback Party did very poorly in the 1884 election and was officially disbanded in 1887. A Union Labor party was organized for the 1888 election from former Greenback and labor elements. But they failed to get much of the labor vote and were still mostly a farmer party.

Towards the end of this era, another party for the common man arose, the Populists. As Figure 2.2 shows, times had not improved for farmers and the monetary issue still resonated with them. Industrialization had produced an urban proletariat, who shared a common enemy with farmers in the financial elite. Populists called for a laundry list of farmer and labor friendly policies: coinage of silver, abolition of national banks, a graduated income tax, plenty of paper money, government ownership of all forms of transportation and communication, election of Senators by direct vote of the people, nonownership of land by foreigners, civil service reform, a working day of eight hours, postal banks, pensions, revision of the law of contracts, and reform of immigration regulations. In their opposition to national banks, calls for monetary expansion and postal banks they were similar to the Greenbacks and the earlier Jacksonians. In their anti-foreigner and immigrant views they recalled the Know Nothings. They had also adopted a number of issues from socialist and labor parties. This combination of views proved potent as the Populists polled nearly 1.5 million votes in the 1894 Congressional elections.

In the election of 1896, the Democrats adopted some of the Populist platform and mounted a vigorous campaign. Republican McKinley won, and it would seem the conservative era would continue. But a new reform movement had begun, represented politically by such men as social reformer John Peter Atgeld, elected Democratic governor of Illinois in 1892, Theodore Roosevelt, elected

Republican governor of New York in 1898, and Robert LaFollette, elected Republican governor of Wisconsin in 1900. Roosevelt's mildly progressive policies were enough to earn him the opposition of Senator Platt, boss of New York's Republican political machine. Platt arranged for Roosevelt to get the Republican vice presidential nomination in 1900 as a way to get him out of the governor's office. But when McKinley was assassinated in 1901, Roosevelt became president, ushering in the liberal Progressive era.

## Liberal period, the "Progressive Era" 1901-1918

The Progressive era saw two items off the populist wish list implemented: direct election of senators and a graduated income tax. Prohibition of alcohol was initiated after many decades of temperance agitation and women's suffrage was achieved. A number of other regulatory actions by the Federal government including the establishment of the Food and Drug Administration and "trust busting" by the Department of Justice round out the list of governmental activism pursuing progressive goals. The era ended with a massive foreign war and a period of panic about subversives. The country wished for a "return to normalcy" and voted in a conservative Republican in the election of 1920.

The beginning of the Progressive era in 1901 appears to the result of a random event, an assassination. Had McKinley lived it would seem that the Progressive era wouldn't have begun. It wouldn't have begun right in 1901, but it would have started soon after. As described above, certain reform-minded politicians had begun to win office at the end of the nineteenth century. Interest in liberal politics had been sparked by provocative articles and books by a number of social critics. Jacob Riis exposed the dirt, disease, vice, and misery of New York slums in his 1890 *How the Other Half Lives*, which heavily influenced Theodore Roosevelt. In 1894, Henry Demerest Lloyd wrote *Wealth against Commonwealth*, a book critical of Standard Oil, which is considered one of the first examples of investigative reporting. In 1902, *McClure's* magazine began to run series of investigative articles on various social and political topics by a number of hard-hitting reporters who came to be called "muckrakers". Examples include Lincoln Steffens' *Shame of the Cities*, which documented the corrupt alliance between big business and municipal governments and Ida Tarbell's devastating expose on the Standard Oil Company. Upton Sinclair's novel *The Jungle*, which contained graphic depictions of the unsanitary conditions at meat-packing plants, sparked an outcry which led to the Pure Food and Drug Act of 1906.

Along with social critics there were social reform movements that had appeared in response to industrialization. One of these was the settlement house movement in which university graduates lived amongst the urban poor and organized clubs, recreation and education programs for neighborhood people. One of the first American settlement houses was Hull House in Chicago, founded by Jane Addams in 1889. Lillian Wald founded the New York Henry Street settlement in 1895. Later, the Social Gospel movement grew out of these early efforts at private provision of social services.

These movements provided the backdrop through which progressive politics played its role. Had Roosevelt not become president, the outcry over the meat packing industry following publication of *The Jungle* would still have given rise to something like the FDA. Following *McClure's* lead, other magazines such as *Cosmopolitan, American Magazine and Colliers* began publishing muckraking articles on abuse against workers, widespread corruption, and misuse of land by big business. With all this attention to issues needing reform, and the spirit of reform already awakened in the land, governmental attention would necessarily follow, regardless of who was in power.

The emphasis on reform of the excesses of industrial society created a new class of liberal politics. In Jefferson's time, liberalism had meant protection *from* government, because government was the servant of the wealthy elite. In the eyes of Jeffersonian liberals, federal government revenues were largely used to pay interest to wealthy bond owners and bankers, to pay for a military to protect the property of the wealthy, and to buy assets for the benefit of wealthy special interests. Revenues came largely from regressive taxes, mostly tariffs and excise taxes. Tariffs were set higher than required for revenue purposes in order to keep prices of domestic manufactures high, maximizing profits for rich business owners. So liberals were anti-tax, particularly, they favored lower tariffs. Finally, liberals favored expansion of democratic rights to a wider population.

Conservatives would argue that government debt was used to pay for highly popular national expansion like the Louisiana Purchase and the Mexican war (both undertaken by Democratic administrations). A military was obviously necessary to provide for the common defense as shown by the War of 1812. Finally internal improvements created infrastructure that would build prosperity in the nation, benefiting all. In the early years of the Republic, activist government was a conservative viewpoint, largely because the kind of policies undertaken by the government were favored by the wealthy elite. Conservatives were opposed to increased democracy precisely because it raised the possibility of government pursuing unconservative policies.

The meaning of liberalism began to change in the years leading up to the Civil War. Although the Jeffersonian concepts remained, the liberal bias in favor of increased democracy began to be applied to slavery. Abolitionists were a kind of liberal who favored positive government action to free slaves. Big government conservatives in the North did not have a philosophical objection to abolition and so abolitionists formed the "liberal wing" of the new conservative Northern party, the Republicans. Pro-slavery Democrats largely made up the conservative wing of the liberal Democratic party. Thus, during the liberal 1860-72 era it was the liberal wing of the Republicans that set the agenda, while during the conservative 1872-1901 era it was the conservative wing of the Democrats and middle-of-the-road Republicans that set policy. Thus both Democrats and Republicans held the Presidency or Congress at various times without having a significant impact on the dominant ideology, which remained solidly conservative. In this way the post Civil War era was different from the early years of the republic when ideology was associated with parties: Federalists and Whigs conservative, and Democrats liberal.

As industrialization proceeded in the late 19th century, social conditions arose that were beyond the ability of individuals to remedy. Liberals believed these conditions were morally wrong, like slavery, and would require some form of governmental action to remedy, like slavery did. Gradually, the idea of liberal activist government developed in both parties as part of the Progressive movement. Progressive liberals considered a wide variety of nostrums to fix what they believed to be society's ills. Some of these were clearly self-serving such as calls for "free silver" by farmers and suffrage by women, while others were not, such as the calls for temperance and civil service reform. Conservatives were able to hold off much of this proposed reform for a long time. For example, prohibition took nearly 50 years to become law after the Prohibition Party ran their first campaign in 1872. It was nearly 60 years after the first Greenback campaign before a more expansive monetary regime was installed.

The phenomenon of a rising activist liberal agenda meant that conservatism increasingly involved defending the property rights of the elite against activist liberal challenges, much as slavery had been defended, rather than advocating an active agenda of its own. Conservatives remained in support of high tariffs and governmental assistance to big business by arguing that it promoted prosperity. But mostly they fought to keep the status quo: the gold standard, non-interference with business, and suppression of labor unions. Although regulatory laws like the estab-lishment of the Interstate Commerce Commission or the Sherman Antitrust Act were passed, they were not enforced.

Nevertheless, as described above, the work of social reformers and the con-scious raising by the muckrakers created a "demand" for liberal politics amongst the general populace, which could not be held off indefinitely. The conservative dam began to crack during the Progressive Era, and completely broke during the New Deal, the next liberal era. Jeffersonian or "classical" liberals came to be con-sidered as conservative because they opposed the liberal activist policies that pro-gressivism was all about. There wasn't a complete break between the two kinds of liberals, progressive liberals generally agreed with classical liberals that tariffs should be reduced. Both tended to be pacifist and anti-imperialist.

Liberal activist government required funding, which was to be provided by increased taxes on the wealthier members of society. Thus, the idea of a progres-sive income tax, advocated by the Populists and various labor parties before them, morphed from a radical leftist idea with no chance of implementation into a liberal position that was implemented in 1916. Liberalism ceased to be anti-tax, as long as they were *progressive* taxes. Hence the establishment of a flat income tax in 1862 is labeled as conservative in Appendix A, but the establish-ment of a progressive income tax in 1916 is labeled as liberal.

Similarly, the 1913 establishment of the Federal Reserve, the third central bank of the U.S., is labeled as a liberal event, whereas the first two central banks were labeled as conservative. The establishment of the Federal Reserve came in response to the Panic of 1907. Its purpose was to ameliorate the severity of cycli-cal depressions, reducing their impact on Americans. This goal was quite differ-ent from earlier conservative goals of easy financing for conservative national projects and making capital readily available to capitalists. By this time potential national projects were not necessarily going to be conservative in nature and pri-vate business had more than sufficient access to capital. Stabilization of financial panics usually means loose monetary policy, which is inflationary. Inflation is bad for lenders and good for debtors. As wealth holders tend to be lenders rather than debtors, conservatives abhor inflation. Thus the establishment of the Federal Reserve did not aid conservative causes or individuals and cannot be con-sidered as a conservative event

Republicans were the majority party during the progressive era, much as they had been during the last liberal era. The progressive Roosevelt was succeeded by the less progressive Taft, who nevertheless engaged in more trust busting that did his predecessor. Taft was not progressive enough for Roosevelt, however. Roosevelt challenged Taft in the 1912 Republican primary and when he was denied the nomination, went on to run as a third party candidate, outpolling Taft in the general election and handing the election to Democrat Wilson. It was under Wilson that the most significant of the Progressive achievements occurred: establishment of the Federal Reserve, passage of the income tax, women's suffrage and prohibition.

With all this change, including a major foreign war with its associated inflation and the social unrest afterward, the American electorate had had enough of crusades and reforms and was ready for Harding's "return to normalcy". A conservative "new era" had begun.

## Conservative period: the "New Era" 1918-1931

The New Era didn't have an overarching theme such as slavery for the antebellum conservative era. It also didn't reflect the nation building of the post-Revolutionary era. Finally it wasn't a time of major economic change like the post Civil War conservative era. The nation was largely industrial with a declining agricultural sector at the beginning and end of this era. The new concept of liberal activism was well established. In many ways, the New Era was a conservative breather in one long liberalizing trend. Like the previous two conservative eras, liberal sentiment during the New Era was expressed in minor parties, particularly the 1924 Progressive Party campaign headlined by Robert LaFollette.

There were two new developments during this era that makes it important. The first was the New Era bull market in stocks. The stock market had wandered between 2 and 6½ throughout the 19th century (market values here are expressed in terms of the S&P500 and its precursors). In the early 20th century it rose several times to around 10, but by early 1921 it had fallen below the 19th century high set forty years earlier. In the next eight years the index soared to over 30, a "take-off" unprecedented in history.

This great bull market reflected euphoria and "bubbleheadedness", of course, but it also represented the ascension of the United States as the premier nation in the world. Prior to WW I, Britain had still held pride of place as the greatest of powers. Although the U.S. had long before surpassed Britain in GDP and even per capita GDP, Britain was still the dominant financial and naval power, as well has possessing the most extensive empire. When the world war came, Britain liquidated many of her overseas investments, paving the way for the U.S.

to take on the role of greatest financial power. U.S economic growth during the New Era was greater than most of the other great powers. Accumulating gold reserves in Fort Knox underlined this American strength. It was truly the entry into greatness for the American republic.

This brings us to the second development. The U.S. had emerged from the First World War as the strongest nation in the world. Not only was it richer than any other nation, it had a larger population and more arable land area than any other great power except Russia. Thus the U.S. could bear the military and diplomatic burdens of world leadership better than any other nation. But, the foray of the US into hegemony had occurred under liberal leadership. Hegemony was rejected by the resurgent conservatives after 1918. This decision was to have serious consequences for the conservative party as the Credit Anstalt crisis shows.

Austria's major bank, Credit Anstalt, went bankrupt in 1931. Its deposits were so large that freezing them through bankruptcy proceedings would have destroyed the Austrian economy, hence the government stepped in to guarantee deposits. The resulting expansion of the currency was inconsistent with the gold standard. In order to keep its banking system from collapsing and to defend the gold standard, the Austrian central bank needed more gold to meet incipient capital flight. Austria was a small country; there was not that much capital to flee. A sizable loan to Austria's central bank would have allowed it to prop up its internal banking system and maintain convertibility. Speculators would observe that the world's governments were serious in their commitment to the gold standard and be leery of betting against currencies.

But the substantial loan was not made. Speculators observed that the international financial community did *not* support currencies that came under pressure. They wondered which country would be next to devalue. The wave of bear speculation moved on to Hungary, Germany, and Britain. By the Autumn of 1931 Britain had abandoned the gold standard. In response to the British abandonment of gold, the Federal Reserve *raised* interest rates in the middle of depression. It is possible that this tightening in an already depressed economy caused economic collapse in 1932.

Before World War I the gold standard had remained on track because there was a single, dominant power in the world economy, Britain. Everybody knew that Britain was the "hegemon", and so everyone played by the rules of the game as laid down in London. Similarly, after World War II the US was hegemon. Both times, the existence of a power that had the capability (and will) to take effective action *on its own* to shape international finance, led to a relatively stable system of international finance. But between the wars, Britain was too weak to continue in this role and the Americans, although certainly capable of acting in this role, did not do so. Ruling conservatives had rejected internationalism launched under liberals in the previous cycle. The resulting economic collapse created a tremendous backlash against conservative rule that nearly obliterated the Republican party in the 1930's.

Had the stock market bubble not have occurred, the financial problems in overseas banks would probably have worked themselves out and there would be no Great Depression. Had the US intervened financially to stabilize international finance, the Depression would likely have been moderated. But with both, the shocks to the global economy were just too great.

Figure 2.3. Federal government spending as a percent of GDP 1900-2003

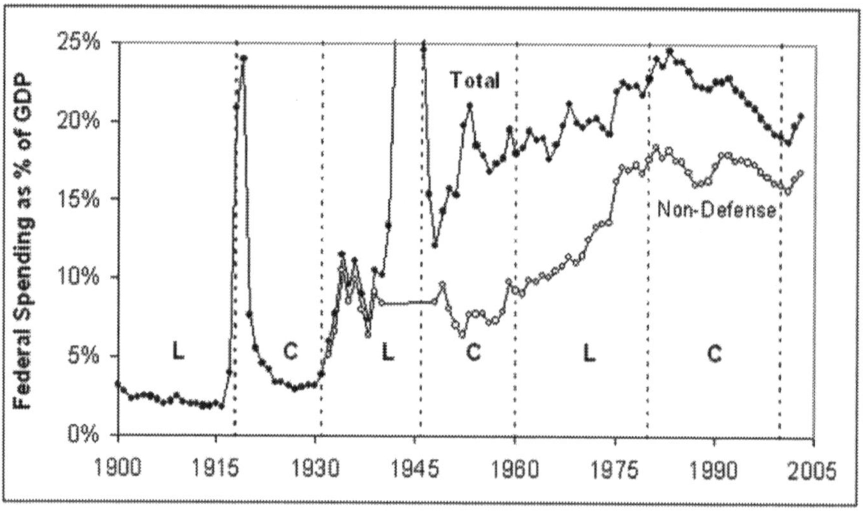

## Liberal period: the "New Deal" 1931-1946

The New Deal era was a time of sweeping change. Government grew tremendously. Figure 2.3 shows Federal government expenditures as a percentage of GDP since 1900. This graph vividly illustrates the concept of liberal government activism. The idea first appeared during the Progressive era, but it reached fruition during the New Deal. Federal government spending rose from about 3%

of GDP in the middle-to-late 1920's to about 15% by the end of the New Deal era. Non-defense spending grew as well. Spending grew strongly over the subsequent conservative era, but non-defense spending did not. Both overall spending and non-defense spending rose steadily in the next liberal era. In the following conservative era non-defense spend held roughly constant, while overall Federal spending declined. In recent years both have again been on the rise, providing evidence that we entered a liberal era around 2000.

A great many new initiatives were launched by the New Deal. Six of the 13 Populist demands listed earlier were met during the New Deal. In 1933 the US went off the gold standard and the US government ran large deficits during peacetime. These policies had the same effect as the Populist prescription for silver coinage and plenty of paper money. Beyond that, the New Deal implemented policies specifically designed to boost farm prices. Social Security met the demand for pensions, and Federal deposit insurance that for postal banks. The 8-hour day was implemented along with a minimum wage. With income tax and direct election of senators enacted during the Progressive era and immigration restrictions during the New Era, just about all of the radical Populist agenda had become reality.

All this rapid change meant that what had been radical 40 years earlier and liberal 20 years earlier had become mainstream politics. The nation as a whole had made a shift towards the political left. The boldness of the New Deal program rivals that of the Radical Republicans, but unlike the latter, the New Deal did not go too far. The short duration of the post-New Deal conservative era, half that of the post-Civil War era, shows that the appetite of the electorate for liberal politics had grown over the previous 80 years.

The Republican Party was nearly destroyed. After Hoover's crushing loss, it would be 48 years before a Republican would run and win on a conservative platform. When Hoover won his landslide victory in 1928, the Republican Party had been in existence for 74 years. It had been 68 years since they had elected their first president and they had held the presidency and the Senate for 52 of those 68 years. They had achieved a level of dominance similar to that of the antebellum Democrats.

This level of dominance had allowed the Republicans to ably defend their business constituents against progressive challenges. In this way they were similar to the antebellum Democrats, who had used their political dominance to protect slaveowner interests for a very long time. Eventually events moved against both parties and they suffered a long night of political near-irrelevance as a result.

## Conservative era 1946-1960

After the end of World War II, President Truman desired to expand the New Deal. The 1946 congressional elections produced a landslide Republican victory that Republicans interpreted as a mandate to reverse the New Deal. As a result, Truman was forced to go on the defensive against Republican assaults on New Deal accomplishments and was unable to promote his own program. Foreign affairs also turned against the Democratic coalition. Increasingly provocative behavior on the part of former ally Soviet Russia led Truman to announce the Truman Doctrine, in which American aid was pledged to free peoples who were resisting attempted subjugation by armed minorities or by outside pressures. Truman specifically requested aid for Greece in its fight against communism. Left-wing Democrats, alarmed at the aggressive stance taken by the Truman administration, formed their own party led by former vice-president Henry Wallace, which would oppose Truman in the 1948 election.

Truman's embrace of civil rights reform after 1946 also fostered opposition from within his own party. After the war, blacks who had served in the military and in the defense industry demanded the right to vote, which provoked white resistance in the South. Truman, conscious of the deleterious effect of Jim Crow segregation on U.S. prestige abroad, established the President's Committee on Civil Rights to investigate race relations in 1946. The Committee's report was issued the next year. It called for a ban on lynching, abolition of the poll tax, a civil rights division in the Department of Justice, desegregation of the military, and efforts to attack segregation in education, housing, and interstate transportation. In 1948, Truman requested that Congress enact most of these measures and issued a presidential order desegregating the military. Southern segregationist Democrats denounced Truman's action as a "stab in the back" and split to form their own party, led by South Carolina governor Strom Thurmond.

Thus, the Democratic Party was split three ways in 1948, yet Truman was still able to narrowly defeat Republican Thomas Dewey. Not only that, but Congress shifted back to Democratic control. Truman interpreted his victory as a mandate for liberalism. He introduced an ambitious social and economic program, the Fair Deal, asking Congress to widen the scope of the New Deal. Congress was distinctly uncooperative, reflecting low public enthusiasm for more reform. In addition a climate of anticommunist hysteria was rising, which spelled the end for social change. After 1949, the administration abandoned reform, focusing on fighting Communism and rearming the nation instead.

These events show the development of a conservative zeitgeist after the war, despite general Democratic success at the polls. A key factor in this shift was the conservative Southern wing of the Democratic Party, which increasingly co-operated with Republicans to thwart liberal legislation. Another key factor was the development of anticommunist hysteria. Rapidly decaying postwar relations between the US and the Soviet Union culminated with the Berlin crisis of 1947 and the start of the Cold War. The Truman Doctrine had identified that a threat existed whereby Communism could "spread" to countries like Greece or China, almost like a disease. Americans had once ignored the problems of foreign extremist politics and had paid a serious price in WW II. People did not wish to let Communism spread to threaten the nation and the world. Hence, it had to be contained. The spread was believed to be facilitated by an international conspiracy of Communists who undoubtedly had bases within the United States. The American Communist party had claimed 80,000 members during World War II, and no one knew how many occupied sensitive government positions.

These fears led to a hunt for subversives. President Truman launched a massive "loyalty" program in 1947. More than 3 million federal employees were investigated. About 3,000 either resigned or were dismissed as a result of these investigations. The probe uncovered no evidence of subversion or espionage, but it spread fear and discouragement among government employees. The House of Representatives Committee on Un-American Activities (HUAC) was re-activated. HUAC had been established in 1938 to root out Nazi sympathizers, but now it was to look for Communist agents. HUAC member Richard Nixon accused Alger Hiss, a prominent New Dealer who had been part of the American delegation at the 1945 Yalta Conference, of being a communist agent. Hiss was convicted of espionage and served 44 months in prison. [Evidence obtained after the fall of the Soviet Union suggested that Hiss had indeed been a spy.] Having found an agent, the search intensified.

The Communist victory in China in 1949 and the successful detonation of an atomic bomb by the Soviets in the same year increased the fear that America might be losing the struggle against Communism. Although the Communist insurgency against the Nationalist government had gone on for two decades, Americans reacted to the Communist victory as if the United States had suddenly "lost" China to international Communism, which was now frighteningly strengthened by acquisition of nuclear weapons by the USSR. Feeling reached a fever pitch in the next year when the nation went to war against Soviet-supported North Korea.

Grandstanding Wisconsin Senator Joseph McCarthy created a furor in February 1950 when he told an audience he had a list of 205 Communists working in the State Department and betraying America. For the next four years, he hunted for Communists in the U.S. government, making wild accusations and sullying the reputation of many innocent civil servants. He met his Waterloo in the Army-McCarthy hearings in which he displayed his odious personal character in front of an audience of 20 million Americans. In the end, he had not found even a single Communist.

It was through anti-Communism that Republican conservatives rebuilt their party. They could not compete with liberals on domestic agenda. Their record in the Depression was fresh and with unparalleled prosperity arguments that New Deal programs would bankrupt the nation held no water. Conservatives began to realize that to win politically they required an activist program of their own. The program they settled on was national defense and anti-Communism.

Figure 2.4. Defense spending as a percent of total Federal outlays

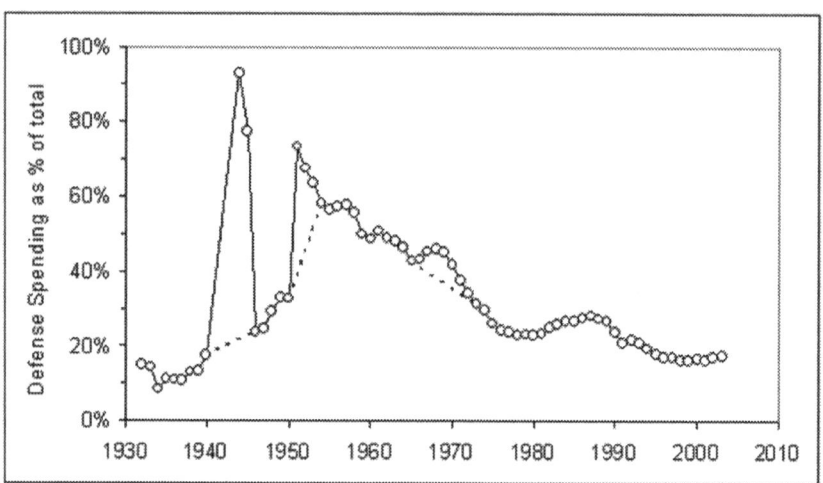

Figure 2.4 shows a plot of defense expenditures as a percentage of total government expenditures. This percentage had run at about 15% during the 1930's and then skyrocketed to over 90% during WW II. After the war it ran about 20-30%. There was a large increase for the Korean War, but afterward spending hardly decreased and was in the 50-60% range for the rest of the 1950's. Thus, during

the 1946-1960 period overall government grew, providing jobs and stimulus to the economy, which was politically popular, yet all of this growth was in defense, the one category of government gigantism acceptable to conservatives.

The Federal spending trends shown in Figures 2.3 and 2.4 illustrate the conservative strategy during the 1946-1960 conservative era. After the frontal assault on the New Deal failed in the 1947-49 Congress, conservatives focused their attention on foreign policy issues. By doing so they were able to prevent the growth of progressive government. This successful halt to the expansion of progressivism is what makes the period conservative. Most of the conservative events in Appendix A for this period reflect the conservative preoccupation with foreign policy that defines this era. Although conservative views on domestic policy were very much alive and ably represented by men like Senators Robert A. Taft and Barry Goldwater, such views were thought to be too far out of the mainstream to be politically workable in the post-Depression era. Expressing this belief, Republicans ran moderates, with one exception, for nearly half a century after Hoover's landslide defeat.

## Liberal Era 1961-1980

The liberal era began with the inauguration of John F. Kennedy in 1961, who instituted a number of liberal policies while in office. But the 1960 election, like the two before, was primarily a personality contest. Both Republican Nixon and Democrat Kennedy were moderates and ran as such. Both framed their campaigns in terms of anti-communism, the dominant issue of the previous conservative era. What was actually responsible for the shift in zeitgeist in the early 1960's was the growing intrusion of the civil rights movement into national affairs.

After the sacrifices made by black soldiers in WW II, black leaders were determined to force the acknowledgement of blacks as American citizens, entitled to the rights granted citizens under the 14th Amendment. The first milestone of this program was achieved through Presidential order, the desegregation of the armed forces, which became reality in 1950. The next step was achieved in the landmark *Brown v the Topeka Board of Education* case in 1954, which declared segregation unconstitutional, overruling the *Plessy v Ferguson* case from 1896. An early test of this ruling was the Montgomery Alabama Bus boycott. Rosa Parks, a black seamstress, was arrested in Montgomery for refusing to give up her bus seat to a white man. Black leaders organized a bus boycott that resulted in a 65% revenue loss for the bus company. Eight months later, the Supreme Court decided that bus segregation was unconstitutional based on the school segregation cases.

School desegregation received its first test in Arkansas. Little Rock Central High School was to begin the 1957 school year desegregated. On the first day of school, nine black students were kept from entering by National Guardsmen sent to the school by governor Faubus. After a court injunction was obtained, the students returned to Central High School, where they were prevented from entering by a mob of 1,000 townspeople. President Eisenhower then ordered National Guardsmen to Little Rock and the school was desegregated.

Civil Rights activism increased in the 1960's with "sit ins" and "freedom rides" designed to provoke racist opposition to perfectly legal and inoffensive behavior. A sit-in involved a group of students who would go to a lunch counter and ask to be served. If they were, they would move on to the next counter. If they were not, they would not move until they had been. If they were arrested, a new group would take their place. The students always remained nonviolent and respectful. Freedom Rides involved integrated groups of activists riding segregated transportation. White activists would sit in the back of the bus and black activists in the front. At rest stops, the whites would go into blacks-only areas and vice versa. In various places these actions provoked violent response which reflected negatively on segregationists.

The campaign reached an ugly peak in Birmingham in May 1963. A crowd of over a thousand children began a march into downtown Birmingham to protest segregation. The previous day a similar march had met with police opposition and some 900 children had been jailed. Public safety commissioner "Bull" Connor was determined not to let them get downtown, but he had no space left in his jails. He brought firefighters out and ordered them to turn hoses on the children. Most ran away, but one group refused to budge. The firefighters turned even more powerful hoses on them, hoses that shot streams of water strong enough to break bones. The force of the water rolled the protesters down the street. In addition, Connor set police dogs on protesters. Pictures of the confrontation between the children and the police shocked the nation.

After Birmingham, President Kennedy proposed a new civil rights bill. Civil rights groups united to organize a March on Washington to show support. Over a quarter of a million people from all over the nation descended on Washington, DC on August 28, 1963. They heard speeches and songs from numerous activists, artists, and civil rights leaders, culminating in Martin Luther King's famous "I Have a Dream" speech.

Congress passed the Civil Rights Act of 1964 in response to demonstrations of support such as the March on Washington and to rising popular anger with segregationist behavior. But this bill was still not sufficiently strong to circumvent state efforts to thwart black suffrage. After additional incidents of murder and terrorism directed against civil rights workers and an unprovoked attack upon civil rights marchers in Selma Alabama, President Johnson and Congress concluded they could no longer duck the issue of black disenfranchisement. The result was the Voting Rights Act of 1965, which effectively implemented black suffrage nearly a century after the 15th Amendment had tried to do the same thing.

The Civil Rights movement was the first of several major movements that characterized this liberal era. Another one was the environmental movement, launched by the 1962 publication of Rachel Carson's *Silent Spring*. Extensive environmental legislation was passed in the two decades after its publication (see Appendix A). The modern women's movement dates from the publication of Betty Friedan's *The Feminine Mystique* in 1963. This movement was a resumption of feminist activism after four decades of relative inactivity. It had a more direct connection to the Civil Rights movement, which helps explain the timing of this "second wave" of feminist activism.

Title VII of the 1964 Civil Rights Act prohibited employment discrimination on the basis of sex as well as race, religion, and national origin. The category *sex* was included as a last-ditch effort to kill the bill, which failed. An Equal Employment Opportunity Commission was established by the Act to investigate discrimination complaints. The commission received 50,000 sex discrimination complaints in its first five years of existence. It quickly became obvious that the commission was not very interested in pursuing these complaints and activists decided to form a civil rights organization for women similar to the NAACP. The National Organization for Women (NOW) was organized in 1966, which was to address civil rights issues for women.

Title IX in the Education Codes of 1972 provided for equal access to higher education and to professional schools. As a result of this act, the number of women doctors, lawyers, engineers, architects and other professionals soared as quotas actually limiting women's enrollment in graduate schools were outlawed. The women's movement also addressed reproductive rights in continuation of earlier efforts made by Margaret Sanger and others in the years after Women's suffrage was achieved. In 1965 the Supreme Court struck down state laws prohibiting contraceptive use by married couples, and in 1973 the court struck down state laws prohibiting abortion.

For the rest of the 1970's largely liberal policies continued to be pursued. But as the decade drew to a close, popular feeling was rising against liberal excesses and particularly against Democratic president Carter. Inflation was steadily rising amidst high unemployment, a combination called stagflation. The loss of the Vietnam War had created a sense of malaise that suggested the country's best days were behind it. Voters were becoming tried of crusades on the behalf of this or that underprivileged group and it was starting to show with tax revolts like Proposition 13 in California. Opposition to abortion rights was on the rise and complaints about "reverse discrimination" began to be heard. Then in 1979 radical Iranian students took some 50 American embassy workers hostage and held them for 444 days while President Carter stood by helpless. By 1980, Carter's approval ratings had sunk to levels rarely seen and the electorate was ready for a change. Ronald Reagan, the first openly conservative Republican to win the Presidency since 1928 was elected in a landslide. His coattails gave the Republicans control of the Senate for the first time in 26 years and ushered in a new conservative era.

## Conservative Era: The Age of Reagan (1980-2001?)

In the election, Reagan promised to restore the nation's military strength, to end "big government", and to restore economic health by an experiment known as "supply-side" economics. Reagan's 1981 program was a collection of programs designed to appeal to his conservative supporters. Inflation hawks were placated by tight controls of the money supply; cold warriors were pleased by large increases in the defense budget; wealthy taxpayers won sweeping three-year tax rate reductions on both individual and corporate taxes; and the middle class saw that its pensions and entitlements would not be targeted. The natural consequence of this policy was enormous budget deficits. Though normally inflationary, tight money policy counteracted the deficit spending and the nation fell into its most severe recession since the Great Depression. When the economy recovered in 1984, inflation had been defeated, and Reagan was re-elected in one of the most lopsided electoral contests in American history.

Reagan's foreign policy was consistently conservative. Early on, he displayed antipathy towards the Soviet Union, labeling them an "evil empire" and called for the development of a ballistic missile defense system that came to be called "Star Wars" after a popular science fiction film. The Reagan administration attempted to oppose Soviet gains by supporting right-wing dictators against left-ist insurgents wherever possible.

Although US military power was substantially increased during the 1980's, both the Reagan and Bush administrations were careful to avoid major military commitments. Their preference was for quick strikes such as the invasion of Grenada in 1983, the air attack against Libya in 1986 and the invasion of Panama in 1989. When Iraq invaded Kuwait in 1990, President Bush lined up an impressive coalition and drove Iraq back out in a war whose ground phase lasted only four days. Democratic President Clinton, who succeeded Bush, followed the same basic model with a successful air war against Serbian forces in Kosovo and a series of air attacks against presumed terrorist targets in Sudan and Afghanistan and against the regime of Saddam Hussein in Iraq.

The election of a Democratic President in 1992 with a Democratic majority in Congress led Arthur Schlesinger Jr. to announce the beginning of a new liberal era. The Republican capture of both houses of Congress two years later (which they have continued to hold) suggests that Schlesinger's announcement was premature. Figure 2.1 also suggests that the Reagan era continued under Clinton. Clinton's first two years were liberal in nature with 9 of 13 events in Appendix A listed as such. Nevertheless, the centerpiece of the Clinton administration's program, his health plan, was rejected. After the 1994 Republican capture of Congress the record in Appendix A turns decidedly conservative showing that a conservative zeitgeist remained.

Another indicator of the essentially conservative nature of politics in the 1990's is shown by Figure 2.3. Under Reagan, who identified big (domestic) government as the problem, non-defense spending averaged 17.3% of GDP, about the same fraction as under Carter. Yet under Carter, domestic spending had risen substantially from the 15.1% it had averaged over the previous four years. Under Clinton, federal domestic spending averaged 17.0% of GDP, slightly lower than under Reagan. Thus, Reagan's goal of halting the growth of domestic government programs, which he accomplished in his own administration, was preserved under Clinton. This was not because the Clinton administration desired this outcome, but because the political zeitgeist would permit no alternative.

# Chapter Three

## Alignment of the political cycle with other cycles

Having described the political cycle, the next step is to look for relations between this cycle and other cycles described in chapter one. Table 3.1 shows several other cycles compared to the political cycle. Secular bull markets (in italics) and secular bear markets are listed in the column marked stocks. Prior to 1861 entire Stock Cycles are listed rather than the secular trends. Recall that whole Stock Cycles correspond to Kondratiev waves so the comparison being made before 1861 is between the K-cycle and the other cycles. Kondratiev upwaves are denoted in bold.

Table 3.1. Liberal-conservative cycles in American politics compared to other cycles[1]

| Type | Political | Stocks [2,3] | Stress [4] | Turnings | Class [3] | Party |
|---|---|---|---|---|---|---|
| L | 1765-1787 | 1770-1787 | 1761-1793 | 1773-1794 | -- | *1788-1800 (Federalist)* |
| C | 1787-1800 | **1787-1815** | *1793-1817 (falling)* | 1794-1822 | 1805-1823 (rich) | |
| L | 1800-1816 | | | | | 1800-24 (Dem-Rep) |
| C | 1816-1828 | 1815-1843 | 1817-1840 (rising) | 1822-1844 | 1823-1843 (poor) | *1824-28 (Nat Rep)* |
| L | 1828-1840 | | | | | 1828-40 (Dem) |
| C | 1840-1860 | **1843-1861** | *1840-1861* | 1844-1860 | *1843-1879 (rich)* | *1840-44 (Whig)* / 1844-1860 |
| L | 1860-1872 | *1861-1881* | 1861-1903 (rising) | **1860-1877** | | *1860-1884 (Republican)* |
| C | 1872-1901 | 1881-1896 | | 1877-1896 | 1879-1896 (poor) | 1884-1894 (Democrat) |
| L | 1901-1918 | *1896-1906* | *1903-1908* | 1896-1917 | *1896-1911* | *1894-1912* |
| | | **1906-1921** | 1908-1919 | | 1911-1921 | 1912-1918 |
| C | 1918-1931 | *1921-1929* | *1919-1931* | 1917-1929 | *1921-1938* | *1918-1932* |
| L | 1931-1946 | 1929-1949 | 1931-1946 | **1929-1946** | 1938-1952 | 1932-1952 |
| C | 1946-1960 | *1949-1966* | *1946-1960* | 1946-1964 | *1952-1965* | *1952-1960* |
| L | 1960-1980 | **1966-1982** | 1960-1981 | **1964-1984** | 1965-1982 | 1960-1980 |
| C | 1980-2000 | *1982-2000* | *1981-????* | 1984-2001 | *1982-1999* | *1980-1992* |

[1] Data to support cycle dates from Alexander, 2002.

[2] Prior to 1815 the K-wave is employed as a proxy for the Stock Cycle. Between 1815 and 1861 whole Stock Cycles (K-waves) are shown. After 1861 secular trends (Kondratiev seasons) are shown

[3] Values in italics represent conditions favorable to conservatives: conservative politics, secular bull market, capital returns rising relative to wages, falling unrest. Bold indicates Kondratiev upwaves.

[4] Stress is based on popular unrest, alcohol consumption and crime indicators (see Alexander, 2002)

Also shown in the table are cycles in social stress, which is defined as the composite of cycles in popular unrest, alcohol use and crime as described in chapter one. A correspondence between unrest and the Kondratiev wave is evident before 1900. Falling unrest (bold italics) correlates with Kondratiev upwaves (bold). After 1900, there is a correspondence between unrest and Kondratiev seasons or secular market trends. Falling unrest (bold italic) is correlated with secular bull markets (italics) and both are associated with conservative eras after 1921.

With the end of a secular bull market in 2000, if the post-1921 correlation between conservative eras and secular bull markets is still valid, a political shift towards liberalism should occur after 2000. Such a shift seems rather counterintuitive with the electoral victories by Republicans in 2000 and 2002, and by the conservative views of President Bush. Of course, the whole purpose of cycle analysis is to spot developing trends before they become obvious. But before I will explore the idea that we have entered a liberal era with the election of President Bush, further investigation into the validity of the proposed cycle timing is warranted.

So far I have shown that the Schlesinger political cycle corresponds to cycles of social unrest and secular market trends over the past 80 years. This correspondence extends over too-short a period for it to be statistically significant. It may be that the cycles just happened to align over the last eighty years and are now in the process of deviating again. If this is the case, there will be no shift from conservative to liberal zeitgeist co-incident with the stock market peak in 2000.

I could have more confidence in my political prediction if I could find other cycles that also align with the political cycle (and which project the same thing as the Stock Cycle projects). Table 3.1 also presents the generational turnings. Since the 1820's, when the modern saeculum emerged, social moment turnings (bold) have been associated with liberal political eras. Assuming that a Crisis turning did begin with the terrorist attack on September 11, 2001, the alignment with the saeculum also supports the idea of a liberal political era beginning in 2001. The problem with using the saeculum to project political cycles is that the saeculum lacks real-time (or close to real time) markers for cycle position. That is, it is difficult to know whether or not we have entered a new turning for quite a long time. Strauss and Howe were able to detect the beginning of the Millennial generation in 1982 nine years after the fact in *Generations*. They identified the 1984 beginning of the recent unraveling 13 years after the fact in *The Fourth Turning*. In that same book they projected the start of the next Crisis turning for about 2005, which is still a year away. As early as 2002, the idea that we began a secular bear market in 2000 was not controversial amongst stock market analysts, whereas the idea that a Crisis era began in 2001 is still hotly contested amongst generation cycle enthusiasts today.

One way to deal with this uncertainty is to apply the 18-year standard generational length as a ruler to measure out elapsed time from earlier cycle markers for which there is no disagreement. Laying out four 18-year rulers from the uncontested beginnings of the previous Crisis in 1929 and eight rulers from the beginning of the Civil War Crisis gives estimates of 2001 and 2004 for the start of a new Crisis. Looking at the most recent turnings of each type, if I lay out three rulers from the beginning of the High in 1946, two rulers from the 1964 beginning of the Awakening and one ruler from the 1984 beginning of the Unraveling, I obtain 2000, 2000, and 2002 as estimates for the beginning of a new Crisis turning. Thus, there are five projections, all clustered in the 2000-2004 time frame, with a median and average value of 2001. The appearance of the unsettling terrorist attack in that same year provides an excellent "trigger event" for dating the start of the Crisis turning.

Direct application of the ruler to the political cycle itself also suggests that the Reagan conservative era had grown "long in the tooth" by 2001. Assuming the Reagan era has extended beyond 2001, this era is longer than all but one of the seven previous conservative eras. Extending the conservative era beyond this year (2004) would make the 43+ year length of the most recent political cycle longer than all but one of the 12 previous political cycles. If the Reagan era continues, it will become the longest cycle in history in 2008.

Even better than using cycle rulers would be some sort of a model that explains why the political cycles occur when they do. One approach might be to look for evidence of class struggle. A number of political struggles in American history have been framed as a battle between the (poor) common man and the wealthy elite. Conservatives tend to prefer to defend the existing (natural) order against ill-conceived change. Such views naturally favor society's economic winners, who have a vested interest in the perpetuation of the existing social order. To the extent that government policy intersects with economic outcomes, periods of relative good times for wealth should align with conservative eras.

Figure 3.1. Cumulative portfolio value compared to actual top U.S. fortunes over time

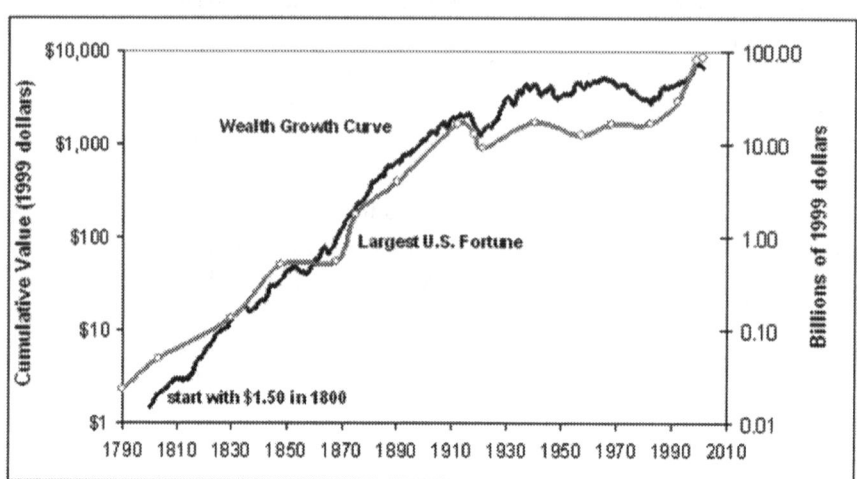

We can look into this idea in greater detail by considering how wealth-holders fare relative to wage earners over time as a function of the political cycle. Wealth holders seek an optimum return on their capital. Periods which feature higher returns to capital relative to returns to labor would be wealth-friendly (presumably conservative) eras.

The return on capital can be estimated using the projected return on a hypothetical portfolio of investments. Before 1971, a mix of 50% stocks and 50% bonds was used. Stocks were represented by an index analogous to that used by Jeremy Siegel in his book *Stocks for the Long Run*. Bonds were long-term government bonds before 1857 and a 4:1 ratio of long-term corporate bonds and short-term debt (commercial paper and t-bills) after 1857. After 1971 a 10% investment in gold was substituted for part of the long-term bond component. This portfolio is designed to reflect an intelligent asset allocation that might be used by an investor attempting to maximize her return in all kinds of markets over the long run. After 1916, the top income tax rate is applied to all interest and dividend income and the top capital gains rate is applied to all capital gains. The portfolio is assumed to be completely turned over once per year with all capital gains and losses taken (and taxes paid) in each year.

Figure 3.1 shows a plot of the growth (in constant dollars) over time of a $1.50 investment in this portfolio in 1800. Also shown is the largest U.S. for-

tune over the same period of time. From 1800 to 2001 the hypothetical portfolio grew some 4500-fold. The largest fortune today (Walton family) is some
4300 times (in constant dollars) that of Elias Derby, the first U.S. millionaire in
the first years of the republic (Phillips, 2002). The shapes of the two curves are
quite similar, both showing the sudden decrease in rate of wealth growth after
1910 due to the onset of income tax and WW I inflation. Both show the level-
ing of wealth growth in the decades after the New Deal, and the resumption of
wealth growth after 1980. The correspondence shown suggests that the hypothetical portfolio does a reasonable job of representing how great wealth has fared
over time.

Figure 3.2. Returns to capital relative to labor over time

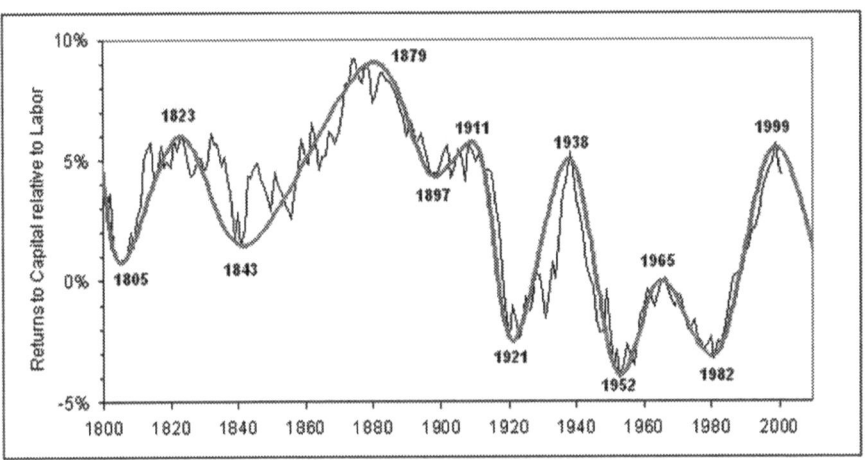

Figure 3.2 shows a plot of returns to capital relative to labor. Returns to labor
are represented by the annual rate of wage increase. The plot is an average of 18
years of annual returns (the current and prior 17 years) minus the average rate of
wage growth over the same period. Thus, a peak in the plot indicates the end of
a "wealth-friendly" period during which capital was faring relatively well. A
trough indicates the end of a "wealth-unfriendly" period during which capital
was faring relatively poorly. The general trends were sketched in by eye and
approximate dating for the cycle given. The trends are shown in Table 3.1 in the
column labeled "Class", with wealth-friendly eras denoted in italics.

Comparison of the Class entries in Table 3.1 with the secular trends under the Stocks column shows that wealth-friendly are roughly co-incident with secular bull markets and wealth-unfriendly eras with secular bear markets after around 1880. This is not particularly surprising, as stock market returns are an important component of capital returns. Wealth-friendly periods are roughly aligned with conservative eras after 1921. The end of a wealth-friendly period in 1999 is consistent with the beginning of a liberal era afterward. However, as the cause of this development is the serious downturn in the stock market beginning in 2000, this measure provides no additional timing information beyond that provided by the Stock Cycle.

A different alignment is seen between the class cycle and party power. Figure 3.3 shows a plot of party power from 1788 to the present. Party power is defined by as the sum of the branches of government controlled by the conservative party or the liberal party. A party power of +1 is scored for conservative party control of the executive branch and +½ for control of one of the houses of Congress. The conservative party is successively the Federalists, National Republicans, Whigs, and Republicans. Similarly, a party power of -1 is scored for liberal party (Democratic) control of the executive branch and -½ for Democratic control of one of the houses of Congress. Power is simply the sum of the scores and ranged from -2 for complete Democratic control of the government to +2 for complete conservative party control of the government. Based on this graph, conservative party and Democratic-leaning periods were determined as labeled in the figure. Control is assigned in two-year allotments beginning in the year of election, not when the term of office actually begins. The reason I use elections is I am trying to track changes in party preference by voters, not partisan application of government power. Thus the 1980 election, which bought a Republican president and Senate and moved party power from -2 to +1 is seen as the turning point, and not 1981, when Republicans actually took power.

Figure 3.3 Party power 1788-present

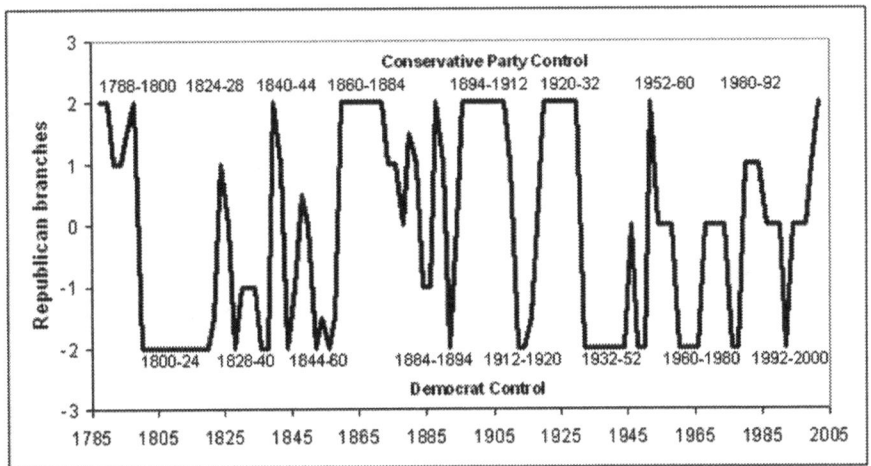

These eras are also presented in Table 3.1. Conservative party eras are in italics. A close alignment between the class cycle and the party cycle is seen between
1860 and 1932. Pro-wealth eras were aligned with Republican eras up to the
New Deal and with conservative eras afterward. Financial wealth was represented primarily through the Republican party up until the New Deal, at which time
the Republican strength was decimated. After the New Deal financial wealth was
represented by conservatives of either party. Similarly, interest groups opposed to
financial wealth were primarily represented by the Democratic party up until the
New Deal and then by liberals afterward. As Table 3.1 shows, party power is not
correlated with the political cycle and electoral returns can say little directly
about whether or not a liberal era has begun.

This analysis of course deals with just economic policy. To the extent that the
liberal/conservative dynamic is economically based we would expect economic
cycles to have an impact on political cycles. Thus we see the Stock Cycle affecting the politics of rich versus poor as described by the class cycle. This class conflict shows up in politics through political party (before the New Deal) and political zeitgeist (after the New Deal). Before WW I political zeitgeist ran independently of class politics and party.

Before the Civil War class politics probably wasn't really relevant, it doesn't
seem to align with either the political zeitgeist or with party. Party power was not

very meaningful before about 1840. Basically, the Federalists were in control up to the election of 1800. Between 1800 and 1860, the party of Jefferson and later Jackson, which eventually came to be called the Democratic party mostly held sway. The exception was two brief periods of dominance by National Republicans and Whigs. But the Democrats of this day behaved like conservatives at times and like liberals at other times and really can't be considered as a consistent entity. Thus, there really wasn't much of a cycle at this time. In any case, there is no evidence for involvement of a class-based cycle in politics before the Civil War.

An involvement of economics in politics before the Civil War can still be recognized. Table 3.1 shows that turnings do align with antebellum political eras. As we saw in chapter one, turnings do have an economic component. One way that economics could be involved in zeitgeist shifts is as a *trigger* for political change. A sudden negative shift in economic fortune can produce a call for political change amongst the electorate. An out-of-favor political party or ideology (if properly organized and presented) can take advantage of this situation and achieve a shift in zeitgeist. If the party or ideology fails, and economic conditions improve afterward, the opportunity is lost and the old zeitgeist can then continue on.

According to the Schlesinger political organization model for political shifts, it is more likely that a shift will be successfully triggered by economic mishap if the challenging party/ideology has been out of favor for a sufficient amount of time for them to have honed their message. The classic example of this is the 1932 election. The Republican's conservative message had been very successful for nearly a decade when the stock market crashed in October 1929. The economic collapse that followed took everybody by surprise and created an electorate willing to change political horses. The New Deal crafted by the newly elected Roosevelt administration was a radical departure from Hoover's approach. The partial recovery from the depths of the Depression in 1933 and the upbeat tone of the new administration created a reluctance to change in 1936 and a new liberal era was born.

To apply this idea to the pre-Civil War era, it is useful to consider the dominant market at this time, land. Figure 3.4 shows a plot of a ten-year average inflation in agricultural prices (see Figure 2.2) and a stylized plot of the land value cycle. Agricultural price trends reflect the "fundamentals" driving land values, much as earnings constitute the fundamentals behind stock values. Periods of upward-trending farm prices should generate favorable conditions for land values. Falling farm prices would be unfavorable. Periods of crashing land values occurred in 1819-23, 1837-41 and 1857-60 (Hoyt, 1970). The trend in agricultural prices turned negative around the same time. The first presidential election that occurred after this downturn is marked by the dashed lines in Figure 3.4. These elections occurred in 1824, 1840 and 1860. Two of these match precisely with the beginning of a new era of political zeitgeist. The 1824 election was the first attempt by the Jacksonians to win power. Jackson actually won a plurality of votes, but was denied the victory. In the next election he did prevail, launching the new era at this time.

Figure 3.4. Trends in ten-year average farm returns compared to the real estate cycle

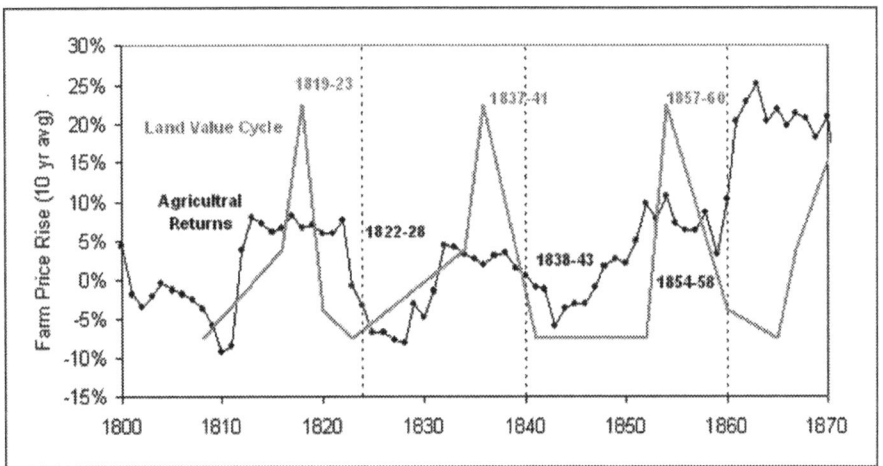

After the Civil War, the land value cycle continued to play a role. The trigger elections defined by it, those in 1876 and 1896, were very close, important elections. Neither introduced a new era of political zeitgeist, however. For the first, the zeitgeist had already turned in 1872. All that might have happened would be a shift towards greater dominance by conservative Democrats, which did happen eight years later. For the second, a shift in political zeitgeist would have accompanied a Democratic victory. The Republican victory served to delay, but not prevent, the shift.

The correspondence between the land value cycle, the saeculum and the political eras in the 19th century shows an involvement between these cycles, but no causative relationship. Shifts in zeitgeist and turning changes occurred around the same time as the economic cycle markers, but could occur before or after. There is no economic determinism here. There are 18-year cycles of social, political and economic behavior that are roughly aligned. The economic cycle length is shown most clearly by the seven financial panics between 1819 and 1929 and the four secular stock market trends between 1929 and 2000, which together define ten economic cycles between 1819 and 2000 that average 18.1±0.8 years in length. The social cycle is shown by the Strauss and Howe dates for the beginning of the Transcendental Awakening in 1822 and the beginning of the New Consciousness Awakening in 1964, that together define two contiguous saecula with average turning length of 17.8 years. The political cycle is shown by the ten Schlesinger cycles between 1828 and 2001, which define an average period length of 17.3 years.

More can be said about the relation between economic, political and social cycles after 1929. At this point they are aligned with the Stock Cycle in such a way that stock bull markets, good times for stock owners (mostly wealthy people), are also times of conservative politics and a relatively calm social scene. A causative relation can be hypothesized. When economic times are good there is less incentive to rock the boat. Such times are thus calmer and favor conservative "status-quo" politics. When times are tougher, people rock the boat; the times feature labor and social unrest; and liberal politics gets a run.

Before 1929 this kind of dynamic didn't seem to happen. Economics was still involved in periodization, but it didn't seem to set the agenda for a given era. Hence, the 1881-1896 secular bear market, which shows up as a bad time for wealth, falls completely inside of a conservative era, that nevertheless saw a degree of dominance by the liberal party. Furthermore, the entire period is a time of rising unrest, yet is a High turning. Moving forward, there is the start of a secular bull market and a Republican era that sees the beginning of the liberal Progressive era.

What seems to be happening in the 19th century is that the concerted action of these cycles creates 18-year periods in which a certain kind of politics is favored. The changeover between these periods occurs either at or around the time of the trigger elections defined by the economic cycle. What kind of period one gets is simply defined by the period before. If a trigger period arrives and the political era had been in progress for a long time, forces arise to change it to the opposite kind of era. If the existing political era has only recently arisen, no change occurs. For example, after the Panic of 1819 ushered in bad times in the early 1820's, there was a "demand" for a new type of politics. Jacksonism arose, was turned back in 1824, but triumphed in 1828. After the Panic of 1837, the next election saw a shift to the Whigs and conservatism. Although the Whig dominance was short-lived, the Democratic policies that followed were also conservative in nature. The Panic of 1857 created an environment for a change as well. The dominant Democrats split and the new Republican party, largely comprised of the old Whigs, but fired by the spirit of abolition, rose to dominance. The next Panic in 1873 saw the change already accomplished. Finally, the aftermath of the Panic of 1893 saw a critical realignment election in 1896, in which the Democratic forces of change were utterly defeated. The political cycle change occurred anyway, but through a different agency altogether.

Changes in political zeitgeist do not march in lockstep with other cycles. An excellent example is the shift from the conservative Gilded Age to the liberal Progressive Era. The Gilded Age had originally arisen from exhaustion from the perceived excesses of the Civil War liberal era. The shift to the Progressive Era did not slavishly follow economic cycles; it was not triggered out of an associated critical election like those of 1828, 1860, 1896 or 1932. Instead, it arose more out the rise of progressive sentiments within *both* parties than with any economically-assisted liberal electoral challenge. There is a school of thought that a new Republican majority has emerged with the elections of 2002. This could well be true; after all, the Progressive Era was accompanied by the rise of a dominant Republican party in 1896. But most proponents of this view have in mind a Republican majority that will follow a conservative agenda. That is, it is an argument for the continuation of the Reagan conservative era. The political cycle argues against the idea that a wave of conservative feeling will power Republicans to electoral dominance for the simple reason that the Reagan era would then have to continue for much longer, destroying the idea of a cycle. If the Republicans are beginning a period of electoral dominance, cycle arguments suggest they will not be following the same sort of small-government conservatism they espoused during the Reagan conservative era.

# Chapter Four

## *Model for the political cycle*

Politics involves repeated contests between coalitions of citizens to advance one set of governmental policies over another. These coalitions are built around interest groups and ideology. An interest group is a collection of citizens united in support or opposition to policy that directly impacts their lives. An example of an interest group would be 19th century manufacturers who supported high tariffs on imported manufactures because it helped provide a higher price for the products of their businesses. Similarly, cotton growers were an interest group opposed to these tariffs because retaliatory tariffs hurt their export business.

A second factor, ideology, is needed to wage political contests. An ideology is a common set of abstract political beliefs held by a group of people. Neither manufacturers nor growers made up a sizable portion of the electorate. They could not obtain their desired policy on the strength of their votes alone. They could do so by allying with other interests and disinterested citizens bound together by a common ideology. Growers cultivated the free trade ideology, which held that tariffs were bad because they force everybody to pay higher prices for the benefit of a few. They are elitist and undemocratic. Manufacturers, for their part, argued that without tariffs, there could be no industrial development. Industrial development would provide a more prosperous future for all Americans, without it, America would remain a backward nation. High tariffs represent progress. Thus a conflict between manufacturing and grower interests becomes a conflict of ideologies: democracy vs. progress.

Ideology often intersects with self-interest, but indirectly. A low tariff meant a larger market for American agricultural output meaning higher prices and more revenue for a farmer's labor. Thus, even small-time farmers could perhaps benefit from lower tariffs, and so they tended to support free trade. Similarly, higher tariffs meant more profits for industrialists, which could lead to more investment and more manufacturing jobs, which could benefit urban workers. High tariffs also meant reduced foreign demand for US agricultural goods because of retaliatory tariffs, leading to lower food prices for American urban consumers. Hence, urban workers tended to hold the industrial development ideology.

Ideologies can be combined into larger, more abstract ideologies that are no longer directly related to self-interest of the individual believing the ideology, and might even be opposed. The concept of liberalism and conservatism that I have discussed in the previous two chapters are examples of these larger ideologies. In this chapter I will present a conceptual model for how the dominant ideology shifts between liberalism and conservatism. The idea of ideology will be related to the paradigm, which I believe is the driver for the modern saeculum.

The first thing to note is the trend. Over time there is a trend towards more and more features of society coming under question by liberals—and then being changed so that future generations of conservatives view them as natural. An excellent example of this is suffrage. When the Constitution was written in 1787 the consensus was that suffrage should be restricted to white men who owned property. Fifty years later suffrage had been expanded to just about all white men. Eighty years later suffrage was expanded to white women, a decade later to Native Americans and thirty years after that to all black men and women. Two hundred years ago the fact that women and blacks had no voice in government was seen as just and natural by both liberals and conservatives. The fact that both groups have a voice in government today is seen as just and natural by both liberals and conservatives. About a hundred years ago conservatives believed that it was natural that women lack the vote. Women were simply too emotionally unstable to vote like men. Liberals at that time believed that women's lack of suffrage was arbitrary; it did not represent a fundamental inability of women to grasp matters of state.

What this means is liberalism and conservatism are relative to each other. The absolute positions taken by either side changes with time, but the relationship of the two ideologies to each other remains fixed. Liberals consistently try to push the envelope, while conservatives resist trends they believe to be dangerous, immoral or just plain wrong-headed. Sometimes their opposition is justified by history; not all ideas that liberals adopt about what is wrong with society have stood the test of time (e.g. Prohibition, Marxism).

The idea of liberalism and conservatism being relative may not sit well with conservatives. Recall that the central task of conservatism is to uphold much of the way things are (or used to be) as right and natural. To do this, conservatives often appeal to an external standard of right to make the case that the way things are (or were) is the way they should be. Hence conservatives will appeal to tradition, to religious authority, and to concepts like natural law to make their case. They will use measured reasoned arguments to argue their case from authoritative tradition or self-evident precepts. Conservatism finds a place for everyone in society and a rational, self-consistent justification for that place. For those whose place is an elevated one, conservatism is a very self-affirming ideology. Even for those who place is lower, conservatism can be an appealing philosophy in a changing world.

## *The ideological dissatisfaction model for the political cycle*

Conservatism is considered the "default" zeitgeist in the model. Liberal eras are considered as deviations from the conservative norm, which decay at a fairly consistent rate. As a result, liberal eras since 1787 are shorter and more uniform in length than conservative eras: 15.3±3.1 years for liberal eras as compared to 18.0±5.3 years for conservative eras. Focusing on just those eras since 18-year generations arose in 1822, the average liberal era length is unchanged at 15.2±3.4 years, while the conservative era is even longer at 19.8±6.1 years. A pair of such eras averages 35 years, close to the 36 years expected for 18-year timing.

Liberals seek to ameliorate the lot of the "disadvantaged" by imposing government on their behalf to change outcomes from what would occur naturally. When the natural process being circumvented is market economics, this intervention is what economists would term rent-seeking. Conservatives generally abhor liberal rent-seeking as unnatural and counter-productive. But rent-seeking isn't only sought on the behalf of the disadvantaged. Often it is sought by the well-connected for personal gain. Rent seeking by powerful conservative interests is particularly corrosive to the appeal of conservative ideology. Conservatives unconnected with the interest seeking the favor generally frown on it.

Liberal eras necessarily involve rent-seeking, which is distasteful to the conservative sensibilities of the majority of the American electorate. As a result, liberal eras end as soon as opposing conservative forces can assemble a case against them. As a result, liberal eras average close to the 15 years Schlesinger maintains is typical for organization of political movements. Once the force of the original liberal impulse is expended, liberal eras shift into conservative eras, sometimes with no effort at all on the part of conservatives (e.g. 1816).

On the other hand, there is no upper limit to the length of a conservative era. Only conservative eras can extend for much beyond the 15-year liberal average. The longest liberal era since 1787 was the 1961-80 liberal era that lasted 19 years. This era was likely extended by disgust over the Nixon scandals and resignation, which temporarily raised the threshold for a liberal-to-conservative shift. Conservative eras show a minimum length similar to that for liberal eras, which reflects the same organizational time factor, but no upper bound on length; the longest so far has been 29 years. Conservative eras switch to liberal eras when the degree of dissatisfaction with conservative rent-seeking exceeds the opposition to liberal rent-seeking for a majority of the electorate. A critical proportion of the electorate begins to look favorably on the liberal ideology and a zeitgeist shift occurs. Human nature mandates that rent-seeking behavior is a constant feature of political life. Dissatisfaction with conservative rent-seeking will tend to rise with the length of the conservative era. Thus, a principal factor controlling the length of the era will be the relative attractiveness of the liberal alternate policies. The more appealing the liberal alternative, the quicker the shift will occur, and the shorter the conservative era.

This model proposes that the reforms suggested by Thomas Jefferson in 1800 and the Civil Rights marchers in the early 1960's were so well-received that their respective preceding conservative eras ended in just 13 and 15 years, respectively. On the other hand, the reforms suggested by the abolitionists were so extreme that one might think the conservative era would have never ended. In this case, however, the liberal reformers were allied with northern pro-business conservatives. The normal conservative support for private property rights (for slaveholders) was fatally weakened. Even so, the 1840-1860 conservative era lasted 20 years, longer than any post-1787 liberal era.

The longest conservative era lasted 29 years. In this case the liberal policies offered over most of the era were particularly unappetizing. The inflationary program advanced by the Greenbackers in the 1870's had no appeal for urban workers or the middle classes. In fact, it smacked of special pleading for farmers. By the 1890's the liberal program under the Populists had expanded to include a number of things urban workers wanted and so the program had much greater appeal, which led to the adoption of populist planks by the Democrats in 1896. The monetary elements of the populist program still worked at cross-purposes, helping one liberal interest (farmers) at the expense of another (labor). Investments had fared poorly over the previous decade (see Figure 3.2) so the middle classes as well as the affluent were not disposed to look favorably upon the inflationary and now quite radical liberal program. Nevertheless, the tipping point was close in 1896 (24 years into the conservative era) when frightened corporate interests funded an all-out effort to defeat Bryan in a close election.

As 1896 was the Kondratiev trough, an inflationary upwave began afterward, which took pressure off farmers and took the wind out of the free-silver sails. What actually bought about a liberal era was a new set of liberal offerings crafted by the progressives. Things like breaking up the great trusts, child labor restrictions, consumer protection laws and direct election of senators were targeted at a narrow elite, and did not discomfit the middle class, farmers or labor.

Another factor that can speed up the switch to liberalism is a perceived gain. The Jacksonian program of national expansion promised gain to a fair chunk of the electorate willing to move to newly opened lands. Figure 4.1 shows a plot of the rate at which the nation grew per 1000 people. The rates were smoothed using a centered 15-year moving average. Also shown are public land sales (Hoyt, 1970) as a measure of land speculative activity, which is tied to the 18-year Kuznets real estate cycle.

This figure shows that pre-Civil War liberal eras saw increases in the rate of national expansion, an example of liberal rent-seeking (at Indian expense). The first such expansion was associated with Jeffersonian liberalism (1800-1816) and was paralleled by rising land sales. National expansion fell during the subsequent conservative era, which also saw the Panic of 1819, following the peak in public land sales in 1818. As described earlier, this panic was politicized by the Jacksonians, who blamed the central bank for the subsequent hard times.

Of particular interest is the next period of national expansion from 1828 to 1845. After the start of the liberal Age of Jackson in 1828, national expansion rose hand-in-hand with public land sales, just as it had during the 1800-1816 liberal period. Land sales peaked in 1836, 18 years after the last peak. The peak was followed by the Panic of 1837. The depression aftermath probably helped bring in the conservative victory in 1840. National expansion continued into the 1840-1860 conservative era, but land sales remained moribund. Before the panic of 1837 national expansion was a liberal welfare program that provided land for landless white settlers and made speculators rich. After 1840, national expansion continued, but nobody was making any money. It was only in 1854, when the Graduation Act slashed the price of public lands by 90%, that money could again be made and this was brought to an abrupt halt by the Panic of 1857.

Figure 4.1 National growth rates and public land sales before the Civil War

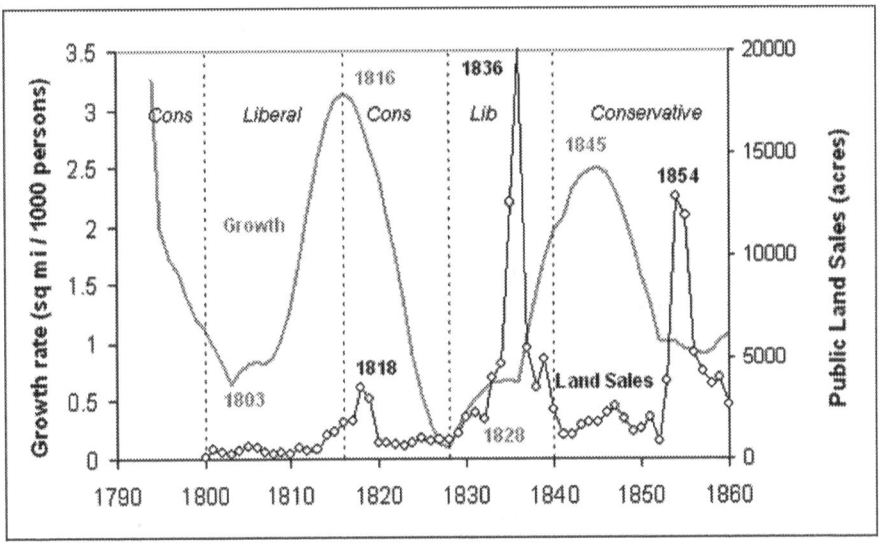

The growth of the abolition movement provided a new interpretation of slavery as an evil system. This new interpretation would see the profitless national expansion under conservative rule as rent-seeking by conservative "slaveocrats" who wished to extend their system into the lands of free men. Democratic liberals continued to support the liberal policy of national expansion, (provision of land to white settlers), they simply demanded it be done in a way that did not promote slavery. One of the responses to this feeling was the Free Soil party which explicitly favored westward expansion, but desired it lead exclusively to "free soil" states. Their standard bearer in 1848 was former president and New York Democrat Martin Van Buren, who had split with his party over the slavery issue.

Figures 4.1 and 3.4 show cyclical rent-seeking by white settlers and speculators in the antebellum era that is correlated with political eras. The correlation suggests a strong component of rent-seeking by both liberal and conservative politicians. In fact, at this early time, liberalism and conservatism could be characterized simply as ideological strategies to try to win votes for one group of interests or another. Although Jefferson's views were surely in part derived from idealism, his supporters probably also relished the opportunity to get rich as the Federalists had done before them. The developing alignment between cycles in land value, turnings and the political cycle in the pre-Civil War era does suggest that *profit* (from speculation in government-provided lands, tariff-protected enterprise, or taxpayer-supplied interest payments) was a driver for the cycle. Each cycle appeared to end 4-6 years after excesses of profit-seeking led to discontent and a desire to change horses. Hence Jackson was challenging Adams six years after the 1818 peak in land sales, the Whigs swept to power four years after the 1836 peak in land sales and Lincoln was elected six years after the 1854 peak.

Just before the Civil War, ideology began to mature. The liberal and conservative sides ceased to be mere collections of opposing interests trying to obtain rent-seeking for their side and bound by a loose sense of ideology. Slavery was the overarching issue that bound disparate interests together. The Republicans, a hodgepodge of conservative and liberal interests, were able to forge a common identity defined by the slavery issue. Later, as Radical Republicans pushed for black suffrage, they became the party of civil rights. Republican conservatism became an ideology in which Jeffersonian libertarianism was combined with high tariffs, national projects like government subsidy of railroads, and Jacksonian expropriation of native lands for distribution to whites (homesteading). Later, when the frontier closed this last policy switched to expropriation of resources from native peoples in foreign lands to American business.

Modern liberalism as an ideology was slower to develop. Jeffersonian libertarianism increasingly served the interests of the elite and so became unsuitable as an ideology for the ordinary citizen. The interest-based politics that I have described as liberal (Greenbackism and Populism) was too unpopular to be a replacement for Jeffersonian liberalism. The emergence of progressivism really was the birth of the modern liberal ideology. Interestingly, the first new liberal ideology (abolitionism and its postwar incarnation as black civil rights) remained part of the conservative party (Republican) ideology. Similarly, it was a Republican Congress that passed women's suffrage. Thus, democracy, the last Jeffersonian concept still consistent with modern liberalism, was not part of the liberal party canon. This explains how a racist like Woodrow Wilson could make a fine liberal Democrat in the early twentieth century.

In the early 19th century, the 18-year land cycle had underlined the cycles of self-interested rent-seeking that were the stuff of politics and helped impress the 18-year timing. By the mid-nineteenth century a coherent ideology had been developed around slavery, which was adopted by the conservative Republican party. After the war, a fully formed conservative ideology emerged. By the end of the century a liberal ideology was also emerging. These two ideologies would battle for dominance in the 20th century, launching political eras of one type or another when the public grew tired of the other ideology. The timing of these switches remained at the 18-year length of the previous cycles. They continued to follow economic cycles, but the Stock Cycle rather than the Kuznets cycle. Unlike the Kuznets cycle, which delivered a boom and bust in each political era, the Stock Cycle delivered a boom during conservative eras and a bust during liberal eras. It is possible that rising stock markets and the prosperity they imply made it easier to tolerate conservative rent-seeking. When times were not as good, such rent seeking was less tolerable and the resistance to liberalism was lowered.

The most extreme demonstration of the ideological dissatisfaction mechanism was the zeitgeist shift in the early 1930's. Here it was economic catastrophe that led to a collapse in support for conservative ideology and a demand for change that might bring relief. It shows how the Stock Cycle can produce such massive dissatisfaction with present ideology that the alternate ideology is preferred. The 1918-1931 conservative era was one of the shortest. There was hardly time for public disgust with conservative rent-seeking to build and besides the most egregious of such behavior had happened early in the cycle under Harding. There was no attractive set of liberal policy alternatives to conservatism that had been advanced by the end of the 1920's; political debate in 1928 and even 1932 was quite sterile. After 1929, the world fell apart and conservatives seemed to think everything was fine. The electorate, perfectly aware that things were not fine, put in the liberals.

## *Interaction of the political cycle with economics*

The New Deal changed another dynamic between the various cycles, although it did not change the basic mechanism of the political cycle. In order to deal with the Depression, the liberal response was to increase spending as if the nation was at war. This was called Keynesian "pump priming". Had it been implemented more aggressively, as in Germany and Britain, the US would have probably been lifted out of the Depression as these other nations were. Instead it required the massive expenditure of WW II to do the job. Nevertheless, the experience of the Depression and WW II created an expectation that the Federal government would now watch over the economy as part of its job. I call this the beginning of the regulated era of the national economy.

One effect of government economic regulation was that economic cycles began to conform to political cycles. The clearest example of this is the four-year cycle in the stock market. Before the New Deal there was a short economic cycle called the Kitchin cycle (Kitchin, 1923) that reflected changes in the inventory of durable goods (Furfero, 2000). The Kitchin cycle was responsible for all of the ordinary business cycles (and bull and bear markets) for nearly half a century before 1929. During that time it had run at an average length of about 40 months. After the start of the New Deal this 40 month cycle was replaced by a four year cycle that was aligned with the four year election cycle. The correlation between election and business cycles is thought to reflect government economic management designed to help re-elect the party in power. Fourteen of the 21 bear market troughs since 1933 fall in non-Presidential election years (Alexander, 2003). The probability of this arising from chance is 0.001%, providing strong evidence for an election-linked cycle in the stock market

Another more subtle effect is the longer Stock Cycle (and Kondratiev cycle) after the New Deal. Prior to 1929 secular market trends had averaged 13 years in length. This length implies a 26 year length for the Stock Cycle (Kondratiev wave) and a 52 year length for the Kondratiev cycle. Since 1929, the average length of the secular market trend has been 18 years (the same length as the political eras, with which it is aligned). Not only did the Kitchin cycle lengthen from a 40 month "economic length" to a 48 month "political" length, but the 13-year secular market trend increased to an 18-year length corresponding to the political cycle. This means the Kondratiev cycle has increased in length from ~53 years where it had been for centuries to a new 72 year length aligned with the political cycle.

Up until the New Deal, the Kondratiev cycle had corresponded to spending for "peak wars" spaced two biological generations apart (see chapter six). The K-cycle was aligned with a long-term cycle in international politics whose timing element was the ~26 year biological generation. Keynesian economics created the possibility of massive deficit spending without waiting for the next "peak war". Such spending could be used to combat cyclical depressions. It would also necessarily alter the Kondratiev cycle because this cycle had previous been intimately related to the war-spending cycle. A peacetime spending cycle would be expected to follow cycles of domestic politics, i.e. the liberal-conservative cycle, and so adopt a new 18-year timing element. And this is what happened. After 1929, secular stock market trends increased in length to 18 years in accordance with the political era, leading to a 72-year Kondratiev cycle.

Evidence for this lengthening effect is seen in the 1997 capital gains tax cut. The purpose of this measure was to promote capital gains, that is, rising asset prices. By 1997 the stock market had already reached valuation levels similar to 1929. The secular bull market that began in 1982 should have ended in that year, but with the boost provided by the cut in capital gains taxes the bull market continued for three more years, making the secular bull market a full 18 years long. A purely political act extended the bull market. Another example was Federal Reserve policy in the wake of the 1987 Crash, which likely held off a recession, lengthening the already long 1980's expansion and permitting a rapid recovery for the stock market.

Similarly, the Kondratiev interest rate peak in 1981 was caused by the Federal Reserve's war on inflation, which sent interest rates to their highest levels in history. This policy crushed inflation by throwing millions of people out of work in the biggest recession since the Depression. It was a conservative policy made possible by the shift to conservatism around 1980. It also happened 35 years after the 1946 interest rate low that marked the start of the Kondratiev upwave that ended in 1981. The Federal Reserve waited until more than 30 years after the upwave began to take action against inflation. Inflation did not suddenly become a problem in 1981. Inflationary pressures had started to rise in the late 1960's, culminating with President Nixon's suspension of gold convertibility in 1971, which ended the gold standard for good. One would expect the authorities to have acted by 1971 (25 years after the Kondratiev trough) to defend the gold standard. Doing so would be consistent with the "natural" length of the Kondratiev cycle (1971 was about 50 years after the last K-peak in 1920). They did not act for the political consequences of doing so would be severe. Lengthening of the cycle in the 1970's reflected political forces.

By 1981 it had been clear that inflation was a major problem requiring a solution. The sort of solution that was required (and employed) dealt out pain disproportionately to working class Americans and was not something that was consistent with liberal politics. Thus, effective action against inflation had to wait until the liberal era ended. This begs the question; why did the liberal era last so long? Why did it not end in the early 1970's when inflation was first raising its head? One answer is shown in Figure 4.2. Until 1973 real wages had been growing at a steady rate and unemployment had been low. Inflicting hard times on Americans when they were accustomed to good times was political suicide, regardless of what was happening with gold reserves.

After 1973 real wages first stagnated and after 1978 started to fall in real terms because of high inflation. Unemployment was trending higher. Now ordinary people were experiencing pain that could plausibly be blamed on inflation. It was no longer just a problem for the financial elite. The nation was now ready to accept the conservative solution, which did end inflation but did nothing to help real wages or employment. But by this time the country was in a conservative era and the public no longer believed government could do anything about the economy anyway.

This begs the question of why did things stay so good for so long? The answer can be found in the decision to have "guns and butter" in the late 1960's and expansionary policy afterward. That is, tax cuts were combined with increasing spending to fund both the Vietnam War and the Great Society programs. As a result, deficits were allowed to rise during a time of prosperity (previously deficit spending had been practiced only during times of economic weakness). This action, combined with the very low interest rates prevalent at the time, was very stimulatory. The result was the longest expansion in history up to that time. A tax surcharge was implemented in 1968, which eliminated the deficit in 1969 and probably also ended the expansion.

Figure 4.2. Wages, unemployment and the deficit as a % of GDP 1950-2003

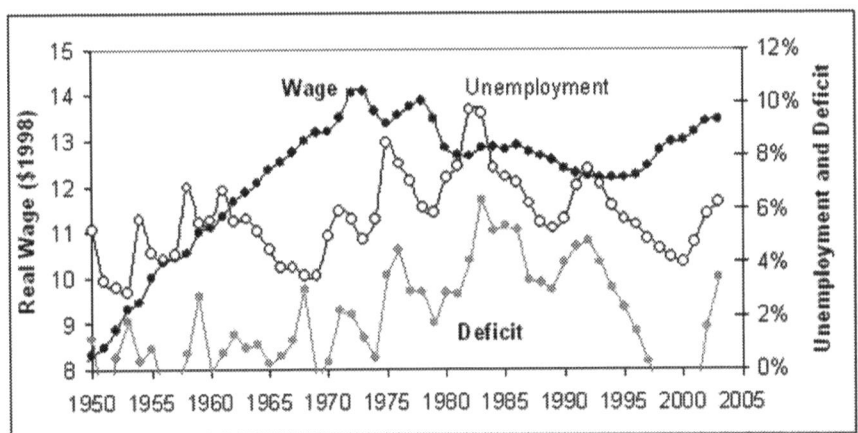

Activist economic policy enjoyed widespread popular and professional support in the early 1970's as expressed by President Nixon's famous proclamation, "We are all Keynesians now". Federal Reserve Chairman Arthur Burns was part of a political, intellectual, and popular environment that expected government to control the economy. During the 1970 recession, Congress and the President relentlessly pressured Burns for an expansionary policy, and he complied.

These actions added a few years onto the long 1960's expansion and tempered the severity of the 1970 recession leading to a powerful recovery. The objective of Keynesian policy was to promote jobs and wage growth at the expense of possibly higher inflation. That is, it was liberal in nature. Liberal economic policy served to extend the postwar boom beyond when it would have ended naturally. The stock market was not fooled by the expansionary policy, however. An inflationary secular bear market began in 1966, in the middle of the 1960's economic expansion. The market had detected that the fundamentals underlying the postwar growth were nearing exhaustion, that is, Kondratiev summer was nigh. Liberal Keynesian-style government economic management was able to continue the good times for seven more years after 1966 at the expense of hard times afterward, which discredited Keynesian economics for the next political era. This action served to delay the Kondratiev peak for as much as 10 years later than it would have occurred had Eisenhower-style conservatism still been in fashion in the 1970's.

But conservatism was no longer in fashion, the country was deep in a liberal era, which explained the popularity of activist economic policy. Prior to 1933 it would not have mattered what sort of era the nation was in, the economic cycles would operate at their natural lengths. But since 1933, each era has promoted policies designed to maintain economic support for continuation of the present era until political exhaustion sets in. The result has been a lengthening of the economic cycles and alignment of them with the political cycle.

The economic cycle feeds back on the political cycle. The best example is how the Great Depression ended New Era conservatism, but stagflation also played a role in weariness with 1970's liberalism. The hangover from the tech bubble collapse will likely play a role in exhaustion with conservatism in this conservative/liberal transitional period. In the postwar era, because of the expectation that government take responsibility for the economy, economic conditions are of considerable importance to politicians. Attempts are made through policy to enhance economic outcomes in a fashion that aids re-election chances. Thus, the four-year cycle and the alignment between the Stock Cycle and political eras has emerged.

Economics can act as a catalyst in changing the political zeitgeist by lowering the threshold for acceptance of liberal ideas during conservative eras or increasing exhaustion with liberal politics during liberal eras. The alignment between serious recessions and zeitgeist shifts described earlier shows the results of this catalytic effect. The conservative victory in 1896 despite a serious recession shows that economic hardship alone cannot produce a shift to a liberal zeitgeist, if liberal policies are sufficiently distasteful. On the other hand, an attractive alternate ideology can readily produce shifts without any serious economic downturn, as the 1946 and 1960 political shifts show.

## The paradigm model for the generational cycle

Having described a model for political change and shown how economic cycles can reinforce the model, I now come to the action of the generational cycle. Prior to 1820 it was the biological generation that provided the timing for long-term social, political and economic cycles. The first political era was a liberal era that ran from 1765 to 1787. At 22 years, it was longer than any other liberal era; the next three liberal eras averaged 13 years in length. This era was the time of the Revolutionary Crisis social moment and was a typical example of rising stress associated with the Kondratiev downwave (see Table 3.1). It was longer than subsequent liberal political eras because it was associated with a turning that was still governed by generations of biological length. The ideological dissatisfaction mechanism for the political cycle only became active after 1787.

After 1820 turnings became shorter than biological generations, only 18 years long on average. They became aligned with the Kuznets cycles as opposed to Kondratiev waves. They continued to be aligned with political eras, with liberal eras and social moments running concurrently. The mechanism I propose for the 18-year turning is the *paradigm*. A paradigm is a model of the world that people use to make sense of the social, political, economic and cultural world they inhabit. It is similar to an ideology, except it incorporates a lot of real-world experience and is less theoretical and idealistic. A person's behavior is influenced by his paradigm, which acts as sort of a road map for life. A paradigm is largely based on personal experience and everyone's is different.

According to the paradigm model, social, economic and political trends, as the collective behavior of society, reflect its collective paradigm. A collective paradigm is the "average" paradigm of a group of people and as such, many differences between individual paradigms "cancel out" leaving those features that are widely shared. Social trends reflect the changing nature of commonly held ideas in individual paradigms. For example, the decline in crime rates over the last decade represents a change in attitudes towards crime amongst young people. Although there are still plenty of individual paradigms that hold that crime does pay, they are less common than in the past. The collective paradigm of the young today is less pro-crime than in the past and as a result they engage in less crime

A group of people sharing a common collective paradigm due to the proximity of their birth years is called a generation. What separates generations is the influence the past has had on their collective paradigm. A younger generation only knows the recent history through which they have lived, whereas an older generation's paradigm is influenced both by the recent past and an earlier time that they know but the younger generation does not. Current events and the recent past will necessarily affect the paradigms of the young adults more strongly than those of older adults.

When recent history has been particularly eventful, the impact on paradigms is heightened. A momentous era in history (i.e. a social moment) will strongly imprint the paradigm of those coming of age during the social moment, binding them together into a common generational outlook. People coming of age just before and just after the social moment will fall into different generations. The recent film *Seabiscuit* illustrates this concept. One of the film's characters, the jockey, was raised in an erudite, professional household. His course in life was changed dramatically by the Depression. In ordinary times he would have gone to college, gotten a professional job and led a comfortable middle class life. But the Depression wiped out his family's finances and he was left on his own to make his way as a small-time pugilist and eventually as a jockey. The common experience of coming of age in the Depression and WW II shared by those born in the 1908-1924 period is what binds them together as what Tom Brokaw calls "The Greatest Generation" and Strauss and Howe call the GI Generation.

Generations formed by the experience of coming of age during a social moment are called dominant generations, while those coming of age during the other turnings are recessive. Thus, the GI generation is a dominant generation while the Silent generation that follows them is recessive. Similarly, the Baby Boom generation who came of age during the tumultuous "New Consciousness" Awakening is similarly dominant while the subsequent Generation X is recessive. It is the paradigms of dominant generations that shape the political zeitgeist.

For example, the GI generation was tempered by the fire of depression and war. They knew that long-term unemployment was something that can just happen to people through no fault of their own. In addition, the experience of the GI's with the New Deal and WW II had created faith in government as part of their collective paradigm. It is not difficult to see why an electorate dominated by the GI generation would not countenance sacrificing jobs for financial rectitude in the early 1970's. As a result of the effect of this dominant generation on policy, the Kondratiev peak was delayed and the cycle lengthened to fit the generational saeculum.

The experience of the dominant Boom generation coming of age during the tumultuous New Consciousness social moment from 1967-1980 created a very different view of government in their collective paradigm. Between these dates they saw the nation defeated in war for the first time, a president resign in disgrace, and an economy seemingly running out of control with something called stagflation. The first wave of Boomers (1943-60) came of age protesting the government while the last wave came of age with a popular president proclaiming "Government is the problem". The Boomers came to put their faith in the free market and in private action rather than public action. That is, their paradigm is opposite from that of the GI's. Indeed, their paradigm was formed by their counter-reaction to policy reflecting the GI paradigm.

Free market economics and a respect for financial values became part of the Boomer paradigm. A soaring stock market was seen as evidence for the correctness of the 1980's economic policy. The 1990's added falling interest rates to a soaring stock market to support this view. This paradigm resulted in policies that favored financial and corporate elites as shown by the enormous rise in executive compensation of the 1980-2001 conservative period. These policies culminated in the 1997 capital gains tax cut and the stock market insanity that followed.

The speculative excesses of the 1990's boom did not just happen. They reflected the Boomer paradigm, with assent from the Silent generation (1925-42), whose portfolios were the chief beneficiary of Boomer cheerleading. Stock market valuation at the end of the secular bull market in 2000 was the highest in history. In contrast, the 1966 peak, when GI paradigms ruled, had the lowest valuation of all secular bull market peaks.

Thus, the conservative policies of the 1980-2001 conservative era were supported by the paradigm of the Boomer generation, just as the liberal policies of the era before was supported by the GI paradigm. Paradigms cannot be the whole picture as neither generation's paradigm was dominant at the time of the zeitgeist shift in 1980. In general, zeitgeist shifts are best explained by the ideological mechanism described earlier. The paradigm model is most useful for explaining why political eras, once established, continue on. For example, the 1992 recession could have acted as a catalyst for zeitgeist shift. Disgust over years of Republican deficits fired the third party bid of maverick candidate Ross Perot, who laid responsibility for the deficit and a broken economy at the feet of the Bush administration. A Democratic president was elected for the first time in 12 years. Not only that, but a Democratic Congress was elected as well. All this looks a lot like a shift to a liberal zeitgeist in accordance with the ideological dissatisfaction model. But the shift did not occur as shown by the "Contract with America" landslide Republican victory in 1994.

The paradigm model has the Boomers as too young in 1992 for the shift to have occurred. Historically, liberal eras begin when the older of the two dominant generations reaches an average age of about 50 (see Table 4.1). In 1992 the Boom generation ranged from 32 to 49 years in age, with an average of about 40, suggesting a shift in 1992 would be about ten years early.

The paradigm model holds that social moments occur because of generational momentum. Dominant generations (like the GIs and Boomers) form their initial paradigms during social moments. Recessive generations (like the Silent and GenX) form their initial paradigms during the turnings between social moments. Dominant generations see their paradigms supported by events in the turning after the social moment that originally created them. Dominant generations tend to lend their support to the recessive generation in power during that turning. As a result, these eras are fairly quiescent and conservative. They have their dark side. The policies carried out during these quiescent turnings end up setting the stage for trouble later on, which brings about the social moment. For example, bubble friendly-policies in the 1920's and 1990's created a major stock market collapse, which produced problems in the next decade.

Dominant generations' paradigms are *not* well suited to deal with events in the next turning. This is why they are social moments. The paradigm of President Hoover's Missionary generation (also dominant) did not support the types of market interventions that could have averted catastrophe. Thus, they were not done and the result was catastrophe. In the wake of the collapse of the 1990's bubble, authorities have avoided the mistakes made the last time. History has provided new problems, however. One is the virulent new strain of international terrorism made all too real on September 11, 2001. Existing paradigms are inadequate for this problem, just as those of Hoover's generation were for the problems he faced. There are other problems lurking as well, as will be discussed in subsequent chapters.

Table 4.1 Dominant generations and liberal eras

| Dominant Gen (type) | Birth Years | Liberal Era | Age at start (avg) |
|---|---|---|---|
| Awakening (idealist) | 1701-1723 | 1765-1787 | 42-64 (53) |
| Republican (civic) | 1742-1766 | 1800-1816 | 34-58 (46) |
| -- | -- | 1828-1840 | -- |
| Transcendental (idealist) | 1792-1821 | 1860-1872 | 39-68 (53) |
| Civil War (civic) | 1839-1856 | 1901-1918 | 45-62 (53) |
| Missionary (idealist) | 1874-1890 | 1931-1946 | 41-57 (49) |
| GI (civic) | 1908-1924 | 1960-1980 | 36-52 (44) |
| Boom (idealist) | 1943-1960 | 2001- | 41-58 (50) |
| Average | -- | -- | 40-60 (50) |

As described earlier, the pro-government Keynesian paradigm of the GIs, successful during the 1950's and 1960's, led to stagflation during the 1970's which helped produce the free-market and financial orientation of the Boomer paradigm, which lent support to the Reagan conservative era. This pro-government GI paradigm had also supported the anti-communism crusade of the 1950's conservative era and the result had been peace. In the next decade it led the nation into the disastrous Vietnam War, which created the anti-government bent of the Boomer paradigm.

So far I have discussed social moments as being similar in that they are times of liberal zeitgeist in which a dominant generation's paradigm collides with reality. There are two kinds of social moments, spiritual awakenings and secular crises, and they have important differences. The liberal eras for awakenings tend to begin because the liberal offering is seen as attractive. That is, the start of liberal eras in 1828, 1901 and 1961 all occurred because the proffered liberal ideology, Jacksonian democracy, progressivism and civil rights, was seen as an improvement over the conservative ideology of the time. Conservatism was not discredited. In contrast, the liberal eras for crises begin because the conservative ideology is discredited. Thus, virulent opposition to British taxes at the start of the Revolutionary liberal era resulted in rejection of colonial rule. The Civil War era was about utter rejection of slavery. And the Depression discredited Republican laissez faire in favor of New Deal action. None of the liberal ideologies adopted in the Crisis eras were chosen by the electorate because of their appeal. In two of the cases, these ideologies hadn't even been formulated at the start of the era.

Because we are now entering a Crisis turning, the paradigm model would have the shift in zeitgeist reflect a loss of credibility for conservative ideology as opposed to a positive affirmation of what liberals are offering. The fact that the zeitgeist did not shift to liberal under Clinton means that no attractive policies arose. But the anti-government nature of the still-rising Boomer paradigm ruled out any action on the part of the government from being viewed as favorable.

It was the pro-government paradigm of the GIs that permitted governmental action on civil rights to be viewed favorably. The paradigms of Civic generations like the GIs, are open to improvement reflecting their pragmatic "can-do" ethos. Similarly, the paradigm of the Civil War Heroes was also open to the experimentation of the Progressive era. In contrast, the paradigms of Idealistic generations like Hoover's Missionary generation and Lincoln's Transcendental generation are based on inflexible principles and are more rigid. They tend to break and be replaced rather than be reformed. Thus, appropriate action on the issues surrounding the secular crisis is not taken by conservative leadership and their ideology becomes discredited, paving the way for the liberal era. This argument suggests that the Boomer-supported conservative ideology of the 1980's and 1990's will also break rather than bend.

## The cycle position in economic, generational and political cycles

The interaction between economic, political and generational cycles produces a tighter alignment between the cycles after 1929. Before 1929 the standard deviation of the political cycle was 35% of its average length. Secular stock market trends showed a standard deviation that was 36% of their average length. Finally, turning length showed a standard deviation equal to 21% of average length between 1822 and 1929. Since 1929 the standard deviation of the political cycle has been 20% of its average length, that of the secular market trend 10%, and turnings only 8%. This greater precision in the modern era suggests that trend changes in stocks and turnings should be identifiable using the 18-year "ruler" within a precision of two years today as compared to 3-7 years before 1929. Trend changes in politics should be identifiable to within 4 years as compared to up to 7 years before 1929.

We can apply this idea to the current era. It was obvious in 2002 that a new secular market trend had appeared. The terrorist attack on September 11, 2001 has likely begun a Crisis turning only 13 months after the S&P500 peak on a monthly average basis. The political situation is not yet clear. History suggests a roughly two-thirds probability that we will know whether the zeitgeist has shifted by the end of 2004.

Assuming that a liberal era is beginning, the model can be applied to provide insight into what sorts of issues and factors will be important in this transition. Adopting the 2001 date for the shift in era, this gives the length of the previous conservative era as being not less than 21 years long (and it could be longer if the shift in eras ends up being later than 2001). According to the ideological dissatisfaction model this length means that liberal ideology failed to make an appealing argument in the 1990's for a switch to liberal politics as, for example, the civil rights movement did. The closest thing to a rights movement today is the gay rights movement, which lacks the sort of graphic imagery provided by the civil rights movement. Barbara Ehrenreich (2002) in *Nickel and Dimed: On (Not) Getting By in America* has written a modern version of *How the Other Half Lives*, but I note that it was eleven years after the publication of that book before the Progressive era began. Although one can certainly argue that a liberal case for redress of social ills is growing it has hardly met the level of public interest as previous efforts.

The generational paradigm model argues that a successful case for liberalism will not be made. That is, the beginning of the progressive era, which ended the longest conservative era, is not a good model for today. The generational paradigm model would have us look at past liberal eras with respect to dominant generations for guidance. Table 4.1 lists all past liberal eras and the associated dominant generation. With one exception, each liberal era begins around the time a dominant generation turns 50, as the Boomers did in 2001. The exception is the Age of Jackson, for which the Republican generation was too old. However, the 50 rule even held for this social moment as the analysis in Table 4.2 shows.

Table 4.2 uses the paradigm idea to create generations out of social moment turnings and liberal political eras. The first column in the table contains composite liberal era/social moment turnings created by averaging together the dates that define each. The next column contains the dominant generation whose paradigm was developed by living through this era. The first entry in this column is the Republican generation of Strauss and Howe that came of age during the Revolutionary Crisis turning. The spacing between the liberal Revolutionary Crisis era and the Republican generation is about 25 years, implying that paradigms of people in their mid-twenties were forged during the Revolutionary period. For the rest of this column, the birth dates for the generation whose paradigm was created in the period on the left was obtained by subtracting 25 years from the dates of that period. Column 3 shows the actual dominant generations from Table 4.1 for comparison to the ones inferred by application of the paradigm model to political eras/social moment turnings. The correspondence is pretty good, except there is an additional generation, created by the 1800-1816 liberal era.

Table 4.2. Appearance of the 18-year cycle after the Revolution

| Liberal Era/ Social Moment | Paradigm- Based Gen | Dom. Gen. from Table 4 | Turns 50 | Next Liberal Era | Associated Turning |
|---|---|---|---|---|---|
| 1769-1791 | 1742-1766 | 1742-1766 | 1804 | 1800-1816 | -- |
| 1800-1816 | 1775-1791 | -- | 1833 | 1828-1840 | 1822-1844 |
| 1825-1842 | 1800-1817 | 1792-1821 | 1859 | 1860-1872 | 1860-1877 |
| 1860-1875 | 1835-1850 | 1839-1856 | 1893 | 1901-1918 | 1896-1917 |
| 1898-1917 | 1873-1897 | 1874-1890 | 1932 | 1931-1946 | 1929-1946 |
| 1930-1946 | 1905-1921 | 1908-1924 | 1963 | 1960-1980 | 1964-1984 |
| 1963-1982 | 1938-1957 | 1943-1960 | 1998 | 2001- | 2001- |

As shown in Table 4.1, a liberal era arises when a dominant generation reaches age 50 on average. The next column in Table 4.2 shows the year in which the paradigm-based generations reach age 50. Right about this time a liberal era develops with its associated social moment turnings as shown in the rightmost two columns. This period then creates a new dominant generation and the process continues.

I started with the Republican generation, born 1742-1766. This generation's paradigm was created by the experience of living through the Revolutionary War Crisis, which itself was created by the war-mechanism of the Kondratiev cycle. The Republican generation is the first dominant generation to come to power (turn 50) after the birth of the American nation. Until democracy was established there was no way for dominant generations to express their paradigms; the saeculum followed the war model.

When the Republicans came to power, the result was the Jeffersonian liberal era (1800-1816), which created a new politically-defined paradigm amongst young people. Young Jeffersonians in the 1800's resurfaced as middle-aged Jacksonians in the 1820's and 1830's. The rise of the Jacksonians helped bring about the Transcendental Awakening, and this rise was necessary for the Awakening to develop properly. Thus, while the war model for the saeculum would have the Transcendental Awakening turning begin shortly after the end of the War of 1812, it did not. Instead the postwar period was the politically quiescent "Era of Good Feelings". The Jeffersonian generation (1775-1796) had not yet come to power. When land values collapsed at the end of the Kondratiev plateau in 1819 and agricultural prices began a long slump (the fall from plateau), people were hurting, but the paradigms of those in power then did not provide any way to understand what was happening. The Jeffersonian generation's anti-elite paradigm did provide an actionable explanation for the hard times, but they were as yet too young to act in 1819. As they aged into power, they became Jacksonians, and a liberal era got underway. The turning change in 1822 can be thought of as a compromise between the old Kondratiev forces that would begin the Awakening around 1814 and the new political forces that would have the Awakening begin with the liberal era around 1828.

The combined Transcendental Awakening turning and Jacksonian liberal era influenced the paradigm of another dominant generation, with approximate dating 1800-1817. This generation collectively turned 50 around 1859, close to the 1860 start of the Civil War Crisis turning and liberal era. The generation whose paradigm was shaped by this liberal era/social moment turned 50 around 1894.

An awakening turning and liberal era followed shortly after. The process continues down to the present era as shown in Table 4.2.

The nature of this mechanism has a social moment/liberal era creating a generation that was born 25 years earlier. This era is then followed by another liberal era/social moment that begins 50 years after the mid-point of that generation. This means that the spacing between liberal eras/social moments should be (25 + L/2) years, where L is the typical length of a liberal era/social moment. That is, L is (paradigm-based) generation length. Because there are two social moments in a saeculum, the length of a saeculum should be equal to 50 + L years. Since a saeculum contains four generations of length L, 3L should be equal to 50. This implies L is about 17, which is quite close the 18-year length of post-1820 generational trends.

Tables 4.1 and 4.2 support the timing for a liberal shift underway today. This shift will be caused by a loss in faith in conservatism. The Civil War precedent shows one way this can happen from a "culture war" that has gone out of control. Although Straus and Howe call the recent conservative period the Culture Wars it is hard to see how the issues contested in the modern culture wars would lead to a conflict and liberal victory as in the Civil War. In the Civil War case the issue was slavery, which was a long-standing practice that had only recently become widely seen as wrong. Thus, an entrenched, well-financed conservative elite was defending it. When they lost, the victory went to the liberal side making the 1860-72 era a liberal one. The modern culture wars about abortion, gun rights, affirmative action, school prayer etc. are mostly about reaction against liberal policy changes made since the last awakening. That is, they are basically conservative in nature. It is unlikely that culture war issues will be the issues about which this liberal era is established.

The Revolutionary precedent involved a schism in the British Empire. A geographically discrete portion of the Empire decided it would be better off with out the central government and rose in revolt. A modern version of the Revolution might be some kind of tax revolt. Superficially, this idea seems plausible. The 1765 tax revolt was against taxes to pay for the recent French and Indian War. Because the colonists had no representation in Parliament, the colonist position was that they had not authorized the debt and thus could not be expected to pay for it. These taxes would go to pay wealthy European financiers who had loaned the money for the war, no benefit would come to the colonists. In a way, it was tribute from subjects rather than taxes paid by citizens. This is one reason the colonist's cause in the Revolution is considered liberal.

A modern tax revolt would curtail expenditures on government services received by taxpayers. As Federal taxes are paid disproportionately by the wealthy, most people receive more back than they pay into government. Thus tax revolts tend to serve the interests of the elite rather than the common man and so are a conservative cause today. A tax revolt is an unlikely issue over which a shift to liberalism would occur. It would seem the Revolutionary precedent is not very useful either.

The Depression precedent has a number of similarities to today. Both the 1918-1931 and 1980-2000 conservative eras featured "new era" bull markets and a brash, "in your face" popular culture. Our current position in the Kondratiev and Stock Cycle is analogous to the early 1930's. A third similarity is our position in the hegemony cycle (see chapter six). At both times the US had triumphed over a Great Power challenger for global dominance (Germany in 1918 and the USSR in 1991). But the fundamental political issue of the last Crisis, the failure of the US to act as hegemon, is not the problem today. In the War on Terror, the Bush administration appears to be making a reasonable effort to live up to the requirements of hegemony. The problem this time is the shortage of leading sectors (chapter five), which was not a problem for any of the three previous American secular crises.

Because the position in the Kondratiev and War cycles today correspond to those for the last Crisis, there will be some similar themes. The various cycles can be used to provide insight. Each cycle rules out certain classes of events. For example, the stock market will not make a sustained new high in constant-dollar terms for at least 20 years. Other combinations of events are inconsistent with logic. Under a weak economy following a long conservative era the electorate will not tolerate increases in conservative rent-seeking. Thus, although the hegemonic cycle indicates that imperialistic practices may be successfully implemented today, to the extent they reflect rent-seeking, they will be unsuccessful politically.

American attempts to install client regimes in Afghanistan and Iraq should be successful from a geopolitical standpoint (no foreign power will object in an effective manner to stop it, and with a bit of cajoling, might actually help). But they could easily fail politically, (e.g. the Bush administration loses the 2004 election) if these actions are revealed to reflect conservative rent-seeking. Dissatisfaction over rent-seeking would be exacerbated by a weak economy.

The Bush foreign policy in Afghanistan and Iraq has been justified as self-defense. Afghanistan was justified by the need to destroy Osama bin Laden and his terrorist network. For Iraq, it was the need to disarm Iraq of its weapons of mass destruction (WMD). Both operations toppled an unfriendly regime, but Osama bin Laden and his organization remain intact and no WMD were found in Iraq. Neither of these objectives is discussed anymore, yet US troops remain in both countries with a new objective of nation building. These observations suggest to some that self-defense was not the only purpose for action in Afghanistan and Iraq and may not even be the primary purpose, suggesting that rent-seeking by interests close to the administration (e.g. oil and oil service companies) may be a factor here. If the "nation-building" operations go well his won't matter, but if things go poorly the ideological dissatisfaction model suggests a shift away from Bush-style conservatism would be the result. This would likely be manifest as a Bush defeat in 2004. This issue will be discussed in greater detail in chapter seven.

# Chapter Five

## *Economic cycle issues*

In this chapter, I will discuss the economic situation to be expected based on the Kondratiev and other economic cycles. The Kondratiev cycle is a wavelike movement in commodity prices, interest rates and certain production indices that was first described in detail by the Russian economist Nikolai Kondratiev. Figure 5.1 shows this wave in the PPI commodities price index from 1785 to the present (in gray). Wave troughs appear in 1787, 1843 and 1896 and wave peaks in 1814, 1864 and 1920. These waves are spaced an average of 54 years apart. The latter half of the period between wave peak and trough (the downwave) generally showed severe depressions. Kondratiev, writing in the 1920's, forecast that a depressionary crisis for capitalism would begin as the post-1920 downwave progressed, a forecast consistent with Marxist theory of the self-contradictory nature of capitalism (and favorably received by his Soviet masters). Kondratiev also maintained that capitalism would emerge from the crisis restructured and stronger than before, a forecast much to the distaste of Joseph Stalin. Kondratiev went to the gulag for his belief and died there in 1938. Kondratiev was right about both the depression and the eventual recovery. His hypotheses received a favorable reception from Western economists in the 1920's through 1940's, particularly from Joseph Schumpeter.

Figure 5.1 The Kondratiev cycle in terms of prices

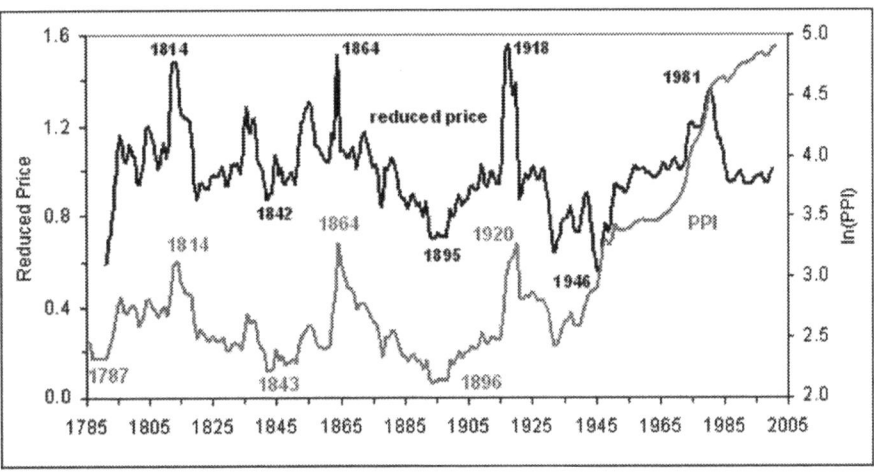

After 1932 the Kondratiev wave in prices seems to have stopped happening. Prices began a nearly monotonic rise after 1932, which still continues. Interest in Kondratiev waves amongst economists faded away after the 1940's, partly because of the disappearance of the price wave. I developed a tool to track the progress of the Kondratiev cycle after 1932 when it no longer could be seen from the raw price data. This tool is the reduced price; its construction is described in my book *The Kondratiev Cycle*. Reduced price gives an indication of what prices would do in the absence of monetary stimulation by government deficit spending and Federal Reserve manipulations. When applied to price data before 1933, reduced price shows the same Kondratiev up and down waves as do the unmodified prices (see black line in Figure 5.1). But when applied to data after 1933, it shows the K-cycle movements that lie "underneath" the raw price behavior that has been distorted by monetary simulation.

In this way, a Kondratiev trough in 1946 and a peak in 1981 can be seen where neither is visible in the raw data. Prices (before 1933) and reduced prices match up with the Kondratiev cycle as defined by interest rates. Figure 5.2 shows that peaks in interest rates in 1812, 1861 and 1920 lined up with peaks in prices in 1814, 1864 and 1920 and with peaks in reduced prices in 1814, 1864 and 1918. Troughs in prices/reduced prices are also times of low interest rates although the exact bottoms do not align as precisely as the peaks. I note that the interest rate bottom in 1946 and peak in 1981 line up very well with the reduced price trough in 1946 and peak in 1981. This suggests that the reduced price transformation is capturing the same dynamic after 1933 that was noted by Kondratiev in the 1920's.

Figure 5.2 Reduced prices and interest rates 1791-2000

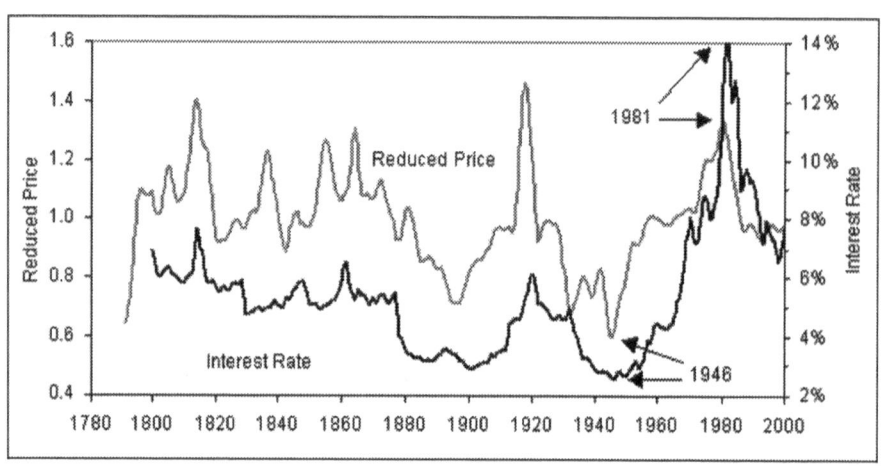

I also learned of another tool, *ex ante* real interest rates, which provides additional insight into monetary behavior over the K-cycle. The *ex ante* real rate is a measure of investors' collective beliefs about the future value of money. It cannot be measured directly, but it can be inferred from measurable data using complex mathematical models that are beyond my understanding. One such model, based on a regime switching framework (Hamilton, 1989) and implemented following Garcia and Perron's (1995) three-state interest rate model, has been recently proposed by Kolari and Viale. This model shows investor beliefs about future real interest rates shifting between high-level (4-6%) and low-level (negative) regimes. Figure 5.3 shows a plot (in gray) of the quarterly *ex ante* real rate obtained from Mr. Viale, which has been smoothed using a running nine-quarter moving average.

Shown with the *ex ante* real rates in Figure 5.3 is the reduced price. Both plots are labeled to identify key structural features of the Kondratiev wave. The period of rising prices between the Kondratiev trough and the Kondratiev peak is the Kondratiev upwave. Conversely, the decline from the peak to the trough is the downwave. Examination of the downwave in reduced prices shows a sharp drop after the Kondratiev peak and then a leveling-off. This level spot in the reduced price plot is sometimes called the *plateau*. The plateau ends with a second precipitous drop, the *fall from plateau,* which bottoms at the *vortex* (Berry, 1991). Figure 5.3 shows plateaus ending in 1818, 1872 and 1929, with a fourth possibly ending now. The vortices following the fall from plateau for the first three Kondratievs occurred in 1820, 1878 and 1932. Following the vortex, there is a temporary rise in prices to an intermediary peak, before prices fall still further to the Kondratiev trough. I call this peak the "deflationary growth peak" or DG-peak in accordance with Berry's (1991) nomenclature. DG-peaks occurred in 1836, 1881 and 1937 (a second larger peak in 1942 due to the start of WW II could be considered the DG peak instead of 1937; I prefer 1937 as it was more endogenously generated).

Figure 5.3. Reduced price and *ex-ante* real rate 1790-present

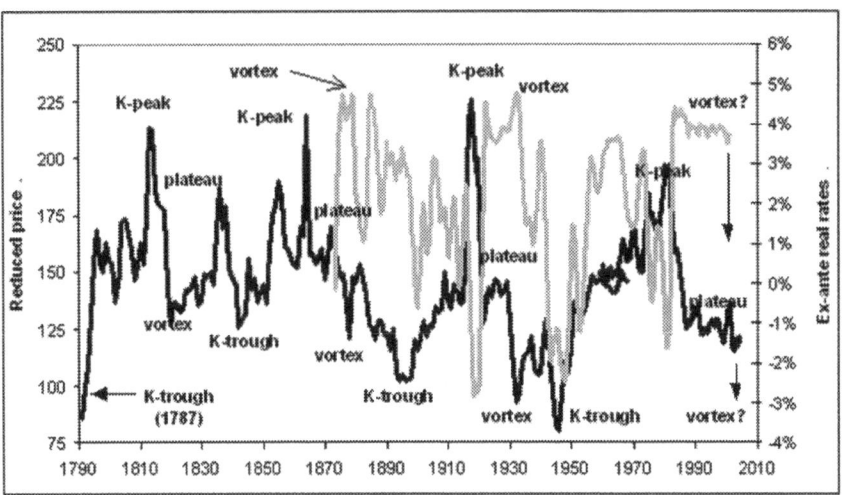

The key feature of interest in the *ex ante* real rate is the rise from a trough close to the K-peak to a broad plateau. This plateau ends right around the time of the vortex in reduced prices, and then falls to a trough roughly around the time of the DG-peak. This trough is followed by another even deeper trough, which denotes the K-trough.

Examination of reduced price in Figure 5.3 shows the K-peak in 1981 and then a decline over 1981-86. Since 1986 reduced prices have been largely flat, suggestive of a plateau. *Ex-ante* real interest rate shows a major trough in 1980, corresponding to the K-peak and then a sharp rise over 1980-83. Since 1983 it has remained in a flat zone. The shape of these graphs shows what looks very much like a plateau period beginning in the mid-1980's. At the beginning of 2001, reduced prices began a major move downward that looked like it might be the start of the fall from plateau. Since the beginning of 2002 this fall has stalled out, however. As of February 2004, the reduced price has yet to dramatically move to lower levels. Such a drop would confirm the fall from plateau. If the past pattern continues, *ex-ante* real rate should begin to fall again at some point in the near future and eventually reach a vortex bottom, which is still in the future.

The picture portrayed by Figures 5.1 through 5.3 suggests that our current position in the Kondratiev downwave is between the end of the plateau and the vortex. This corresponds to the 1929-1932 period in the last cycle. Politically, this is significant because it suggests that 2004 might be a critical realignment election like 1932 was. Previous critical elections are often given as 1800, 1828, 1860, 1896, 1932 and 1968 (Phillips, 1990). The next election in this sequence would be 2004.

Figure 5.4. Relative price changes after 2000

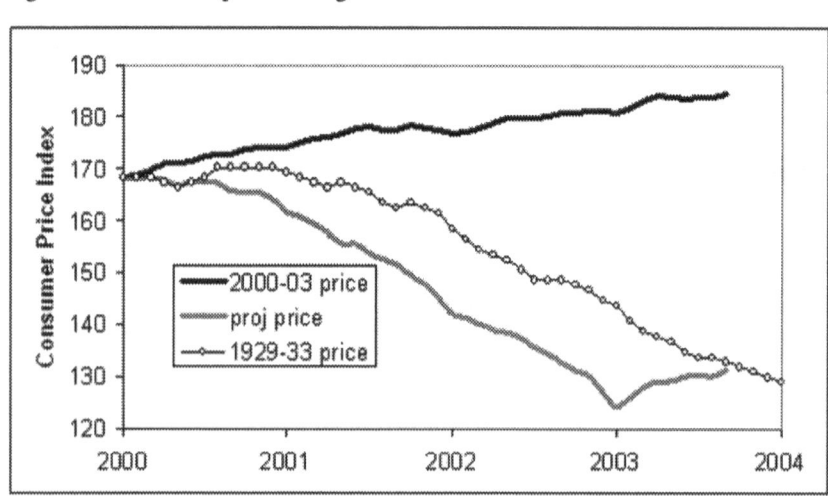

Comparison to the last cycle also suggests that we should be in a depression now. A detailed examination of the fall from plateau era in the early 1930's and today reveals some key differences between then and now. The most important difference, and a large factor in why there is no depression this time, is deflation. Figure 5.4 shows the consumer price trend since the beginning of 2000. Also shown (scaled to today's price) is what happened in 1929-1933. Finally a hypothetical price trend is shown, which corresponds to what would likely have happened if monetary stimulation had played out after 2000 like it did after 1929.

Figure 5.5 shows a plot of the changes in money supply after 2000 compared to that after 1929. M3 and M2 money are plotted as a ratio to their values in 2000 and 1929, respectively. Also shown is the accumulated federal deficit after the stock peaks in 1929 and 2000 as a percentage of the GDP in those years. Federal deficits behaved similarly. Both periods began with a surplus, which quickly turned to deficit. Actual policy was different. President Hoover raised taxes in order to balance the budget, while President Bush cut taxes. Large deficits appeared in both cases, and so federal fiscal stimulus was not greatly different between the two eras. The big difference has been in money supply. Money supply has continued to grow after 2000, while it contracted sharply after 1929.

The effect of this change in money supply can be put into the reduced price model and used to project what prices might have done if money supply had fallen after 2000 like it did after 1929. The money supply profile shown in Figure 5.5 was used to calculate the projected price profile in Figure 5.4. This analysis suggests that it was the decrease in the money supply after 1929 that led to sustained deflation and (probably) the Great Depression. This idea is not new; it is basically the same idea advanced by Friedman and Schwartz (1963) in their classic *Monetary History of the United States*.

Figure 5.5. Money supply and deficits after the 1929 and 2000 stock peaks

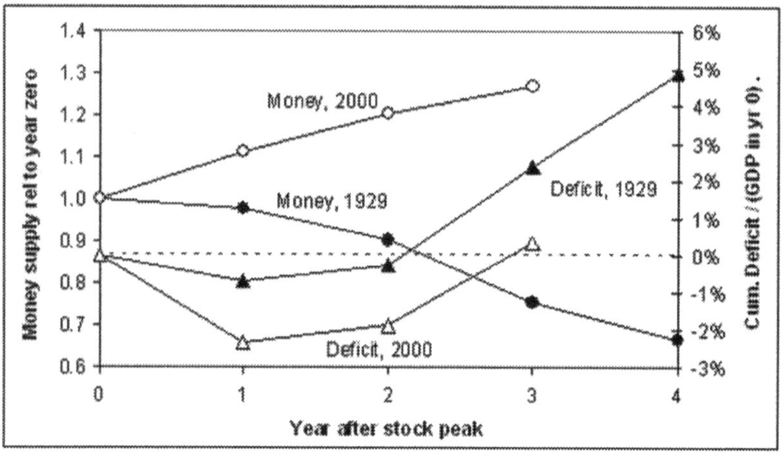

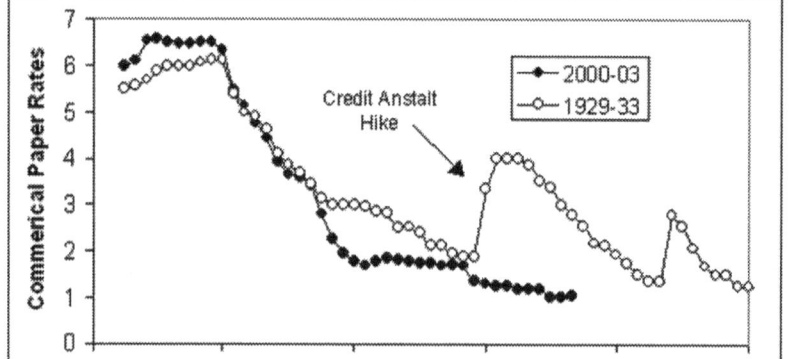

Money supply is one of the economic variables that comes under the purview of the Federal Reserve. The key tool of Fed policy is manipulation of short-term interest rates. Figure 5.6 shows the effects of Fed policy over the periods of interest in terms of commercial paper rates, the cost of short-term loans for businesses with good credit.

Figure 5.6. Commercial paper rates after the start of easing in 1929 and 2000.

Figure 5.6 shows that the Fed cut interest rates dramatically in response to the bursting of both the 1929 and 2000 stock bubbles. The Fed cut more deeply initially in 2000 than they did in 1929, but by two years after the crash the cumulative declines were similar. The most dramatic difference was the sharp hike in rates due to the devaluation of the pound in the aftermath of the Credit Anstalt bankruptcy in 1931, which was discussed in chapter two. The story told by the previous three figures suggests that the persistent low rates established by the Fed after the collapse of the stock market and the September 11, 2001 terrorist attacks has helped prevent the deflationary outcome of the last fall from plateau.

Figure 5.7. Deficit spending and reduced price trends

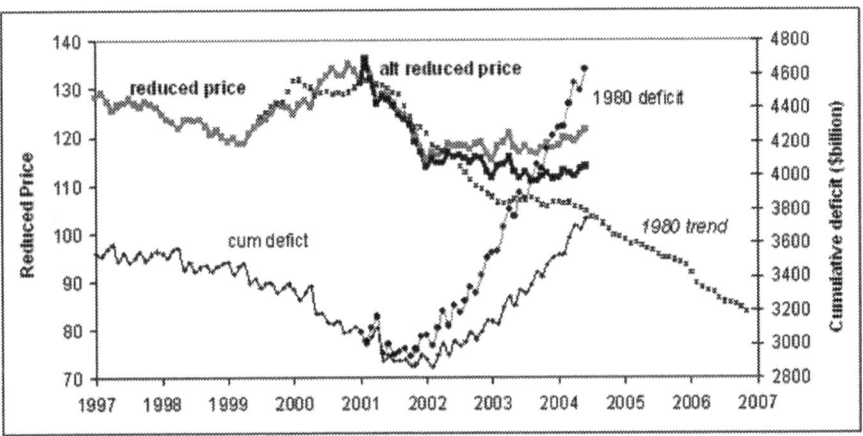

It has also served to delay the fall from plateau itself. Analogy with the fall to plateau over 1981-1986 suggests that a sustained decline in reduced prices will happen as the large Federal deficits continue. Figure 5.7 shows a plot of cumulative deficit from 1997 to the present. Also shown as "1980 deficit" is what that cumulative deficit would look like had President Bush run deficits of the same relative size as President Reagan. Such a cumulative deficit is coming, but it is not here yet. As shown in the figure, the cumulative deficit is lagging far behind where it would be with Reagan-style deficit spending. Also shown is the reduced price plot, which shows more or less a continuation of the plateau. Reduced prices have yet to move strongly below the levels at which they have been since the mid-1980's. Figure 5.7 also shows an alternate version of reduced price (called alt reduced price) that employs the alternate deficit trend obtained by using Reagan deficits instead of Bush ones. Had deficit spending developed as quickly under Bush as it did under Reagan, a lower trend in reduced prices would be evident that is closer to how reduced prices actually fell in the early 1980's. This trend is shown in the figure as the 1980 trend.

Because sustained high deficits are on the way, it is expected that reduced prices will start to move downward in the near future and by the end of 2005 will be significantly below the levels of the plateau. This development would then confirm the fall from plateau and establish Jan 2001 as the end of the plateau. Assuming this comes true, one can tentatively conclude that we have passed through the treacherous early stages of the fall from plateau era without serious economic mishap. We have not been completely unscathed. Today (February 2004) there is much talk about the jobless recovery, the term used for the employment-based recession that is still in progress.

With this, the Kondratiev-informed analysis of the present economy is complete. The findings are summarized as follows: 1) Today is cycle analogous to 1929-1933. 2) There was no depression because of timely action by the Federal Reserve. 3) The growing Federal debt will grow much larger; there will be no serious inflationary consequences from the deficit, just as there were not for the 1980's deficits. 4) Adverse economic consequences have not been avoided, merely spread out.

There is more that can be said by consideration of the *ex-ante* real rates and other economic cycles, but these effects will play out in the *next* recession and are not relevant for today. I now wish to turn to another economic aspect of the Kondratiev cycle that has relevance as a possible great defining issue for the coming liberal era. This aspect is the innovation wave or leading sector model for economic growth.

The Harvard economist Joseph Schumpeter attempted to build a theory for the Kondratiev cycle (Schumpeter, 1939). His view was that the Kondratiev cycle reflected the impact of periodic concentrated bursts of innovation that transformed the economy. He coined the term "creative destruction" to describe how the creation of new industries and superior business methods in existing industries partially replaced (destroyed) old industries and methods. These new industries and methods can be described as a "new economy" that both adds to and partially replaces the old one. The development of a new economy creates new areas of economic activity (leading sectors) that did not exist previously. These leading sectors can then grow strongly for decades as they spread into every part of the economy. This growth can occur readily because resources formerly employed by the old economy are freed up by productivity enhancements resulting from the adoption of new methods. The period during which this replacement takes place is the Kondratiev downwave.

Schumpeter's writings are rather difficult to follow. Since his time, his ideas have been extended and formulated in different ways by a number of researchers. Gerhard Mensch (1979) has developed a more explicit model for Schumpeterian innovation that fits an *innovation wave* into the Kondratiev wave. The business consultant and popular financial writer Harry S. Dent (1993) describes a four-step economic cycle that is similar to Mensch's model for the Kondratiev wave, but with a number of new twists. I have developed my own version of the innovation wave. I will use Dent's terminology and conceptual scheme as it is easy to understand, but will come up with a somewhat different detailed formulation, and will use it to discuss one of the important issues facing the nation over the next decade or two.

## *The Product Innovation Cycle*

New products and technologies typically go through three stages of growth: an innovation phase, a growth phase and a maturity phase. These three stages are shown graphically by what is called the S-curve, an example of which is shown in Figure 5.8. The vertical axis in the figure refers to the degree of market penetration for the new product or service. Dent defines the period during which penetration increases from nothing to 10% as the innovation phase of the S-curve. The period from 10% to 90% penetration is called the growth period. Finally the period from 90% and up is termed the mature phase.

Figure 5.8. The S-curve for market penetration of new products

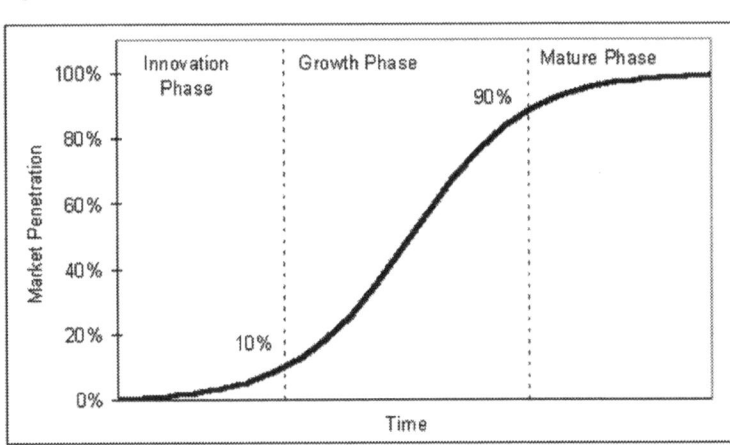

## The Innovation Cycle for the Economy

Dent extends the S-curve concept to the entire economy. He notes that some periods are richer in entrepreneurial activity than others. One such period was around 1900, when many of the common mass-market brand-name products like Gillette razors, Coca-Cola or Ford automobiles were introduced. Following Mensch, Dent calls the innovations associated with these entrepreneurial periods "basic innovations" because they form the base for a new economy. He calls periods when the basic innovations appear the innovation phase for the new economy. The period around 1900 would then be the innovation phase for the "mass-market" economy.

Initially, the basic innovations operate on the margins of the old economy. Gradually, they are adopted by a small, but significant, fraction of the economy. At this point, the nascent new economy enters its growth phase, during which the basic innovations move into the mainstream. Thus far, the development of the new economy follows the same S-curve as does the development of an individual product or technology with an innovation period (0-10% adoption) followed by a growth boom (10-90% adoption).

The next phase of the developing economy is the shakeout. The shakeout occurs when many firms, attracted by the opportunities of the growth phase, enter the business and encounter increased competition as the market becomes saturated. Saturation results in increased price competition and business failures. The shakeout is a period of deflation and depression. It is also a period of innovation, but of a different sort.

During the shakeout, new technologies and products are developed that complement and improve upon the basic innovations. Dent calls these "maturity innovations". Of the many new-economy companies that existed at the end of the growth period, only a few successfully employ the complementary maturity innovations and products to win the competition and survive the shakeout. Following the shakeout, a new growth period begins, during which improved versions of otherwise mature products are sold. This period is called the maturity boom.

Another way of describing the maturity boom is the growth phase of the mature-type innovations. In this concept the shakeout is the overlap of the basic innovation's mature phase and the mature innovation's innovation phase. Figure 5.9 shows a diagram of this concept. The S-curves for the basic and maturity innovations are combined into a composite "double-S" curve that Dent calls the innovation wave.

Figure 5.9 Diagram of Dent's innovation wave

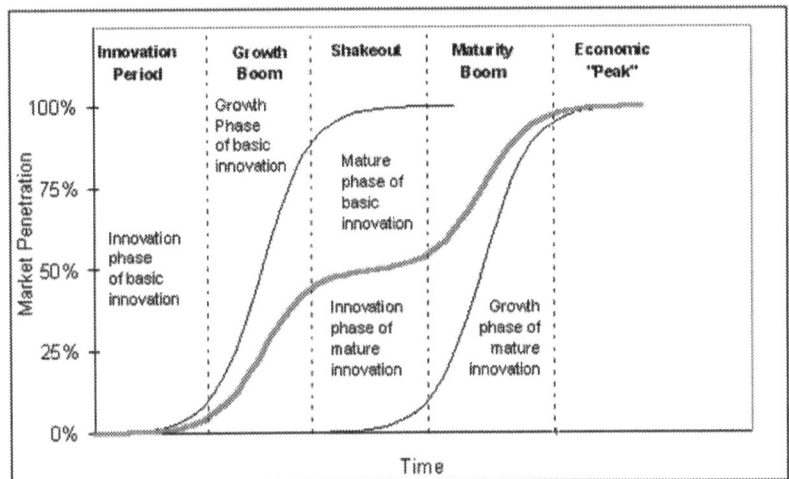

# *Detailed assignment of historical innovation wave to the mass-market economy*

I will start with what Dent called the mass-market economy that got its start around 1900 as described earlier. He implies that there was a growth boom during the 1910's and 1920's that was associated with what he calls "the Henry Ford generation" and a maturity boom from the late 1940's to late 1960's that was associated with what he calls "the Bob Hope generation". Although he introduces the concepts of the S-curve and the "four stroke" economic cycle, he never explicitly applies it the previous economies. So I will try to do so here.

First I identify important industries that became important during the first three quarters of the 20th century. The scheme shown in Figure 5.9 can then be applied by compiling S-curve data for these industries. The market penetration for a particular product can be expressed as units possessed or consumed per household or worker. Alternately, the growth in importance of a new industry, measured in terms of units of output per unit of GDP, can be used as a measure of extent of growth or "penetration" into the economy. Once a number of innovation waves for industries characteristic of a particular economy have been obtained, they can be averaged together to produce a composite innovation wave that defines that economy. The growth boom and maturity boom are obtained by analogy to Figure 5.9. By looking at the timing of the basic innovations underlying that economy, an estimate for the innovation period can be obtained as well. I will start by applying these ideas to a couple of single industries. Then I will move on to the entire economy.

My first example is broadcasting. Broadcasting started with the development of voice radio transmissions in the 1906-1917 period. The first radio station went on the air in 1917 and the dominant radio company of the era, Radio Corporation of America, (RCA) was spun off from General Electric in 1919. RCA and others developed television during the 1926-1939 period. The first US television station went on the air in 1939 and the first major television network (NBC) was established by RCA in 1941. A second wave of growth in broadcasting got underway after this. Figure 5.10 documents this entire process by showing the growth in the percentage of households with radio and television sets over the 1922-1995 period. The growth curves for radio and television resemble Figure 5.8. In Dent's terminology, radio would be the basic innovation and television would be the maturity innovation. If I average the two curves together I get the broadcasting innovation wave, which shows an initial growth period up to around 1940, a flat period to 1946 and then resumption of the trend upwards to a peak in 1970. By analogy to Figure 5.9, I denote the radio growth phase as the growth boom and the television growth phase as the maturity boom. The flat period in the composite curve (1940-46) becomes the shakeout and the second growth period (1946-1970) the maturity boom. By analogy with Figure 5.8, I denote 1925 as the beginning of the growth boom, since that is when the composite growth curve reached 10% of its 1940 level, giving 1925-1940 as the broadcasting growth boom.

Figure 5.10. The innovation wave for the radio and television 1922-1995

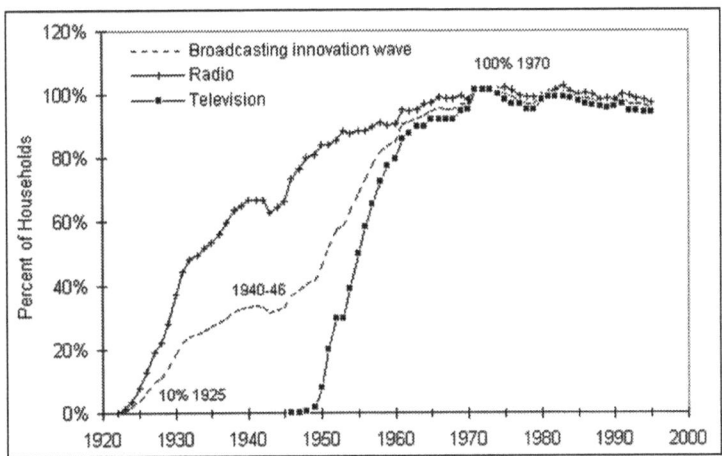

I will now try to apply this idea to the auto industry. Figure 5.11 shows two kinds of growth curves. The first is a plot of the total automobile fleet divided by the labor force. This shows the growth of the auto in terms of market penetration. The shape of this curve is shaped much like the prototypical innovation wave in Figure 5.9. There is a definite growth boom up to 1929, a shakeout from 1929 to 1949 and a maturity boom from 1949 to 1973. Unlike with radio and TV, where the basic and maturity innovations reflect distinct products, the maturity innovations for the car reflected such things as automatic transmission, power features and the interstate highway system, which made using a car for personal transportation more appealing to a broader spectrum of the public.

The second curve in Figure 5.11 shows the annual production of vehicles per million 1996 dollars of GDP. This ratio indicates the importance of the auto industry relative to the economy as a whole. As a major economic element, the auto industry peaked in the 1920's. The initial growth in the auto industry reflects the growth boom in market penetration. I can date the beginning of this growth boom as the point when production of cars reached 10% of the importance it would have at the growth boom peak in 1929. Thus, I would date the growth boom for the auto as 1907-1929, the shakeout from 1929-1949 and the maturity boom from 1949-1973.

Figure 5.11. The innovation wave for the automobile

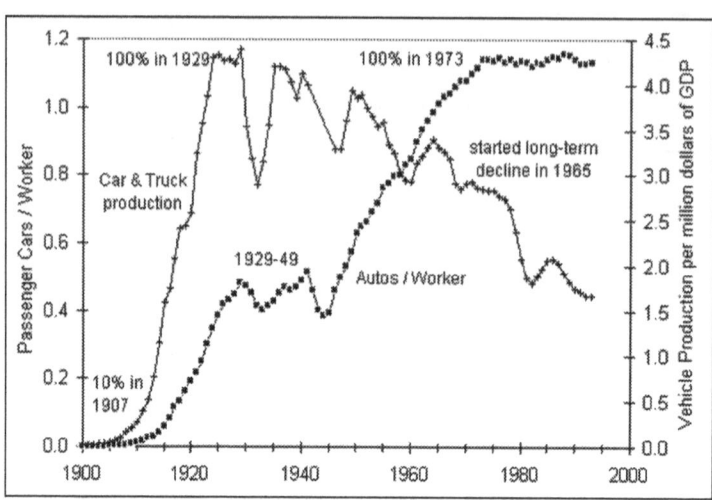

These examples illustrate the use of market-penetration and production-volume curves. Market penetration curves are those that measure the extent to which the innovation has saturated a market. The broadcasting innovation wave is of this type. Volume curves use the levels of physical output relative to GDP (in constant dollars) as a measure of the extent to which the new economic activity has diffused throughout the economy. It measures the economic penetration of a new innovation (or cluster of innovations). To apply this graphical analysis to a whole new economy I obtain as many curves of either sort as I can for important industries in that economy and average them together to produce a composite curve. This curve is then inspected to obtain the dates of the growth boom, shakeout and maturity boom.

Innovation waves were constructed for nine industries and estimates for growth and maturity booms obtained (see Table 5.1). Production volume data were averaged together to form a composite output curve. Similarly, market penetration data were averaged into a composite innovation wave. Both curves are shown in Figure 5.12.

These curves show the growth of the mass-market economy in terms of both output (economic penetration) and market penetration. The output curve shows a broad top in 1973-1979 after which it starts to decline. The market penetration curve shows a plateau after 1973 indicating that the mass production economy industries as a whole saturated their markets after 1973. With these observations, I would put the "economic peak" or end of the maturity boom of the mass-market economy in 1973. The output curve shows a dip from 1937 to 1944 that can be interpreted as the shakeout, making 1944-1973 the maturity boom. For the start of the growth boom I use 1908, when output reached 10% of the 1937 level.

Table 5.1 Mass-market economy industries

| Industry | Innovation Date | Growth Boom | Maturity Boom |
|---|---|---|---|
| Airline | 1909 | 1951-1967 | 1967-1987 |
| Broadcasting | 1917 | 1925-1940 | 1946-1970 |
| Education (Secondary) | -- | 1910-1940 | 1940-1970 |
| Electric Power | 1882 | 1905-1941 | 1945-1976 |
| Electric Appliances | 1901 | 1909-1937 | 1943-1960 |
| Motor Vehicles | 1893 | 1907-1929 | 1949-1973 |
| Petroleum | 1859 | 1889-1937 | 1943-1956 |
| Synthetic Fibers | 1884 | 1921-1936 | 1943-1978 |
| Telephone | 1876 | 1907-1929 | 1945-1980 |
| **Composite** | **1895** | **1908-1937** | **1944-1973** |

Figure 5.12 Composite innovation waves for the mass-market economy

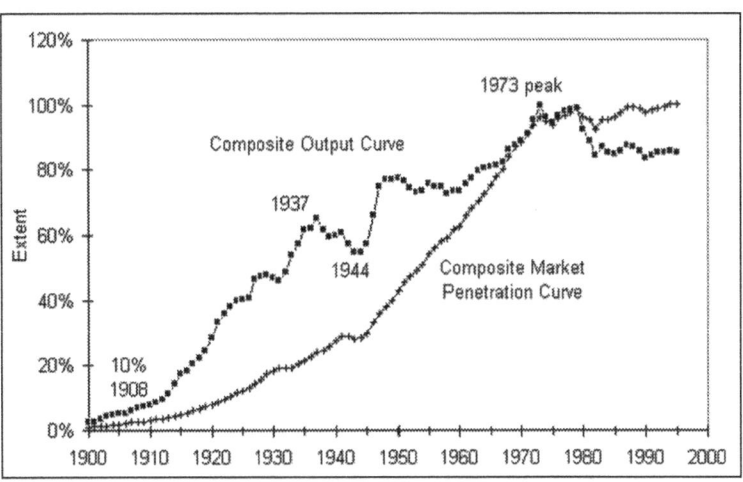

Thus far there has been no discussion of the innovation period. By Dent's construction, the innovation period ends when the growth boom began in 1908. Since I employed average growth curves to obtain the other periods, I average the innovation dates in Table 5.1 to estimate the center of the innovation period. The average of these dates is 1895, which I will denote as the center of the mass production innovation wave. This gives dates for the innovation period as 1882-1908. The output curve in Figure 5.12 appeared in Figure 1.1 as the mass-market innovation wave. This analysis (Alexander 2000a) and a related method (Alexander 2002) were used to construct the earlier innovation waves shown in Figure 1.1.

## Today's Economy

Today's new economy is the information/networked economy, or just information economy. Figure 5.13 shows the growth in market penetration of cable television, personal computers, cellular phones and the internet. Also shown is the ratio of college to high school students (from four years before) minus 0.38, the value of the ratio in a base year. The year 1954 was selected for this base year as it fully reflected the growth in college attendance resulting from the GI bill. This measure then shows a growth curve beginning at zero in the mid-1950's and growing from there to about 0.6-0.7 today. It is a rather crude indicator but it should suffice for my purposes here. The composite penetration S-curve appears in Figure 5.14. Based on this curve, the growth boom began in about 1980. Using innovation data: the integrated circuit (1958), the founding of Intel (1968) the Arapanet and Unix operating system (1969), the PC (1974), genetic engineering (1976), the founding of Microsoft (1977) and the founding of AOL (1985); I get an average value of 1972 for the cluster of innovations leading to the information economy. The period 1964-1980 was selected as the innovation period.

Figure 5.13. Information economy market penetration 1970-2000

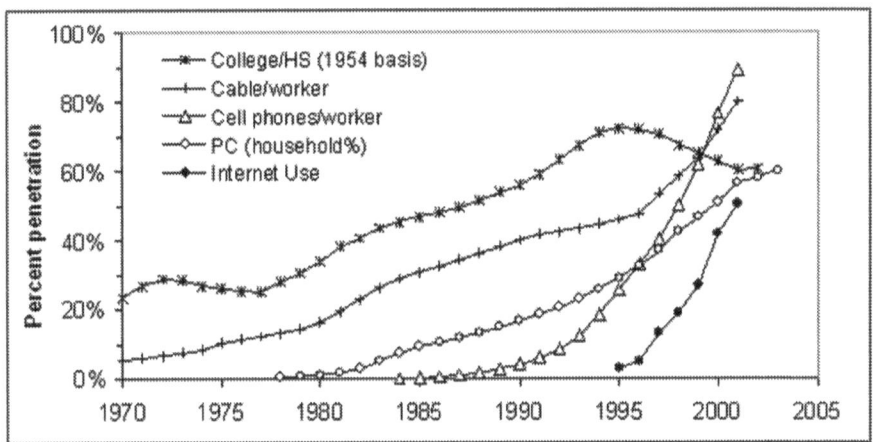

The most striking feature of this presentation of the information economy is the paucity of data series examined. Compared to the mass-market economy, for which lots of data are available, the analysis for the information economy looks barren. Some of this can be explained. Because we do not yet know how the information economy will turn out, nobody knows which industries will end up being the important ones. As a result, economic statisticians have not yet produced a collection of data series suitable for studying this economy, as they have for the previous ones. Secondly, unlike the previous economy, which was characterized by the appearance of a wide range of startling new products and services (e.g. cars, broadcasting, air travel) the information economy is a largely hidden phenomena. The impact of the information economy goes far beyond the handful of new products shown in Figure 5.13. It reflects new ways handling the information management aspects of existing businesses, such things as the supply chain, inventory, marketing and distribution management (in general, any activity that involves exchange of information between multiple parties). To accomplish these changes requires not only new communications and information-processing technologies, but also a new kind of information-savvy worker. Tracking these sort of changes through existing data series is difficult at best, so I settled for tracking some of the communications and information technology products that have grown into importance during the last twenty years. To track the appearance of the information-savvy worker I used the growth in college-level education. The early date of 1980 for the beginning of the information economy growth boom partially reflects the acceleration of college attendance in the late 1970's.

Figure 5.14. Composite innovation waves for the information economy

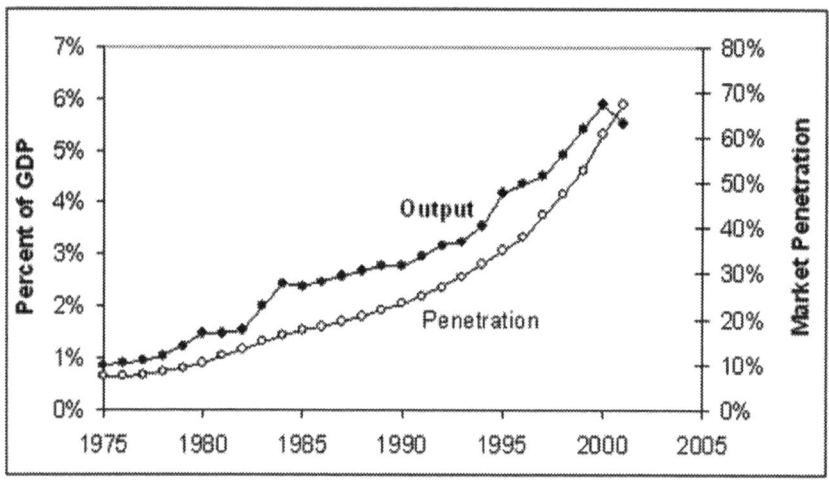

Even with these factors the information economy is not as large as the previous one, which has important implications for national policy making. Many of the information economy innovations simply accelerate loss of employment in the old industries, without offsetting these losses with an equivalent number of new economy jobs. The lack of new economy jobs reflects the small growth impulse produced by the new products of the information economy. Many new products have been introduced, but these often replace previous products rather than form a new type of spending. For example, personal transportation technology (cars) in the mass-market economy created a new source of revenue for businesses (and new employment opportunities). What was "replaced" by the auto was walking, which was free. Autos created a new *category* of household spending.

New products like cell phones do not create a similar new category of spending. Their revenues, to some extent, come at the expense of older industries. Growth in the cell phone industry and the jobs associated with it are offset by decline in the telephone industry due to declining long distance revenues. Not all of the information economy is like this, personal computers and internet services represent new classes of spending. They didn't replace an old form of spending—we still watch TV for entertainment as well as play with our PCs. This makes them a bona fide leading sector that resulted in net job creation.

The size of the PC industry in the 1990's doesn't compare to that of autos in the 1920's. Figure 5.14 shows a measure of information economy size obtained by summing the total sales of the cell phone, pharmaceutical, cable, software, semiconductor and personal computer industries and dividing by GDP. Total output of these industries has risen to about 6% of GDP. These industries employ a little over 4 million workers. In contrast, the output of the industries selected to represent the mass production economy in Table 5.1 employ about 6.5 million, suggesting that even today, after decades of decline, the mass production economy is still some 50% "bigger" than the information economy. Today, manufacturing employs about 12% of the workforce and contributes 13.7% to national income. In 1973, 24% of the workforce was employed in manufacturing, which contributed 25% of total national income. In 1929 the contribution was about the same. Thus, the mass production economy today is about half as important today as it was back in 1929 and 1973, and yet it is still today about 50% bigger than the information economy. This suggests that the information economy today is only about one-third the size of its predecessor in 1929.

This is a serious problem because as the old economy decays, workers must be deployed into the new economy. If the rising new economy is smaller than the declining old economy where will workers go? Those workers have gone to low-paid service jobs. One source of such jobs is the health care industry, which, leaving out pharmaceuticals (which was already counted as part of the information economy) employs about 10% of the workforce and represents about 11% of the GDP. If the health care industry is added into the information economy its size is now roughly similar to the old mass-production economy in 1929.

One does not think of health care as a dynamic new source of economic prosperity (i.e. a leading sector), but it could be. Much discussion revolves around the need to keep this sector from growing; pundits talk about the crisis of health care and how we as a nation *spend too much* on health care. This is like a 1929 columnist complaining of the vast amount Americans "waste" on stuff (manufactured goods). It was this "wastage" that led to the remarkable postwar prosperity from 1945 to 1973. In other words, growth in the health sector as a percentage of the GDP could be a good thing.

It is not a good thing because health care is a low productivity sector. There is much unmet demand; this sector is far from saturation (unlike PCs and cell phones, for example). But low productivity means that many health workers cannot earn enough to afford the services they provide. Thus, growth in the sector does not simultaneously produce the wealth needed to pay for its products. Normally, leading sectors are autocatalytic; their growth creates the ability to afford their own products, supporting additional growth until everyone has them. If productivity were higher, the health care sector would become autocatalytic and could continue to power economic growth for decades. That is, health care would be a true leading sector.

The development of the healthcare industry as an additional leading sector for the information economy would have significant benefits for the nation. Paul Krugman, in his 1994 book *The Age of Diminished Expectations* extolled the virtues of enhanced productivity: "Productivity isn't everything, but in the long run it is almost everything." Increased productivity, he wrote, "would make many, but not all, of the problems discussed in this book (health care, budget deficit, stagnant standard of living) fade away". At the time Krugman was writing, productivity (expressed as GDP per worker) had increased at only 0.9% per year over the previous 21 years, while over the 26 years before that it had run at 2.3%. Since 1994, productivity picked up, growing at an average rate of 2.0% from 1994 to 2003. One problem, the deficit, was eliminated as a result, only to return with a new President and new fiscal priorities. Productivity growth is no longer a problem. But productivity growth is not enough if employment fails to grow. Manufacturing productivity has grown at phenomenal rates. But manufacturing is now a *shrinking* sector; it has been in decline since the peak in the mass-production economy in 1973. Great productivity growth is offset by declining numbers of workers. In fact, the current jobless recovery is in part due to enhanced productivity growth that permits expansion of the GDP without a commensurate expansion of the workforce.

Rising productivity, though highly desirable, is not enough. Healthy leading sectors are also needed. New economic activities, amenable to productivity improvement by investment, are needed to absorb the workers no longer needed in "old economy" industries experiencing rapid productivity growth. This is the process of creative destruction that is a central feature of the Kondratiev downwave and also Dent's Growth Boom and Shakeout

Farming was once low-productivity work like health care, so low that about 85% of the work force was needed to grow food for the entire population. Today, less than 3% of the work force grows food for the entire population. This enormous increase in productivity came from investments in equipment and know-how over the years. In principal, similar investments in health care could also increase productivity, which would make the healthcare industry a true leading sector. This has not happened. The reason seems to be the difficulty of optimization in the health care industry. The objective for increasing productivity in farming (and most other things) was to reduce cost of production further below selling price to maximize profit. To perform profit maximization one requires a market price, which assumes a well-functioning market exists.

Health care does not have a well-functioning market. In fact, there is hardly any market at all. The primary reason for this is subsidized health insurance, particularly government programs like Medicare and Medicaid. Health insurance makes the out-of-pocket costs for medical procedures much less than their full price. As a result consumers have no incentive to modify their consumption patterns to maximize the value received for money spent. That is, demand does not respond to price, giving inappropriate signals to suppliers. As long as health care is completely run using the current system of subsidized health insurance, healthcare can not develop as a leading sector. Suppliers will have no incentive to provide cost-effective services because consumers don't shop for health care, their insurance company determines what services they can buy. There is no market price for health care services. Insurance companies pay "reasonable and customary" fees no matter how unreasonable they may actually be.

Insurance by itself is not the problem. After all, the market routinely functions for home or life insurance. The market fails to work for health insurance because the risk to be insured is hugely variable from person to person and there is an asymmetry of information between market participants. When an individual contracts for health insurance, he has a better idea of his health problems than the insurer. In general, people whose health is poor will have more need for health insurance than people in robust health. They will be more likely to seek insurance. The insurer, knowing this, will charge higher rates, which will discourage healthier people from buying and reduce still further the health of the average person seeking insurance. It is a vicious cycle that has no resolution until just about everyone has been priced out of the insurance except wealthy people who don't need insurance.

Thus, health insurers tend to insure groups of people whose membership in the group is based on criteria unrelated to health status, such as employees of a particular firm. In this way the population insured will have average health and insurance can be priced in the normal way, using statistics predicated on random samplings from a reference population. But everyone in the group must partici- pate. If it is optional, the healthier will opt out and pricing will escalate until nobody who needs it can afford it. Employers subsidize the insurance they offer their employees so that it is less expensive than private insurance in order to incent full participation.

A central issue for the nascent liberal era could be the transformation of the healthcare sector into a true leading sector. One reason this can happen now is that Kondratiev winter is the traditional incubator of leading sectors. Late down- wave innovations have powered new clusters of leading sectors for hundreds of years. Growth is encouraged by the low cost of capital during Kondratiev winter. Creating a leading sector out of health care would require substantial government intervention, however. It would disrupt the current status quo and so be inher- ently liberal in nature. It could only occur during a liberal era as the failure of the Clinton health plan in the 1990's shows. It would be a government-sponsored leading sector innovation. Such innovations have been common in history.

The very beginnings of our modern capitalistic system were government proj- ects. Prince Henry the Navigator sponsored voyages down the African coast that established a new economy founded on African gold, slaves and spices (Braudel, 1982). Later, the voyages of Vasco de Gama to India and Cabral to Brazil spawned another new economy for Portugal based on Indian pepper, Brazilian dyewood and East Asian trade (Modelski, 1996, Schwartz, 1974). The beginning of Brazilian sugar production in the mid-16th century created another leading sector for Portugal (Modelski, 1996). The Spanish-sponsored voyages of Columbus led to several leading sectors for Spain: gold, silver, and Seville-based Atlantic trade (Modelski, 1996, Goldstein, 1988). Even those early-modern leading sectors not established specifically by government were pursued using political rather than economic means. The growth of Dutch Asian trade and its sugar industry did not result from competition in the marketplace, but from armed conquest of Portuguese trading posts and sugar plantations. Other nations fought trade wars in order to gain access to particularly profitable trade oppor- tunities and to deny them to rivals. It was not until the industrial revolution that leading sectors started to appear spontaneously through commercial means. And even then, many of these new industries received considerable support from gov- ernment from the railroad subsidies and the protective tariff in the 19th century, to the airmail subsidy for the nascent airline industry in the 1920's and to the establishment of the precursor to the Internet as a government defense project in the late 1960's.

A reorganization of the health care industry would be a maturity innovation (health care is not a new industry). The natural time for this is during the Shakeout, which takes place during Kondratiev winter (the era we have just entered). Winter is also a natural time for leading sector development because low interest rates make investment less costly. Also, a restructuring of health care is exactly the kind of reorganization that is typical of a Crisis turning. What I am getting at is the confluence of the various cycles, Kondratiev, political, and generational is creating the environment needed to accomplish a major reorganization of health care in the United States.

It could not happen before now because there was a secular bull market and easy, silly projects like pets.com could make fortunes for entrepreneurs. The coming of a secular bear market means no easy money anymore, would-be moguls will have to actually earn their fortunes through real innovation. It could not happen before now because the government could not afford it, government had to run a surplus to keep interest rates low. Kondratiev winter will provide the low interest rates even in the face of huge deficits. It could not happen before now because there was no political will; it was a conservative era. The political will can be found with the rise of a liberal era.

Finally, it could not happen before now because it was an Unraveling turning, when debate is informed by idealist generational paradigms. Idealist paradigms contain strongly-held ideas of what *should* be done that conflict with one another, making it impossible to *do* anything. Only when the pragmatic paradigm of Generation X gains in strength can anything be *done*, that is, can the institutional change typical of the Secular Crisis happen. What will be done will derive from some of the "shoulds" from the previous era, but only after competing shoulds have been defeated.

Healthcare is not the only potential leading sector that has not developed. The last two Kondratiev/innovation waves have seen major changes in energy production. In the railroad/industrial wave it was coal-fired steam engines that transported cargo and people across a continent and powered an industrial revolution. In the mass-market economy it was petroleum-fueled internal combustion engines that provided transportation and fossil-fuel derived electric power that completed the industrial revolution. In today's information economy, energy is still needed and petroleum is running out. New leading sectors built around alternative energy sources (biomass, nuclear, solar, wind) and more fuel-efficient technologies (hybrid autos, high efficiency appliances, less energy-intensive man-ufacturing processes) are certainly possible.

Such new sectors pose a direct threat to old sectors that currently meet these needs (e.g. the oil industry) through the process of creative destruction. Consider the fate of the "old tech" computer companies during the information economy growth boom: Sperry, Burroughs, IBM and Digital Equipment Corporation. All but IBM have succumbed to the wave of creative destruction unleashed by such companies as Apple, Microsoft, Intel, Yahoo and Dell. Only IBM has remained independent as a business services company. Substitute the oil companies for the old-line computer companies and one can see the situation faced by these firms in a changing energy environment. It is easy to see the appeal of keeping the old "oil paradigm" going as long as possible. Doing so requires access to petroleum deposits in politically unstable areas of the world that are not available through natural market mechanisms. Consider what might have happened had the US government not intervened in Kuwait. It is possible an alternate energy sector could have gotten started in the nineties boom. Today's interventions in Afghanistan and Iraq have the potential to bring additional supplies of oil and gas to the market, extending the oil paradigm still further, and retarding the development of an alternate energy leading sector.

The principal stumbling block to all these potential leading sectors is politics. The transformation of healthcare into a leading sector requires a serious consid-eration of what to do about deathly ill patients who cannot afford treatment. Development of alternate energy will require dealing with the power of the oil lobby. Nuclear power is currently politically unpopular, which prevents any expansion in its use. To get around these stumbling blocks will require a major change to the status quo. It will require a disruption in the natural order that is inherently not conservative.

It would appear that much of what would be necessary to free up leading sec-tors is the same sort of free market economics favored by conservatives. Free mar-ket economics as supported by conservatives must be natural. The free-market characteristics for health care to develop into a leading sector are unnatural, oth-erwise it would have spontaneously happened during the Growth Boom of the 1980's and 1990's. Thus, conservatives will necessarily oppose any efforts at pro-ducing a leading sector out of health care. Similarly, developing alternative ener-gy into a leading sector will require overcoming opposition from the oil lobby, which will not happen with the Bush administration and is unlikely under any administration in a conservative era. Only under a liberal era during a

Kondratiev downwave period of creative destruction can the developments I have discussed become possible.

In summary, this section has presented the concept of leading sectors as the engines of economic growth. Leading sectors are clustered at Kondratiev intervals, forming new economies. During a Kondratiev downwave, the old economy gives way to a new one, a process called creative destruction. The present era features its own new "information economy" that is replacing the old mass market economy as a source of wealth and employment. The information economy is small relative to the mass production economy it is replacing. Hence the actions taken by industry to cope with this period, such as exporting jobs overseas and automation, is resulting in slower than normal wage growth, especially when considered in the context of funding future outlays for old age pensions. The addition of healthcare and alternative energy as leading sectors would create an information economy fully as large as the previous one.

Accomplishing this is more a political than an economic matter. It requires a special environment conducive to government-assisted innovation on a large scale. The convergence of the political, economic and generational cycles to produce a liberal, deflationary Crisis can produce this environment. I will return to these concepts with some specific ideas in chapter eight. But first, there is one more set of cycles to be introduced; the hegemony cycle.

# Chapter Six

## The hegemony cycle

In this chapter I will move into the arena of international politics. A substantial literature exists on cycles in international relations, especially between great powers. Some of these cycles are linked to the Kondratiev cycle and generations are often given as possible timing elements. Thus, the idea that long cycles exist in international politics and economics with lengths that are multiples of a (biological) generation is not new.

One thing that is new is the generational saeculum of Strauss and Howe that gives explicit dates for a cycle of generational mood swings over five hundred years. Another new thing is the concepts of the Stock Cycle and reduced price that together permit a close to real-time determination of position within the Kondratiev cycle. Based on my Stock Cycle indicators I was able to forecast the start of the secular bear market in early 2000 (Alexander 2000a), before it happened. Using the reduced price indicator I will be able to confirm the Kondratiev cycle location as the fall from plateau as soon as it happens. Based on the correspondence between the Stock Cycle and the saeculum, I was able to identify the current position in the saeculum to be on the threshold of the Crisis turning a year *before* the September 11, 2001 terrorist attack (Alexander, 2000b). Although this attack and the War on Terrorism that followed does not confirm that a Crisis began in 2001, it greatly increases the likelihood that my 2000 prediction was correct.

As a result of these previous efforts, I have a reasonable degree of confidence that I have determined our location within the Kondratiev cycle and saeculum correctly. I used this location and the historical correspondence between the saeculum and the political cycle to forecast that a shift towards a liberal zeitgeist began after 2001 (Alexander, 2002). This shift is obscured by the conservative administration now in power, but the evidence suggests that it is happening. I will extend the same sort of reasoning to the cycles of international politics that impact US foreign policy. Before doing so I will first present one of these cycles in war and great power politics.

## Cycles in War

The American political scientist Quincy Wright (1942) was the first to describe the phenomenon of regular cycles in warfare. Although wars themselves are scattered more or less randomly throughout history, the incidence of major wars is not. Wright identified clusters of major wars spaced about 50 years apart. A good way to see these clusters is by looking at total fatalities in wars involving the great powers over time. Today the great powers are the United States, Britain, France, Germany, Italy, Russia, Japan, China and India. These nine nations possess the largest economies or largest populations, and six of them have nuclear capability. India might be thought to have joined the great power club sometime after obtaining nuclear capability in the 1970's. China and Japan replaced the Austrian (Hapsburg) empire after the First World War. Prior to the mid-nineteenth century, Italy and the United States should be deleted and Germany replaced with Prussia. Prior to the nineteenth century Spain was a world power. Before 1715, one would delete Russia and add the Ottoman Empire, Sweden and the Netherlands as great powers.

Using war death data over the 1495-1975 period (Goldstein, 1988), a running generational (25 year) average in war intensity was constructed from 1520 to 1990. War intensity is measured by war deaths in all wars involving great powers (see above) at a particular time divided by total population of the great powers.

Figure 6.1 shows war intensity expressed as death rate per 100,000 population (per 10,000 for the two world wars). Successive waves of greater-than-normal war intensity are evident in the data. The waves up to World War I are spaced 40-65 years apart with an average spacing of 52 years.

Figure 6.1. Generational average war deaths per 100,000 population*

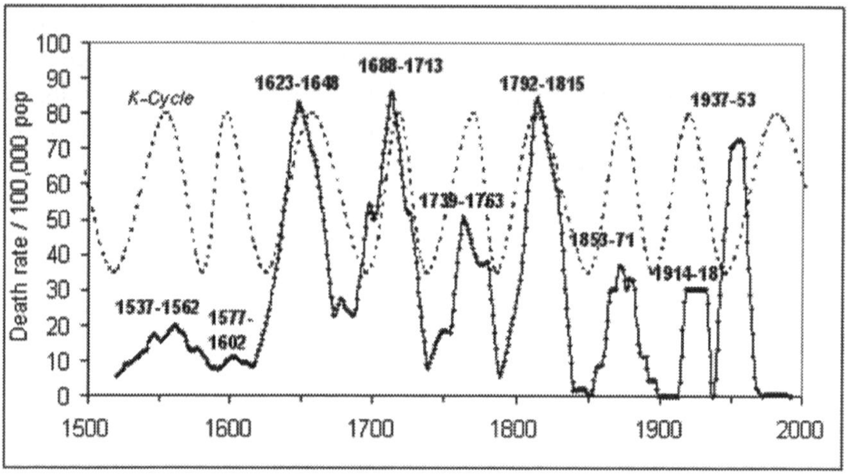

*Deaths per 10,000 population shown for WW I and WW II. (data from Goldstein, 1988)

Wright also advanced the idea that cycles in warfare were related to K-cycles. Figure 6.1 shows that war cycles do appear to line up very well with K-cycles; peaks in war intensity are close to Kondratiev peaks from the mid-16th century up until the First World War. The placement of World War II just 27 years after World War I breaks this neat pattern. Instead of occurring at a K-peak like the other war peaks, World War II occurred at a K-trough. I will return to this "world war anomaly" later in the chapter.

Kondratiev upwaves show more intense warfare than downwaves (Table 6.1). Closer examination of Table 6.1 shows that significant correlation between upwaves and higher war intensity only started in the seventeenth century. The five upwaves from 1625 to 1873 showed war intensities that were about four times higher than those during the six surrounding downwaves. The difference is statistically significant at greater than 99% confidence. In contrast, 16th century upwaves showed war intensities that were not significantly different than those during downwaves. Data for the Hundred Years War shows war deaths at high levels in 1335-44, 1360-89, and 1422-44 (Sorokin, 1957). The first of these is around a K-trough, the second around a K-peak, and the third during an upwave. These observations suggest that the war cycle's relation with the K-cycle was strongest during the period bracketed by the Thirty Years War and World War I. Before the 17th century and after World War I, war intensity and upwaves were not strongly correlated.

An alignment between war and the Kondratiev cycle is to be expected based on the (war) debt model of the Kondratiev cycle described in chapter one. This model holds that upwaves reflect increases in money supply and deficit spending associated with high levels of armed conflict. When the wars finally end, a lengthy period of peace (the downwave) ensues while the belligerent nations pay down their war debts. The Thirty Years War was the first really big war that was decided by the participants' ability to pay for continued war. By the time the next cluster of war arrived in the late 17th century, innovations to finance wars had been made. These innovations constitute the financial revolution, and with them came the rise to dominance of the debt model of the K-cycle. Thus, the alignment between the Kondratiev cycle and the war cycle only emerged in the 17th century.

Table 6.1. Correspondence between the war cycle and the Kondratiev cycle

| Downwave | Deaths per 100000 | Upwave | Deaths per 100000 |
|----------|-------------------|--------|-------------------|
| 1490-1519 | 5.5 ± 0.8 | 1519-1555 | 16.1 ± 1.7 |
| 1555-1581 | 12 ± 1.4 | 1581-1598 | 9.6 ± 1.0 |
| 1598-1625 | 20 ± 4 | 1625-1657 | 69 ± 6 |
| 1657-1696 | 40 ± 6 | 1696-1718 | 66 ± 10 |
| 1718-1738 | 7.7 ± 2.0 | 1738-1770 | 40 ± 8 |
| 1770-1787 | 3.7 ± 1.0 | 1787-1814 | 81 ± 9 |
| 1814-1850 | 3.2 ± 2.0 | 1850-1873* | 32 ± 8 |
| 1873-1895 | 4.1 ± 2.9 | 1895-1920 | 223 ± 98 |
| 1920-1946 | 387 ± 123 | 1946-1980 | 137 ± 62 |

*The British upwave is used here because it is more in sync with the European K-cycle than the U.S. upwave (most of the great powers at the time were European).

Wright advanced a generational explanation for the 50-year war cycles. Basically, there is a "warrior generation" who experienced the ravages of war firsthand and raises the next generation to have an aversion to war. The following generation grows up during relative peace and so learns to romanticize war, becoming another warrior generation upon entering adulthood, starting the cycle anew. Wright's concept provides the (biological) generational timing for the (war) debt cycle mechanism for the Kondratiev cycle in the late 17th to early 20th centuries. It neatly dovetails with the population-food supply mechanism for the Kondratiev cycle that I described in chapter one. This mechanism also employs generations of biological length to explain the timing of the Kondratiev cycle before 1700.

## Hegemony Cycle

Wright also identified a second pattern of unusually big wars that occurred every other cycle. These big wars were associated with the rise and fall of great powers. The historian Arnold Toynbee (1954) proposed specific hundred year cycles of war and peace to explain this pattern. The leading proponents of this cyclic view of war today are the political scientists George Modelski and William Thompson (1996). Modelski and Thompson stress naval power as the key military underpinning of world political leadership. Their choice of successive world leaders: Portugal, the Netherlands, Britain and the United States reflects this viewpoint. All four of these nations projected military power over a world-girdling trading empire through a first rank navy.

Modelski and Thompson (1996) measure naval power by noting the number of capital ships possessed by the world-leader as a fraction of all such ships held by all the great powers. They define capital ships over the 1494-1654 period as any state-owned, gunned, long-range sailing vessel. For the 1655-1859 period, an escalating minimal number of guns carried is employed to qualify vessels as capital warships. From 1860-1945, battleships (also subject to escalating minimal attributes in size and armament) are used as capital ships. After 1945, heavy or attack aircraft carriers, and after 1960 nuclear attack submarines weighted by number of warheads are used in the definition of capital ships. Figure 6.2 presents the fraction of all capital ships of the great powers that were possessed by the leading power. Peaks in naval power for successive leading nations can be seen about every hundred years, corresponding to the hundred year cycles of Wright and Toynbee. The last peak, the American one following World War II, was a bit delayed, occurring some 130 years after the previous British peak. This delay reflects what I call the world war anomaly.

Figure 6.2. Share of total great-power capital ships held by successive world leaders

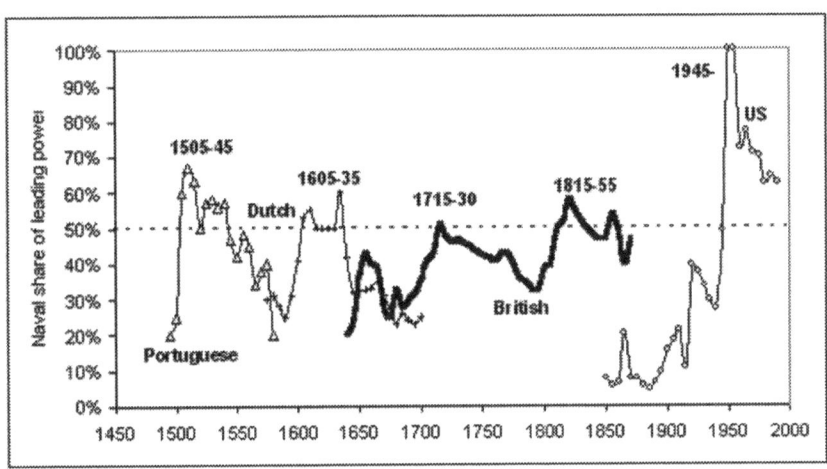

The other major determinant of power is economic and flows from the pioneering of new leading sectors of the world economy. Modelski and Thompson (1996) argue that the pioneering fifteenth century voyages down the African coast, begun under Portugal's Prince Henry the Navigator, set the stage for Portugal's world leadership period early in the sixteenth century. Similarly, the maritime and financial innovations made by the Dutch in the sixteenth century set the stage for Dutch leadership in the seventeenth century. The pioneering of tobacco cultivation in Virginia and the coming of "Dutch finance" to Britain during the Glorious Revolution set the stage for British leadership in the eighteenth century. Britain won another round of leadership in the nineteenth century by their pioneering of the industrial revolution late in eighteenth century. Finally the spread to America of British ideas of liberal democracy in the eighteenth century and the practice of industrial capitalism on a continental scale in the nineteenth led to American leadership in the twentieth century, which continues to this day.

This idea of a nation's pioneering of new leading sectors (what I have called "new economies") leading directly to subsequent world leadership fits in very well with the correspondence between war cycles and K-cycles (see Figure 6.1). I have already noted that the development of new economies is closely aligned with the Kondratiev cycle (Table 1.1). What is not so clear is why leadership cycles should occur every two K-cycles (~100 years) when development of new economies and outbursts of great power war occur every K-cycle (~50 years).

The shift from one world leader to another occurs during a period of what Modelski and Thompson call global war. Although periods of global war do tend to contain big wars, it is the change in world leader that makes them special. In general, the reigning world leader is challenged by another power for leadership. As a result of this challenge, one or more coalition wars are fought between the challenger and her allies and the old leader and her allies. One of the countries on the winning side of this conflict emerges as the new world leader. Sometimes it is the old world leader who comes back for a second round of leadership.

Figure 6.3 Share of total armies held by successive leading land-based great powers

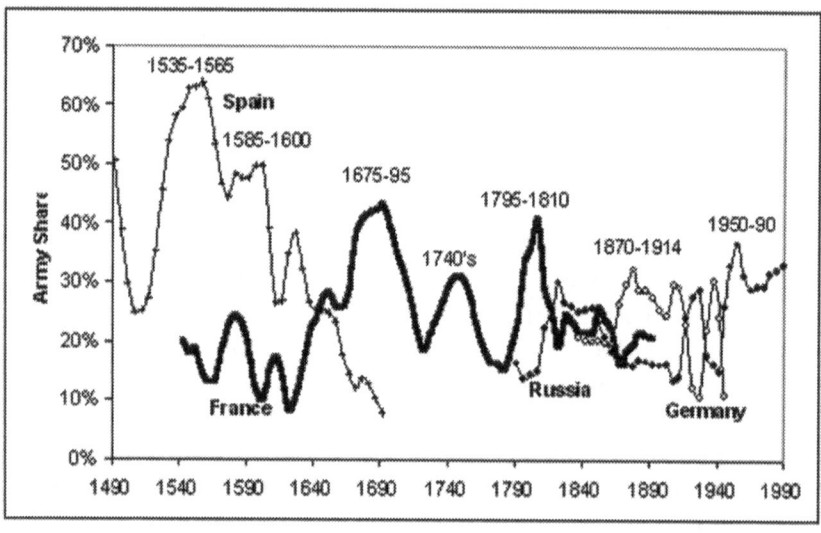

The role of challenger typically is played by a continental power, whose major strength is land-based. Ludwig Dehio (1948) developed a view on war cycles that focuses on these land-based powers. He notes a tendency for peaks in land-based power to occur around the time of low points in sea-based power, and vice versa. For Dehio the key powers have been Spain, France, and Germany. Dehio believed the USSR (Russia) would play the role of the next continental power in the decades after the 1940's. Land-based power can be measured much as was done with naval strength. A simple measure is the size of the regional power's army relative to all great power armies combined. Figure 6.3 shows a graph of land power for the four successive regional powers (Rasler and Thompson, 1994). Since all great powers maintain fairly substantial armies, the degree of dominance displayed by the world leaders in naval power are typically not attained by land-based powers (except for the case of Hapsburg Spain in the early 16th century). Nevertheless, a pattern of fairly regular peaks can be seen, each associated with one of Dehio's key actors. Comparison of Figures 6.2 and 6.3 does show that peaks in land power and sea power do seem to alternate (see Table 6.2).

Modelski and Thompson integrate Dehio's powers (which they call regional powers) into their leadership cycle. The country enjoying the naval power peak is called a world power. The war peak immediately preceding the naval power peak is called *global war* (or *general war* by Toynbee). During the global war period or immediately before, there is an army peak. The country holding land power dominance at this peak becomes the *challenger* during the global war. The country showing a rise to naval dominance after the global war is the new world leader. The concept of global or general war accounts for half of the war/army peaks and all of the naval peaks. The other war/army peaks fall between global/general wars. The war peaks between the global wars are called *supplementary wars* by Toynbee. Typically, an army peak occurs at the same time as supplementary wars. Supplementary wars can be thought of as contests between potential regional powers that decide who will be the challenger during the next global war.

Table 6.2. Peaks in war, navies, and armies compared to the world leadership cycle

| War Deaths | Naval Power | Army Power | Composite Cycle | Modelski and Thompson's World Leadership Cycle | |
|---|---|---|---|---|---|
| | | | | Dates | Name of Period |
| | | | | 1430-1460 | Agenda-setting |
| | | | | 1460-1494 | Coalition-building |
| 1495-1522 | | | 1495-1514 | 1494-1516 | **Global War (France)** |
| | 1505-1540 | | 1514-1538 | 1516-1540 | **Portugal World-Power** |
| 1535-1562 | | 1535-1565 | 1538-1563 | 1540-1560 | Agenda-setting / Delegitimization |
| | | | 1563-1581 | 1560-1580 | Coalition-building / Deconcentration |
| 1577-1602 | | 1585-1600 | 1581-1603 | 1580-1609 | **Global War (Spain)** |
| | 1605-1635 | | 1603-1629 | 1609-1640 | **Dutch World-Power** |
| 1623-1648 | | | 1629-1661 | 1640-1660 | Agenda-setting/ Delegitimization |
| | | 1675-1695 | 1661-1691 | 1660-1688 | Coalition-building/ Deconcentration |
| 1688-1714 | | | 1691-1714 | 1688-1714 | **Global War (Britain)** |
| | 1715-1730 | | 1714-1735 | 1714-1740 | **Britain World-Power** |
| 1739-1763 | | 1740's | 1735-1763 | 1740-1763 | Agenda-setting/Delegitimization |
| | | | 1763-1793 | 1763-1792 | Coalition-building/Deconcentration |
| 1792-1815 | | 1795-1810 | 1793-1814 | 1792-1815 | **Global War (France)** |
| | 1815-1855 | | 1814-1854 | 1815-1850 | **Britain World-Power** |
| 1853-1871 | | | 1854-1871 | 1850-1873 | Agenda-setting/Delegitimization |
| | | 1870-1914 | 1871-1914 | 1873-1914 | Coalition-building/Deconcentration |
| 1914-1918 | | | ? | 1914-1945 | **Global War (Germany)** |
| 1937-1953 | | | | | |
| | 1945- | 1950-1989 | ? | 1945-1973 | **US World Power** |
| | | | ? | 1973- | Agenda-setting/Delegitimization |

The peaks in war, naval power and army share were combined into a composite cycle in Table 6.2. This composite cycle provides the empirical support for Modelski and Thompson's world leadership cycle. The cycle begins with global war, a period of great power conflict in which an economically-advanced sea power and a militarily-strong land power struggle for the role of global power. The sea power wins as measured by a rise in its naval share and a fall in the land power's army share following the conflict. Figure 6.3 shows sharp drops in the army share of the challenger following the global war conflicts that ended in 1609 (Spain), 1714 (France), 1815 (France) and 1945 (Germany).

Following global war comes the world power phase of the cycle, during which naval power is at a peak (Figure 6.2). With one exception (which reflects the world war anomaly) army share of regional powers falls to a minimum during this time. It is the time of maximum hegemony of the new world leader. In time, army power of potential regional powers rises and a series of wars are fought through which a new regional power emerges. The world leader is unable to prevent the emergence of this new regional power; its role as leader is said to be delegitimized. Hence, the period of increased warfare during which this happens is called delegitimization when considered from the point of view of the world leader. When considered from the point of view of the next world leader, it is called agenda-setting, as the groundwork for future leadership is laid during this time.

Following delegitimization/agenda-setting comes deconcentration, which is typified by the development of a minimum in the naval power graph. It is the time of minimum hegemonic power of the old world leader and sets the stage for the coming period of global war. As the power of the world leader falls, the regional power challenger and the future world leader build coalitions for the coming showdown. From their point of view, this phase is called coalition-building. Eventually a new round of global war breaks out and the cycle is complete.

## *The world war anomaly*

The neat correspondence between the Kondratiev cycle and the war/hegemony cycle breaks down after WW I. World War II occupies an anomalous position with respect to the K-cycle. It occurred at a Kondratiev trough rather than a peak like all the other war cycle peaks. This is a direct result of its close spacing with respect to WW I (27 years), half the normal spacing of the war cycle. Another consequence of this anomaly is the overlap of naval and army peaks by the world leader and future challenger right after World War II. In previous cycles, the naval power peak (which defines the world power phase) preceded the army power peak (which falls into the delegitimization or deconcentration phases). Figure 6.3 shows Soviet (Russian) army share rising to a dominant position at the same time as US naval share is rising. The latter is characteristic of the world power phase, while the former suggests a delegitimization phase.

Modelski and Thompson favor the former interpretation, that the post-war era is one of US world power. They treat World War I and II as parts of the same period of global war. Thompson expresses the idea that after the second world war regional leadership in Europe no longer had the meaning it once did, implying that Russian army shares have less meaning (Rasler and Thompson, 1994). Yet if that is so, why did both superpowers and the rest of the European powers form permanent alliances and maintain huge armies in Europe? For decades NATO military planners took very seriously the idea of World War III beginning with a Warsaw Pact thrust into Germany. It is reasonable to assume that the massive army of the Soviet Union (Russia) in the postwar period explicitly reflected the Kremlin's desire that the Soviet Union be a major player in European events, if only to prevent another attack from the West during a future global war.

Table 6.3. Modified world leadership cycle 1870-present

| Deaths | Navy | Army | Period | Leadership Cycle |
|---|---|---|---|---|
| | | 1870-1914 | 1873-1907 | Deconcentration/Coalition building |
| 1914-1918 | | | 1907-1918 | **Global War** (Germany challenger) |
| | | | 1918-1941 | US *de facto* World Power |
| 1937-1953 | 1945- | 1950-1989 | 1941-1964 | US Delegitimization |
| | | | 1964-1983 | US Deconcentration |
| none | | | 1983-1991 | **Global War** (USSR challenger) |
| | | | 1991- | US World Power |

My views diverge from those of Modelski and Thompson (see Table 6.3). I see WW I, but not WW II, as a global war. Thus, I begin the global war era with the Anglo-Russian entente in 1907, which completed the process of coalition-building for WW I. After the war, a curious thing happened, what I call "the world war anomaly". The United States was clearly the strongest nation in the world after WW I and did decisively defeat Germany. The U.S. certainly had the resources to establish naval dominance after the war, but did not. The U.S. certainly could have joined the League of Nations and when Hitler invaded the Rhineland drive him out under League of Nations auspices, just as Saddam

Hussein was driven out of Kuwait under UN auspices. Instead, America turned inward and retreated behind her flanking oceans, desiring a "Return to Normalcy". The result was a postwar "world power" phase with nobody filling the role of world leader. As a result, Hitler's ambitions were unchecked and World War I was replayed as World War II, with virtually the same actors.

I see the period between Pearl harbor and the Gulf of Tonkin resolution as the delegitimization period. World War II is then an early supplementary war in which Germany and the USSR contested for control of Eastern Europe and Japan for control of East Asia. The war is anomalous as it was conducted about half of Kondratiev cycle early. It occurred while the United States (though dormant) was still unquestionably the greatest power. But since the US refused to act as a hegemon, there was no one to dissuade Germany from its objective of European dominance or Japan from its Greater East Asia Co-Prosperity Sphere. Eventually the US did enter the war. Germany was utterly defeated in 41 months and Japan in 44. The war created a power vacuum in East Asia and left the USSR as the strongest power in Europe.

Early in the Cold War, Toynbee, Dehio, and others had identified the Soviet Union as the next challenger, a role that becomes clear only after the world power phase. The rise of this challenger followed WW II immediately. There was no "world power" period of calm after World War II during which the Americans exercised hegemony. With the Berlin crisis in 1947, the Korean War in 1950, and the Vietnam War in the 1960's, the Soviet Union was engaging in regional conflict typical of the agenda-setting phase. The culmination in the delegitimization phase came with the Gulf of Tonkin resolution, when America first committed to the Vietnam War. This marks the start of the deconcentration phase.

After losing Vietnam, America stood by helplessly as Middle Eastern states waged economic war against her and saw the spectacle of her citizens held hostage by a third rate power while she stood by impotent. President Carter spoke of a malaise that had descended upon the nation. Taking advantage of apparent American weakness, the Soviet Union invaded Afghanistan in an effort to prop up a friendly regime. The nadir was reached in 1983, when a seemingly impotent America did nothing after 241 Marines were murdered in Lebanon. All these events suggest a decline in perceived American power and influence, even if the actual military power possessed by the U.S. was still comparatively large compared to her rivals. The 1964-83 period has many similarities to the period of deconcentration.

I suggest that the stage of global war was reached in 1983, when the American President Ronald Reagan proposed the construction of the Strategic Defense Initiative, whose specific intent was to neuter Soviet nuclear weapons. It ended in American victory with the collapse of the Soviet Union in 1991. The collapse of the Soviet Union and economic weakness in Japan has given the United States a dozen years of unquestioned global dominance that very strongly resembles the world power phase. Not only is the U.S. militarily and politically dominant, but economically and financially too. After the fall of the Berlin Wall in 1989, the U.S. began to act as a new world leader, first in the Gulf War, later in Bosnia and Kosovo, and now in the War on Terrorism.

Modelski and Thompson's (1996) 1973-2000 delegitimization period leaves out the Vietnam war (the largest US war in the past forty years) and includes the Reagan buildup and post-Cold War period of revived American status. The overall trend in American power during this time does not suggest the coming of a period of deconcentration.

## *Alignment between the leadership cycle and the saeculum*

The alternate cycle timing shown in Table 6.3 cannot be supported using the approach outlined in Table 6.2 for characterization of the leadership cycle. Neither can Modelski and Thompson's characterization of the post-WW I cycle. My view comes from a correlation with the saeculum that can explain why the World war anomaly occurred and also predict that the leadership cycle should be about 72 years long now. This correlation centers on what I call the "national will" cycle. The national will cycle is simply another way to represent the generational saeculum. The ability of a nation to undertake national projects (national will) is assumed to vary with the position in the saeculum. It is at a maximum during the High and a minimum during the Unraveling. I define the national will cycle as peaking in the middle of the High and bottoming in the middle of the Unraveling. Figure 6.4 shows a graph of the national will cycle compared to the war cycle and the leadership cycle. The war cycle is obtained from Figure 6.1. The leadership cycle is represented by a trough at the midpoint of the deconcentration phase and a peak at the end of global war.

Figure 6.4. Comparison of the leadership, war and "national will" (saeculum) cycles

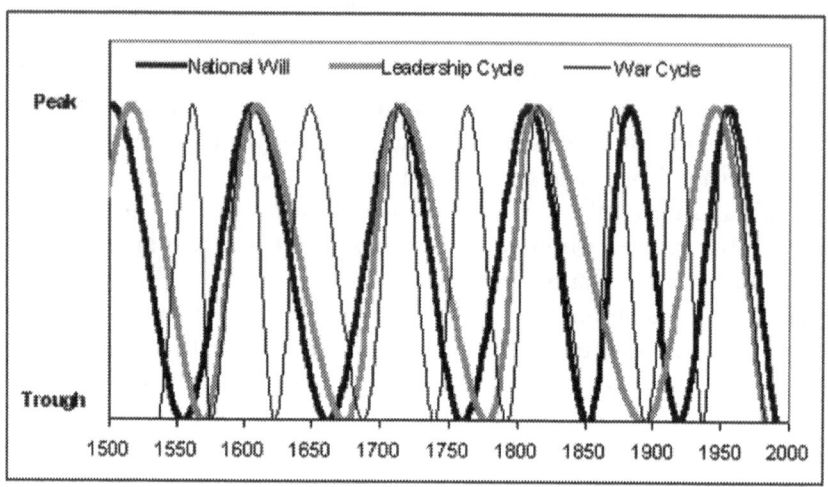

Starting from the left side of the figure there is a leadership peak (bold gray) associated with 1495-1516 global war in the leadership cycle. There was a peak in national will (bold black line) in 1502. The war peak around 1550 was a supplementary war, not a global war, and there was no peak in national will at this time. Looking at the next five war peaks, three (ca.1600, 1700 and 1800) are associated with peaks in national will. All of these are global wars. The intervening supplementary war peaks did not show peaks in national will. So far a pattern between global wars and national will is evident. Every other war peak is associated with a peak in national will. These wars are also considered to be global wars according to the leadership cycle.

This neat pattern breaks down with the next war peak, associated with the U.S. Civil War and the Wars of German and Italian unification. There is a peak in national will at this time, but these wars are not global wars since they occurred at the wrong time in the leadership cycle, during the period of delegitimization, when the old world power is still too strong to be challenged. The misalignment between the national will and world leadership cycles reflects the shortening of generations to 18 years after 1820. As a result of this shortening, the peak in national will came in 1886, about 25 years early. It was not until the next war peak, that for WW I, that the correlation of forces was consistent with a new bout of global war. By this time national will had fallen to a low (see Figure

6.4). Hence, World War I did not produce the outcome typical of a global war. Had the saeculum not shortened, the peak in national will would have occurred around the time of WW I, the US would have arisen as the new hegemon, and there would be no world war anomaly.

What these observations suggest is that what makes a global war are two things, the proper correlation of forces, which is determined by the leadership cycle, and the proper "national mood", which is determined by the saeculum. In order for a period of war to establish a new world leader, the nation taking on this role must be in a time of rising or high national will, that is, in a Crisis or High turning. Also, the correlation of forces must be appropriate, (i.e. the position in the leadership cycle must be right). Hence, the mid-nineteenth century war peak, although associated with a peak in national will, was not a global war. The wars of German unification were fought with singular purpose and effectiveness, consistent with a peak in national will. But Germany was not yet ready to consider the issue of European hegemony, much less challenge Great Britain for global leadership. By the time conditions for the reemergence of global war had arrived, national will was at an ebb. The almost accidental development of World War I is characteristic of supplementary wars fought during periods of low or falling national will (i.e. Awakening and Unraveling turnings). The failure of the war to resolve anything, much less the leadership question, is also characteristic of supplementary wars (e.g. Thirty Years War, Seven Years War). Since nothing was resolved, the conditions for a global war remained in place, and so the next war, when national will was high, finally resolved the issues of the global war.

The national will cycle shows a deep connection between the saeculum and the leadership cycle, implying that they reflect the same underlying dynamic. This is not really surprising. War Cycle theorists have always seen a connection between the K-cycle and the war cycle. In *The Kondratiev Cycle* I showed that there is also a connection between the Kondratiev cycle and the saeculum. Thus, there must also be a connection between the war cycle and the saeculum, which I have expressed as the national will cycle. The tightest connection between the three cycles should be evident over the late 17th to early 20th century period when the financial model for the K-cycle was most valid. During this period the K-cycle is driven by war (debt) and a tight correlation between K-peaks in prices and wars is expected (and observed). During this period High turnings occur during upwaves and national will should peak at the mid-point of every other upwave.

The correspondence between the leadership cycle and the saeculum implies that they should both be of the same length. Since the saeculum has shortened from around a century in length to about 72 years, the leadership cycle should have shortened as well. The next global war period should occur about 72 years after the last one in 1907-1918, or about 1979-1990. This timing is reasonably consistent with the 1983-1991 global war shown in the alternate leadership cycle (Table 6.3).

This analysis shows how combination of the different cycle types can improve the predictive power of individual cycles. Because of the world war anomaly, the most sensible interpretation of the leadership cycle prior to the fall of the Soviet Union was to use the old length of the leadership cycle and interpret World War II as a global war. Using the 100-year "standard" timing of world leadership cycles one would look for the next period of global war to begin in the second quarter of this century. However, once the alignment between the saeculum and the leadership cycle is established by the use of the national will cycle, it could been seen that the length of the leadership cycle must also have changed along with that of the saeculum and K-cycle. Specifically, it must have shortened in length to about 72 years. Strauss and Howe detected this saeculum shortening and called it the Civil War anomaly. Kondratiev experts detected the "Kondratiev anomaly" by their series of failed predictions in the 1970's and 1980's. A Leadership cycle anomaly finally showed up in the 1990's with what appears to be a rise of U.S. hegemony during the late delegitimization phase (something that isn't supposed to occur). The appearance of "anomalies" in all three cycle traditions is strong evidence of an underlying connection between them.

If this reconstruction of the recent leadership cycle is correct, this means that the nature of conflict between great powers has changed. During the 1980's global war, there was no hot war, just a cold one. National will was at a low ebb. The global war was simply a matter of fiscal endurance and the Soviet Union lost. It is likely that great power war is no longer conceivable by any of the great powers because of the existence of nuclear weapons. In fact, a "no holds bared" conflict between great powers is to be avoided. In this sense, the very worst time to resolve questions of leadership is during times of high levels of national will. It appears that the leadership cycle today delivers the proper correlation of forces for global war precisely when national will is at a nadir. The side that can most afford the political cost of continuing the contest will win future global war contests.

The modified hegemony cycle presents an application of the "unified cycle" concept. The original leadership cycle as constructed by Modelski and Thompson in the 1970's and 1980's have the United States currently entering the deconcentration phase, a time of minimal "hegemonic power". This assessment would bode ill for the War on Terrorism. Indeed, some commentators have suggested that the World Trade Center attack may be the beginning of a new multi-decade struggle similar to the Cold War. If the orthodox leadership cycle is active, the US will likely lose the War on Terror and then go on lose World Leadership in the next global war, to begin about two decades from now.

But the alternate cycle, informed by the saeculum, has the United States midway though the world power phase, having won a second run as world leader, just as Britain did after defeating Napoleon. This position implies that the United States should win the War on Terrorism. The outcome of the War on Terrorism can then serve as a test of the unified cycle concept as applied to the leadership cycle.

# The relation between the war/hegemony cycle and other political cycles

Frank Klingberg (1952) proposed the idea that alternating introvert and extrovert moods have shaped American foreign policy. During the extrovert phase, presidential leadership is widely supported and the nation has been eager to bring its influence to bear on other nations. During the introvert phase, Congress reasserts its power and the public is unwilling to venture on any more foreign crusades, preferring instead to deal with problems at home. Dates for the Klingberg cycle are compared to the world leadership and political cycles in Table 6.4. Extrovert mood is correlated with periods of increased war (global and supplementary wars) before 1973. Introvert moods tend to appear during times of reduced warfare such as the world power and deconcentration/coalition-building periods in the leadership cycle. This alignment is significant at the 75% level, meaning that there is a 1 in 4 probability that it could have arisen from chance. The Klingberg cycle is also aligned with the Kondratiev cycle over the same period, with extrovert eras falling into upwaves and introvert eras into downwaves. This alignment is also significant at the 75% level.

Table 6.4. Comparison of political cycles

| War/Leadership* | Klingberg | Political | Saeculum |
|---|---|---|---|
| 1763-1792 (DC/CB) | 1776-1798 (I) | 1765-1787 (L) | 1773-1794 (C) |
| 1792-1815 (GW) | | 1787-1800 (C) | 1794-1821 (H) |
| | 1798-1824 (E) | 1800-1816 (L) | |
| 1815-1850 (WP) | | 1816-1828 (C) | 1821-1844 (A) |
| | 1824-1844 (I) | 1828-1840 (L) | |
| 1850-1873 (SW) | 1844-1871 (E) | 1840-1860 (C) | 1844-1860 (U) |
| | | 1860-1872 (L) | 1860-1877 (C) |
| 1873-1907 (DC/CB) | 1871-1891 (I) | 1872-1901 (C) | 1877-1896 (H) |
| 1907-1918 (GW) | 1891-1919 (E) | 1901-1918 (L) | 1896-1917 (A) |
| 1918-1941 (WP) | 1919-1940 (I) | 1918-1931 (C) | 1917-1929 (U) |
| | | 1931-1946 (L) | 1929-1946 (C) |
| 1941-1964 (SW) | 1940-1973 (E) | 1946-1960 (C) | 1946-1964 (H) |
| 1964-1983 (DC/CB) | | 1960-1980 (L) | 1964-1984 (A) |
| 1983-1991 (GW) | 1973-1991 (I) | | |
| 1991-    (WP) | 1991-    (E) | 1980-2001 (C) | 1984-2001 (U) |
| | | 2001-    (L) | 2001-    (C) |

*Here GW=global war, WP=world power, SW=supplementary war (delegitimization) DC/CB=deconcentration/coalition-building

The alignment with the Kondratiev cycle is understandable in terms of Kondratiev social dynamics. Kondratiev downwaves show a higher frequency of internal unrest due to economic troubles (Alexander, 2002), so it makes sense that a democratic society would shift from an external focus to an internal one as the Kondratiev wave shifted from up to down. For example, the shift from extrovert to introvert mood after 1973 could reflect economic events (stagflation, decline of real wages) as much as post-Vietnam malaise. The 1973 turning point in real wages is a consequence of the peaking of the mass-production economy innovation wave (a Kondratiev feature).

Similarly, the alignment with the leadership cycle makes sense for the time before the US became the greatest power. One would expect non-hegemonic foreign policy to be most active at times when the hegemonic order is being challenged, that is, during periods of global war and supplementary war (agenda-setting). Once the

US became the greatest power, however, one would expect the nation to remain in its extrovert phase during the period of world power because exercise of hegemony requires an extrovert-type policy.

This did not happen after WW I, the US went into an introvert mode just as it had after previous periods of global war, creating the world war anomaly as a result. The development of an introvert era after the US had achieved hegemonic power suggests that the Klingberg cycle does not merely reflect the leadership cycle. Rather, it possesses an internal dynamic of it own. Thus, the Klingberg cycle continued to follow the Kondratiev cycle until 1973 as if the US was not hegemonic. Not only that, but the Kondratiev that the Klingberg cycle followed was still at its old length of about fifty years. The year 1973 is interesting because it represents the time when the Kondratiev peak *should* have occurred, 53 years after the last one in 1920. In chapter four I advanced the idea that the Federal Reserve should have hiked interest rates around 1970 if they wanted to preserve the gold standard. Had they done so, a serious recession would have ensued and the Kondratiev peak would have occurred in the early 1970's (on the fifty-year schedule). For this to happen the liberal era would have had to come to an end with the Nixon landslide in 1972. The Vietnam war would be a "peak war" analogous to WW I, which would mark the end of a 27 year upwave and delegitimization era. It would be followed by a ~27 year downwave deconcentration era of declining American power. Today we would be in the early stages of a global war, in which a new hegemon, probably China, would emerge. Economic elements of this scenario were imagined by Shuman and Rosenau in their 1972 book *The Kondratieff Wave*. They hypothesized that the Kondratiev peak had occurred in 1970 and that the late 1970's would see mild deflation and a stock market boom, with a crash in the early 1980's.

As discussed in chapter four, no anti-inflation action was taken in 1970; it was delayed by 10 years because of the effect of the generational paradigm on policy makers. The effect of the paradigm was to delay the Kondratiev peak by a decade, extending the length of the Kondratiev cycle. Cycle-lengthening actions in the 1980's and 1990's, also the result of the generational paradigm, resulting in further extension of the cycle length. As a result, Shuman and Rosenau's predictions *did* come true, just twenty years late.

The abrupt failure of the Klingberg cycle to align with anything after 1973 resulted from the cycle lengthening caused by the action of the generational paradigm on domestic policy-making. For two decades after Vietnam, the US was undeniably in an introvert mood, yet during this time the USSR was defeated in a global war and the US is now enjoying a new world power era. Since 1991, the Klingberg cycle shifted again to an extrovert mood, this time in alignment with a world power era (as it was not in the last cycle), but no longer in alignment with the Kondratiev cycle. The victory in the Cold War was a very passive activity. There was no great war. Instead the US hegemon simply continued the pressure of the Cold War arms race on the Soviet challenger in the hope that the latter would collapse from internal weakness first. This bloodless struggle worked and it is likely that future great power conflicts will be resolved in a similar way.

Several issues need to be resolved about the interaction between the leadership cycle and the Klingberg cycle after WW I. One is why do these mood oscillations occur? It is one thing when America was not the greatest power, then she was simply dancing to the tune played by the other great powers. But once she became great herself, why did she continue to follow the same tune? Why did post-1918 America reject hegemony after fighting a war to get it? Previous hegemons did not behave in this way, what makes America different?

I believe this did not happen with previous hegemons because they were not democracies when they started playing the great power game. There was no tradition of popular moods having an effect on foreign policy. International politics was originally the "great game" of a handful of European princes who viewed their nations as their personal property. As European nations gradually became more democratically ruled they continued to play the same game by force of tradition, each developing a cadre of experienced diplomats and military leaders to do so. The United States alone among great powers entered the game as a democracy. Thus, US foreign policy has always been influenced by domestic politics to a degree not seen in other great powers.

Domestic politics is the realm of the political cycle. Table 6.4 shows how the Klingberg and leadership cycle align with the Political Cycle. Each extrovert period contains sizable portions of both liberal and conservative eras. Liberal content has ranged from 42-64% of previous extrovert eras. This split is also true of introvert eras, except the proportions are more variable (5-75% liberal). This shows that the extrovert versus introvert mood has nothing to do with liberalism versus conservatism. Both ideologies either supported or did not support an active foreign policy depending on position within the Klingberg cycle. As the nation grew, the extrovert period began to show a pattern of conservative zeitgeist early in the era and liberal zeitgeist at the end.

The beginning of extrovert eras at the end of downwaves in the 1840's and 1890s saw small-scale, profitable wars (Mexican and Spanish-American Wars) consistent with conservative ideology. The US was establishing itself as a regional power, with territorial grabs in Mexico in the 1840's and gunboat diplomacy in Latin America and the Pacific in the 1890's. The late nineteenth century expansion was fundamentally the same kind of colony chasing that the other great powers were pursuing, except the US mostly sought business opportunities rather than territory. America enjoyed a free hand in Latin America, thanks to the Monroe Doctrine, which had staked out that region of the world as a US bailiwick seventy years earlier, when there was little great power interest in the region. American expansion did not produce the kind of great power rivalry that expansion efforts of other Powers did. Hence, America was not part of any coalition-building, even though she was undeniably a great power and in an expansionary mood.

Halfway through these extroverted eras, the zeitgeist shifted from conservative to liberal. Both extroverted periods ended with big liberal wars (Civil War and WW I). Both were followed by conservative eras that were ushered in by ideological dissatisfaction with liberal war policies. This dissatisfaction translates to the start of a new introvert era. The consequences of the conservative/introvert shift after WW I created the world war anomaly. This shift was a luxury no longer affordable for a nation whose economic power had become hegemonic in size. American economic power at the time of WW I was so great that her participation in that European war would guarantee victory to whatever side the US joined.

Thus, once the US declared war on Germany, Germany's fate was sealed. Germany's bid for hegemony was turned back, but not by any of the great powers who had started the conflict. The old hegemon, Britain, lacked the might to exercise hegemony over the more powerful Germany. Only the United States, whose power had crushed German aspirations, could do so.

But the US had not sought hegemony when she entered the war. The US had no territorial ambitions in Europe, or in any European colonies, for that matter. With a continental homeland and an entire hemisphere as her imperial domain, the US desired nothing out of the Old World. The Wilson administration had pursued war for what amounted to idealistic reasons. Entry into war reflected Wilson's liberal internationalist ideas. There was no compelling national interest to continue Wilson's policies after he left power.

Thus, when the shift to a conservative zeitgeist occurred, hegemonic policy (Wilsonian internationalism) was rejected as distasteful liberalism. That is, domestic politics (the political cycle) trumped foreign policy (the leadership cycle), changing it (shortening it to ~72 tears). In chapter four it was argued that domestic politics in the New Deal and afterward trumped the Kondratiev cycle, changing it (lengthening it to ~72 years). The two may be connected; the failure of the US to act as hegemon in the aftermath of the stock market crash may have helped intensify the Great Depression, leading to the cycle-distorting Keynesian policy. The key idea here is intrusion of US domestic politics into the international political economy disrupted the international Kondratiev and leadership cycles, eventually forcing them into 72-year lengths aligned with the 18-year pulse of US domestic politics. This intrusion occurred as the US became the most powerful nation in the world. This view is different from the one I advanced in *The Kondratiev Cycle*, in which I hypothesized that industrialization was the responsible factor.

It was not until late in the 1931-46 liberal era that the US was again able to act internationally, by entering WW II and acting as a hegemon afterward. This was a departure from previous extrovert eras. The 1940-1973 extrovert era began with a big liberal war as well as ending with one. The nation entered a conservative era after WW II, just as it had after WW I. This time the conservative response was different. As discussed in chapter two, conservatives had been unable to roll back the New Deal and reduce the size of government. Conservatives generally prefer defense expenditures to social welfare spending, and so conservatives became supporters of a big defense establishment. There was no retreat into isolationism; instead the US maintained an extremely powerful navy, as befits a hegemon, and a first-rate army and air force as well.

This change in the conservative position with respect to world leadership created alignment on matters of defense between liberals and conservatives in the early years of the Cold War. Defense spending soared, squeezing out new domestic initiatives, which was fine during the conservative fifties. With the onset of a liberal era in the 1960's, liberal leaders wished to expand the role of the Federal government to deal with issues of socioeconomic inequity raised by the Civil Rights movement, not only between races, but also between classes. But they also felt they had to get engaged in Vietnam to stop the advance of Communism. This dual policy led to the "guns and butter" policy of the Johnson administration which helped bring in the stagflation that later discredited liberalism as was discussed in chapter four.

The failure of the Vietnam War disillusioned most liberals with the practice of hegemony. Another factor was the revelation of CIA involvement in removal of elected foreign leaders whose policies went against US corporate interests (another form of rent-seeking). These leaders were replaced with pro-American dictators who often practiced torture and mass murder of their people to suppress dissent. Thus, the shift to an introvert mood occurred under liberal leadership, just the reverse of the last cycle. Defense spending fell precipitously during the latter seventies and the power of the intelligence agencies was reduced. In the decade after Vietnam the nation fell to the nadir of its power with the lack of a meaningful American response to the 1983 bombing of the Marine barracks in Lebanon. That same year saw the beginning of the global war period with Reagan's Strategic Defense Initiative.

There was a switch in position amongst liberals and conservatives between the two global wars. The first war was fought and won under liberal direction, but then had to be fought again by liberals because conservatives had refused to practice hegemony. The second global war against the USSR was won by conservatives who followed up afterward with hegemony. Thus, one would predict no major war for this Crisis turning, a projection contradictory to what Strauss and Howe predict. My projection is also consistent with the Crisis turning falling within the Kondratiev downwave, which is a time of minimal great power warfare.

The entire global war and a goodly portion of the world power phase has occurred during a conservative era. Conservatives have embraced necessary hegemonic functions that they rejected during the last World power era. Partly this is because conservatives learned to tolerate big government in the form of a large armed forces and security apparatus. Another reason is American business interests are no longer concentrated in the Western Hemisphere—they are worldwide. Finally conservatives have bought into Wilsonian internationalism in the sense that if an ordered world is desirable (and it is for the conduct of international business) then the US must sometimes serve as a "policeman" simply because no else will.

The current extrovert era began in a conservative period suggesting a return to the old pattern of conservative early extrovert eras and liberal late extrovert periods. Like the 1844-1871 and 1891-1919 extrovert eras, this one also began with an inexpensive war, of the kind consistent with conservative ideology. Like the Mexican and Spanish Wars, the Gulf War was a very limited (and inexpensive) campaign. US allies paid for a good fraction of the cost. As the extrovert era progresses the demands of hegemony become more demanding and less profitable and less supportable from a conservative point of view, suggesting a shift to a liberal zeitgeist might be required to continue the world power era. Evidence of this can be seen in the Iraq war. The second Iraq is being fought under conservative leadership (many of key players are the same as in the Gulf War). But it is 12 years deeper into the world power phase and the extrovert era. This time the US has had to largely finance the operation itself and the operation has been more divisive domestically.

Not only that, but a lengthy and expensive occupation will likely be necessary. Such large governmental undertakings go against conservative ideology. The decision to go ahead with the war and occupation shows that conservatives now are willing to support America's hegemonic role even if it requires "liberal-like" policies. Recall that the definition of a liberal era does not require that liberals rule, merely that *policy* leans liberal. The Iraq war is the clearest indication so far of how a liberal era could play out in an era of Republican dominance. Even if the Republicans continue to hold power for the next couple of decades, the *environment* created by the various cycles will force them to act liberal much of the time.

# Chapter Seven

## *Bringing it all together*

In the last six chapters I have outlined six cycles in politics, economics and the culture. All of these cycles interact with each other. This interaction tends to produce alignment between them. This alignment is the key idea of this book. I believe that one can track nearly invisible cycles (and make useful forecasts based on them) by following another more easily tracked cycle that is aligned with the cycle of interest. In principal this idea is trivial. The difficulty comes in two places. First, even the easiest cycles to track are often elusive. I wrote *Stock Cycles: Why stocks won't beat money markets for the next twenty years* in early 2000 and filled it with cycle-based reasons a secular bear market had to begin soon. Reading it today, after the 2000-2002 meltdown, readers might wonder why I focused so much on the overvalued market, as if that was not obvious. It was not obvious in early 2000 that stocks would under perform money markets for the next two decades. That is, it was not obvious that a secular bear market was beginning in 2000. In fact, even today this is not obvious; many investors believe the market will head much higher than the 2000 highs over the next decade.

The second reason is that cycle alignment is hard to assess. Establishing the clear-cut dates needed for alignment comparison is difficult for many cycles, even with historical hindsight. Many scholars give different turning point dates for the same cycle. An even more important problem is that previously aligned cycles often abruptly stop aligning.

Over my six years of cycle study, I have developed a number of methods to deal with these two problems. To track the cycles I have constructed tools like reduced price to visualize hard-to-see cycles. I have collected literature data on religious/spiritual events, political events, social unrest events, war casualties, prices, production indices, interest rates, crime indices and army/navy sizes to determine my own set of cycle dates, presenting my results and the methods used in my books. Not all the dating is certain and I have had to make assumptions, which are documented in my books. Some of the results have already been and will continue to be revised by later findings.

To deal with alignment issues I have characterized as many cycles as I could over a substantial amount of time (~800 years). Over this length of time the way the cycles align has changed, but I have been able to detect these changes (and explain them) by having at least two aligned cycles at all times. This has allowed me to track the unity of the social, economic, political and cultural cycles over time without losing my way. I did this by hypothesizing that there was a fundamental cyclical process that underlies the cycles in various types of human behavior we observe in history.

I use the generational saeculum as an approximation for this underlying cycle. The saeculum I employ is largely derived from that of Strauss and Howe, except I use different dates for the 1860-1929 period as was shown in Table 1.4. The saeculum I use extends before 1435, when Strauss and Howe claim the saeculum began. I follow the cycle scheme of historian David McGuinness (2001) for this dating. In the next section I will present an summary of how all these cycles have aligned over time. The emphasis will be on mechanisms for why these cycles align with each other and why this alignment has changed over time. I will simply present the cycle alignments and my proposed mechanisms with no discussion of evidence or alternate theories. This has been discussed in my previous books and earlier in this one. The goal here is to give the reader an idea of the unity of cycles and that the subject of this book is not just a hodgepodge of mysterious cycles that vibrate for a time in unison for no apparent reason. Once a cycle concept is understood and dated it becomes possible for the reader to apply some of these ideas to develop his or her own view of the future.

## A cyclical account of Western history from Medieval times to the early 19th century

At the beginning of this period there were only two cycles that I have studied, the Kondratiev cycle and the saeculum. The two were aligned such that social moments in the saeculum tended to occur during Kondratiev upwaves. I advanced a simple population-based explanation for why these cycles occur and why they align in this way (Alexander, 2002). The upwave is a time of upward-trending prices and increased price volatility. A population that is rising faster than the food supply is growing should produce a rising price trend. Greater population pressure on food supplies should produce more frequent and more severe food shortages (famines), resulting in increased price volatility. Periods of increased famine are obviously more stressful times, and might be expected to show increased social unrest. This is what is observed. Times of increased social unrest are "eventful times", which is the hallmark of the social moment. Thus, increased population pressure on food supplies cause both social moments and upwaves. Having a common cause, the saeculum and Kondratiev cycle would naturally align.

One might further expect that the stressful upwaves/social moments would be times when young adults find it harder to secure a place for themselves and a family. They may delay marriage, reducing fertility, or perhaps reduced fertility results from poor nourishment during the hard times. In either case, increased stress results in decreased fertility. Decreased fertility will, in time, show up as fewer adults in the population and less pressure on the food supply, which brings the hard times to an end. A period of excess food supply relative to population slowly develops and prices respond by trending downward. This is the down-wave, which is a less stressful period consistent with a non-social moment turn-ing. As the downwave continues, fertility rises, which will eventually show up as an increased number of adults and greater pressure on the food supply, complet-ing the cycle.

Population growth creates conditions in which growth either slows when pop-ulation rises above food supply or accelerates when it falls below food supply. This process has a lag; changing fertility will eventually change the number of adults, but not immediately. The system I am describing is a negative feedback control loop. It is analogous to a thermostat and is easier to understand in terms of this analogy. A thermostat measures temperature with respect to a control setting. When the room temperature rises above the set point, the thermostat sends a signal to the furnace controller to turn off the furnace. When the temperature falls below the set point a signal is sent to turn the furnace back on. When the signals are promptly acted upon the system works well to maintain the desired room temperature.

Now suppose the furnace controller had a built-in delay of an hour before it can respond to any signal. In this case, when a rising temperature reaches the set point the furnace remains on for an hour afterward, driving the temperature much higher. Once the furnace turns off the temperature begins to fall, eventually reaching the set point, at which time the thermostat sends a signal to turn the furnace back on. The controller delay means the furnace is turned on an hour later, during which time the temperature falls well below the set point.

The result of this response lag is a temperature that cycles between too hot and too cold. This result is general. Introduction of a delayed response into a negative feedback control loop will produce oscillations. The population cycle is like the thermostat example with the population taking the role of the temperature, the average population sustainable by the food supply taking the role of the set point and fertility taking the role of the signal. The delay between a change in fertility and its effect on the adult population occupies the role of the controller lag. In the same way as the room temperature, the population will cycle between too high in relation to food supply (upwaves/social moments) and too low (downwaves/nonsocial moments).

The lag in the population cycle will reflect the time it takes to affect the adult population by changes in births—that is, one biological generation. Thus, both the Kondratiev cycle and the saeculum, being derived from this lagged negative-feedback loop with population, should show a timing element equal to one biological generation in length. Thus, Kondratiev cycle length has averaged 53 years (two biological generations) for centuries. Average turning length before 1700 was about 27 years, also consistent with the length of a biological generation.

A new cycle was added to this picture around 1500. This cycle was the War Cycle and the related leadership cycle. War has been part of the human condition from the dawn of time and the medieval era was no different. By the late medieval period, wars were no longer largely fought by feudal troop levies. Vassals had increasingly fulfilled their feudal obligations to their overlords by providing funds rather than actual troops. This development reflected the development of a money economy over the 12<sup>th</sup> through 14<sup>th</sup> centuries and the growth of towns which had always preferred to meet their obligations with cash as opposed to personal military service.

As a result of these changes, a "war-fighting" economy arose in which mercenaries were available for hire by anyone with ready money who wished to fight a war. There was no shortage of lords and monarchs willing to go to war with each other, the limiting factor was the wherewithal to pay for one's wars. The monetization of war meant that is was possible for a ruler to temporarily increase the size of the forces under his command by borrowing the funds needed to carry out his plans. Thus war ceased to be a purely political activity in which a charismatic leader could inspire others to support his cause through their personal service, and came to be somewhat of a financial transaction. Any ambitious prince, who could convince the bankers to lend to him, could try to make the world his oyster.

But bankers are a sober lot. They care little about glory or the righteousness of one's cause. Mostly they care about getting a return on their investment and the return of their principal. A good way for a ruler to secure a loan was to pledge certain regular revenues for the repayment of the loan with interest. For example, King Edward III pledged the revenues from the English wool tax to raise loans to fight the French early in the Hundred Years War.

During upwaves, not only food, but all types of prices tended to rise. Thus, upwaves were bullish for the producers of cash crops and other types of goods, because they received more money for their goods over time. Rising prices encouraged increased output of such commodities, which meant increased tax revenues for the taxing authority. Rulers found it easier to repay debts during upwaves and so were better credit risks. This made it easier to finance wars. On the other hand, during downwaves, falling prices discouraged production and tax revenues fell. This often resulted in loan default and bankruptcy of the lenders. For example, Edward III defaulted on his war debt after wool tax receipts declined during the early 14<sup>th</sup> century downwave, leading to the collapse of a string of Florentine banking houses in the early 1340's.

Downwaves complicated matters for would-be Alexander's. One way to deal with them was to encourage new trades that could then be taxed to provide new revenue streams. Such streams could support fresh loans to support additional military campaigns. Thus we see Edward III encouraging the development of a wool textile industry in the mid-fourteenth century. In the next century it was the Portuguese, under Prince Henry the Navigator, who were opening new trading routes to Africa and, later, to the Indies. The discovery of America by Columbus led to probably the greatest revenue-producing leading sector, the "royal fifth" of the silver exported from Spain's Latin American colonies.

During the 14th through 16th centuries the basis for capitalism developed out of the scramble for taxable leading sectors to fuel militarism. Capitalism is an economic system that features private ownership of capital, market-based transactions and a *growth ethic*. A central tenet of capitalism is that capital is mobilized with the objective of maximizing its rate of growth. This is a new development over previous economic systems that resemble capitalism in that wealth is privately owned and market economics practiced, but which lack this growth ethic. For example, 15th century Chinese merchants engaged in more extensive free-market trade than their European contemporaries. Rather than using their surplus profits to grow their business, successful Chinese merchants typically bought land and a title of nobility or education for their children instead, hoping to advance themselves or their offspring beyond the lowly merchant class and into the landed aristocracy or the learned Mandarin class. Fifteenth century Italian merchants also refrained from reinvesting their surplus profits to expand their own business at the expense of their fellow merchants. Doing so would provoke the same from others to the ruination of the trade. Instead they spent their surplus profits on sumptuous living and patronage of the arts. The Italian Renaissance was largely the product of these surplus trading profits.

Merchants, like everyone else, craved status and theirs was lowly. The route to status in China was land and education, in Italy it was lavish spending and patronage of the arts, but in other European countries it increasingly came from financial support of the monarch's war making policies (what might be called patriotism). As Monarchs came to realize the war potential of the income streams generated by a flourishing trade, the status of those who generated such wealth and who pioneered new leading sectors or otherwise brought wealth to the nation (e.g. privateers) was enhanced. In portions of Europe, it became possible for wealthy merchants to gain power and status without giving up their economic function. Rather, they could augment their status it by obtaining more wealth through business. They came to seek ever more wealth, beyond anything they could ever use. In this way Western merchants gradually developed the growth ethic and became capitalists.

The need for wealth to fund wars was insatiable, because rulers would match increased forces by their competitors with their own increases. The cost of war spiraled ever upward, requiring a ceaseless accumulation of capital to fund it all. It is this interaction between capitalism and militarism that propelled Europe from a backwater on the western edge of Eurasia to a world-dominant colossus in just three centuries. As this system developed, certain features appeared in the cycles. As described earlier, funding wars was easier during upwaves because rising prices encouraged business expansion, which increased revenues allowing larger military operations to be funded. Thus, upwaves came to be booms in existing leading sectors and in the warfare they supported. This development tended to make leading sector peaks cluster around the end of the upwave (the Kondratiev peak) as was shown in Table 1.1. It also created the correspondence between big wars and the upwave. That is, it created the War Cycle. Downwaves saw decreased intensity of warfare and the innovation of new leading sectors to replace the ones that peaked in the last upwave.

It was this interaction between the population-based Kondratiev wave and the foreign policy of European rulers that created capitalism and the alignment between both the innovation wave and the War Cycle with the Kondratiev cycle. The innovation wave and War Cycle did not merely get entrained into the Kondratiev cycle and saeculum; they also exerted their own effect back on the saeculum. Development of leading sectors and massive government spending for wars created urban prosperity and a ready market for agricultural goods. Improvements in transportation infrastructure reduced the severity of famines because food could be moved from regions of surplus to famine areas more easily than in Medieval times. The result was a gradual weakening of the population model for the Kondratiev cycle and its replacement with the war model for the Kondratiev cycle over the 16$^{th}$ and 17$^{th}$ centuries.

In the war model it is the economic stimulation by heavy war spending that produces inflationary prosperity during the upwave. Once the nation's capacity to fund wars is tapped out, the wars grind to a halt and the spending stops. Withdrawal of the stimulus produces deflation, beginning the downwave. The need to repay debt depresses economic activity. Business seeks new leading sectors, while workers struggle to find jobs. The social dynamics of the war-powered Kondratiev cycle are the opposite of the population-powered Kondratiev cycle. Upwaves, being times of exuberant economic activity reflecting war-related stimulation, now become the times of low stress and the non-social moments. Downwaves, being times of depression, see the higher stress levels and are aligned with social moments.

The Kondratiev cycle was completely unchanged by this transition. The population-driven cycle morphs into a war-driven cycle with no perturbation in cycle length; it remains at ~53 years. No impact is to be expected because the War Cycle and the population cycle reinforce one another. What is expected is for the two cycles to become tightly aligned, which did happen. The saeculum is changed, however. The old population-driven saeculum was two Kondratiev cycles long and had social moments aligned with upwaves. The new war-driven saeculum was also two Kondratievs long, but it had social moments aligned with downwaves. The saeculum shortened to accommodate the new alignment. The 1649-1844 period contained two complete saecula, but only 3.5 Kondratievs. This means that the saeculum went from 2.0 to 1.75 Kondratievs in length. With Kondratiev cycle length unchanged, this implies a shortening of the saeculum length by one-eighth. Average turning length in the 18th and early 19th centuries was 23.6 years, about seven-eighths of the pre-1700 length of 27 years.

Towards the end of the 18th century a new set of cycles arose. These were the American political cycles: the liberal/conservative Schlesinger cycle and the extrovert/introvert Klingberg cycle. As described earlier, the Klingberg cycle was a reflection of the leadership cycle, which is based on the War Cycle. It was aligned with the war-powered Kondratiev cycle until 1973 when it became clear that the Kondratiev cycle no longer followed its old length and that the War Cycle was no more. As a mere reflection of the other cycles, the Klingberg cycle does not add anything to the cycle picture. It is the liberal/conservative cycle that is more interesting.

This cycle was born out of the Revolutionary War Crisis, which forged the first modern democracy. From its very beginning, American politics has pulsed with a beat of its own that was independent of the other cycles. The Federalists, centrist conservatives originally represented by George Washington, gave way in the 1800 elections to Jeffersonian liberals who favored a decentralized approach to government. Sixteen years later the Jeffersonians had essentially been transformed into the conservatives against which they had originally rebelled. Their conservative rule provoked another liberal rebellion from within their own party, which ended with success in 1828. By the 1840's conservative ideology was again dominant. The 1788-1840 period demonstrated an inherent oscillation in American politics with an average length of 13 years.

# The rise of the 18 year cycle timing

This democratic pulse became enmeshed with another economic pulsation, the 18-year cycle in land values called the Kuznets cycle. By 1840 the two cycles were aligned. Between the Panic of 1837 and the crash of 1929, six Kuznets-linked financial panics occurred, spaced an average of 18.2 years apart. Between 1840 and 1931 five political eras averaging 18.4 years unfolded. The political cycle expanded from its original length of 13 years to 18 years after 1840. After 1931, the political cycle continued to operate at 18 years despite having become uncoupled from the Kuznets cycle. Instead, it has become enmeshed with the Stock Cycle, which lengthened to 18 years from 13 years after 1929.

All seven financial panics (1819, 1837, 1857, 1873, 1893, 1907 and 1929) occur in odd-numbered years. The probability of all seven panics occurring in either all-even or all-odd years is 1 in 64, making it statistically significant. Leaving numerology aside, the only commonality shared by panic years that comes readily to mind is that they occur in non-election years. This coincidence strongly suggests a political dimension between financial panics (a manifestation of the Kuznets cycle in the 19th century) and electoral politics. This dimension could involve efforts by politically-connected actors "to keep the good times going" until after the election.

Recall that a similar statistically significant alignment between bear market bottoms and non-presidential election years was used to demonstrate the involvement of politics in the stock market after 1933 (but not before). Land speculation was a more important financial activity than stock speculation in the 19th century. Interactions between politics and economics would naturally involve land in the nineteenth century and stocks in the twentieth. One interpretation of these relations would be rent-seeking behavior by political actors trying to affect market dynamics.

Panics occur after financial extremes are reached. Such extremes reflect market psychology rather than economic fundamentals. This suggests that the 15-20 year panic cycle reflects market psychology. At bubble peaks, investors *believe*. The belief of otherwise sober and rational businessmen in market silliness suggests an organized belief system underlies irrational market beliefs. This organized belief system I have expanded into the concept of the generational paradigm. New generational paradigms are created approximately every 18 years. This length is too short for the phase of life concept proposed by Strauss and Howe. Their explanation is very powerful and appealing in its elegance, but the cycles it calls for are too long. First, to make it work they have to invoke the Civil War anomaly and the assumption that cycle length has shortened as the pace of life accelerates. Also, as described in chapter one, a rigorous application of 22-year phase-of-life timing would project the start of the Crisis turning well into the next decade, which disagrees with their own 2005 projection.

The saeculum appears to run too fast for phase-of-life timing. According to the Strauss and Howe conception, a key feature of a turning is the generation that is missing. For an unraveling, the missing generation is of the Civic type. Yet when the recent unraveling began in 1984, a member of the Civic GI generation was president. He was replaced by his vice president, also a GI. GI generation member William Rehnquist is still chief justice of the Supreme Court fully 20 years after the Unraveling turning began.

It seems clear that the modern cycles in politics, the stock market and the saeculum all operate with a fundamental length too short to be consistent with a phase of life. Not only that, but this 18-year cycle appeared in the 19th century before "fast-paced" modern life appeared. The paradigm model that I favor is capable of producing political cycles with a natural length of 17 years as was shown in chapter four. Table 7.1 shows paradigm-based liberal eras obtained by adding 17 years onto the 'turns 50" dates from Table 4.2. These eras are purely theoretical. Also shown in Table 7.1 are the corresponding economic cycles obtained from Table 1.4. These cycles are observed. It is not clear how or why 18-year economic oscillations arose after 1819, but it is an observational fact that they did.

Table 7.1. Merging theoretical liberal eras with economic cycles to project social moments

| Paradigm Cycle | Economic Cycle | Composite Cycle | Strauss & Howe |
|---|---|---|---|
| 1833-1850 | 1819-1842 | 1826-1846 | 1822-1844 |
| 1859-1876 | 1857-1877 | 1859-1876 | 1860-1865 |
| 1893-1910 | 1896-1917 | 1894-1913 | 1886-1908 |
| 1932-1949 | 1929-1949 | 1930-1949 | 1929-1946 |
| 1963-1980 | 1966-1982 | 1964-1981 | 1964-1984 |
| 1998- | 2000- | 1999- | -- |

The dates for the theoretical paradigm cycle and the observed economic cycle were averaged together to produce a composite cycle that defines social moments based on the paradigm theory and economics. Also shown are the social moment turnings since 1820 according to Strauss and Howe. The centers of the composite cycle were in 1836, 1867, 1904, 1940, and 1973. The centers of the social moments were in 1833, 1863, 1897, 1938 and 1974. The average spacing between the social moments predicted by the composite cycle is 34.25 years, as opposed to an average spacing of 35.25 years obtained from the Strauss and Howe dates. The phase-of-life model predicts an average spacing of 44 years between social moments. With the added assumption of the Civil War anomaly, the expected average spacing should fall to 38.5 years. Thus, the paradigm-economic model fits Strauss and Howe's own dating better than their own phase-of-life model, even when the Civil War anomaly is factored in.

In *The Fourth Turning*, Strauss and Howe refine their phase-of-life model, suggesting that phase of life has shortened from about 25 years to 20-22 years since the early 19th century. In this case the theoretical spacing between social moments should rise to a Kondratiev-like ~50 years before the early 19th century and to 42 years after. With the skipped generation from the Civil War anomaly factored in, the expected spacing of post-1820 social moments should fall from 38.5 years to 36.5 years. With these modifications, the phase-of-life model fits Strauss and Howe's dating about as well as the paradigm-economic model. To test between the two models one can make a predictions for the timing of the next social moment using both models and then see which made the better prediction. The paradigm-economic model projects the next social moment (a Crisis turning) to begin around 1999 (Table 7.1), while the modified phase-of life model projects 2013 (= 4 x 21 years + 1929). Long before 2013 it will become clear whether or not the Crisis turning began with 911. If it is determined that the Crisis did begin with 911, as I believe, then the phase-of-life model can be rejected in favor of the paradigm-economic model. On the other hand, if six years hence it is *still* not clear whether a Crisis era was entered around the time of 911, then the paradigm-economic model will be rejected.

So far, I have described how a generational population cycle produced aligned Kondratiev and saeculum cycles. The introduction of war finance resulted in the entrainment of warfare into the Kondratiev cycle, which produced the war cycle. This entrainment changed the nature of the interaction between the saeculum and the Kondratiev cycle, shortening the former. Similarly, the introduction of democracy introduced paradigm-based generations, which created the 18-year cycle length after 1820. Thus, in the 19th century there were two parallel long cycles. One was the war-powered Kondratiev cycle with its aligned innovation wave and war cycle. The other was the paradigm cycle composed of the saeculum, political cycle and Kuznets cycle.

The latter of these was a domestic cycle dependent on American democratic traditions, while the former involved an international system that reflected the older autocratic polities of the great powers. When the US became the dominant world power, the international cycle was entrained into the US domestic one. Today all the cycles are aligned with the beat set by a democratic pulse first released by the American Revolution.

## What do cycles say about the 2004 election?

The major cycle to be considered here is the political cycle that says we have already entered an era of liberal zeitgeist that will last for about 18 years. Table 7.2 shows electoral results as a function of political eras since 1856. In the House, Democrats gain seats 59% of the time and lose them 41% of the time during liberal eras. During conservative eras the corresponding figures are 44% and 54%. In the Senate Democrats gain seats 50% of the time and lose them 38% of the time during liberal eras. During conservative eras the corresponding figures are 49% and 41%. In Presidential elections, Republicans are strongly favored (71%) during conservative eras whereas Democrats are only slightly preferred (56%) during liberal eras.

Table 7.2 Electoral results since 1856 as a function of era

| House | Conservative Era | Liberal Era |
|---|---|---|
| Democrat gain (avg # of seats) | 18 (35) | 19 (30) |
| Democrat loss (avg # of seats) | 22 (29) | 13 (34) |
| No change | 1 | 0 |
| Senate | Conservative Era | Liberal Era |
| Democrat gain (avg # of seats) | 20 (4.8) | 16 (5.4) |
| Democrat loss (avg # of seats) | 17 (5.9) | 12 (5.9) |
| No change | 4 | 4 |
| Presidency | Conservative Era | Liberal Era |
| Democrat win | 6 | 9 |
| Republican win | 15 | 7 |

This would suggest a slightly better chance for Democrat Kerry to win in the 2004 election. But Republican candidate Bush is an incumbent. If I focus on just Republican incumbents during liberal eras since 1856 I find that they have won three times and lost twice. This suggests a 60% probability that Bush will win re-election if today is a liberal era. If today is a conservative era, a Bush victory is also predicted. This shows that a Bush victory will give no confirmation of what sort of era we are in. On the other hand, a Kerry victory is only 29% likely (Table 7.2) if the Reagan conservative era is still in operation. Incumbency has had no effect, Democrats have beat incumbent Republicans two out of seven attempts (29%) in conservative eras. So if Kerry wins, it provides some support for the idea that a liberal era has indeed begun. Also, should Kerry win, and a liberal era is in progress, historical precedent suggests he is very likely to win re-election. During liberal eras, five of six Democratic incumbents have been re-elected.

Congressional elections might provide some insight. Table 7.2 shows that Democrats tend to pick up seats in both the House and Senate during liberal eras and lose seats in the House during conservative eras. These correlations are weak and not statistically significant. Nevertheless if the Democrats lose more seats in Congress following their losses in 2002, this does provide some evidence for the idea that the conservative era is still in progress.

Electoral results and party dominance do not correlate well with liberal and conservative eras or with any other cycle. Thus, I have not been able to use the political cycle (or any other cycle) to make valid electoral predictions. As described earlier, a liberal era means that the policies pursued during the post-2001 period will be liberal in comparison to those over 1980-2001. The Bush administration fiscal polices are liberal in that they have reversed the trend to flat or declining domestic spending begun under Reagan. Another liberal trend is the war in Iraq. The next section discusses the Iraq war as a liberal-style war in the mold of WW I or Vietnam, as opposed to a conservative-style war like the Spanish-American War or the first Gulf War.

## *The war in Iraq as evidence for a liberal cycle in operation today*

An excellent example of liberalism under a conservative administration is the occupation of Iraq. President Bush is managing a conflict in Iraq just as his father did. Many of the key players are the same individuals. But the two conflicts have played out very differently. In the first war, the United States was responding to an invasion of Kuwait by Iraq, which cut off Kuwaiti oil from the West. It was clearly an old-fashioned power play by Iraqi leader Saddam Hussein. It was clearly in the interest of the US and the other advanced nations of the world that Iraq should be driven out of Kuwait. A mostly US force was assembled that did just that in a matter of days. President Bush the elder was able to assemble a coalition of rich nations who would largely pay for the cost of the war. The operation was short, relatively inexpensive, and had a tangible payoff—Iraq's attempt to increase its say in the oil market was turned back. It is just the sort of war typically fought during conservative eras.

The second war is entirely different. Beating Iraq in a war is one thing. Occupying the country and installing a new democratic government is a much longer and much more expensive proposition. It was not at all clear how the US, much less the other advanced nations, would benefit from regime change in Iraq. Not surprisingly, President Bush the younger was unable to assemble a similar coalition for the second war. The US proceeded largely on its own, with little financial assistance. Considering that President Bush is a conservative, it is remarkable that his administration has embarked on a program of what conservatives derisively refer to as "nation building".

But nation building is a requirement for installing a democratic government in a country like Iraq. Iraq is rife with ethnic and tribal rivalries and lacks democratic traditions. Much easier would be installation of a brutal dictator like the US did with the Shah of Iran in 1953. Replacement of one murderous tyrant with another is not a politically realistic option today. Today's political zeitgeist reflects the Boomer paradigm of mistrust of government, not the GI paradigm of faith in government that was operative in 1953. Instead, the Bush administration proposes to replace the regime of Saddam Hussein with a democratic government. Before the war, Iraq was said to have large stockpiles of weapons of mass destruction (WMD) which might end up in the hands of terrorists allied with the Iraqi leader. After the invasion, American forces found no WMD. It appears that the potential threat from Iraq was exaggerated to provide a conservative justification for what increasingly looks like an expensive liberal program of nation building.

The obvious question is why would a conservative administration want to engage in such a foreign adventure in the first place? The cycle answer is that we entered a liberal era in 2001 and now large-scale wars for idealistic purposes like "the war to end war" (WW I) become possible. But this tells us nothing about why a conservative like President Bush should start acting liberal simply because a cycle turning point has arrived. Bush has not suddenly become a liberal; he retains his conservative ideology. What has changed is the environment he faces.

The mastermind behind the World Trade Center attack was Osama bin Laden, a Saudi terrorist and Islamic extremist. Bin Laden had issued a call to war (jihad) against the United States largely because he was incensed over the presence of American troops, which he refers to as Crusaders, in the "Land of the Two Holy Shrines" (Saudi Arabia). Other pretexts for war were the US-backed embargo against Iraq, which had caused substantial suffering for the Iraqi people, and the US backing of Israel. The source of most of bin Laden's animus against the U.S. is related to Iraq. Had Iraq not been led by an aggressive leader, there would be no US troops in Saudi Arabia and no Iraqi embargo. There would likely be no jihad against the U.S. and no attack on the World Trade Center.

Anger over Israel would continue, but thirty years of history shows that Palestinian-related terrorism is usually focused on Israeli targets. When Americans are struck it has always been overseas. Bin Laden's group, al Qaeda, does not have a significant Palestinian element. Its origin lay in the jihad against the Soviet Union in Afghanistan in the 1980's. The objective for groups like al Qaeda has been the propagation of conservative Islamic beliefs into government. These groups see the superpowers as the key factor propping up governments they view as insufficiently Islamic (as defined by their extremist brand of Islam). Thus their enemies have been meddling superpowers, first the USSR who was supporting an atheistic Communist government in Afghanistan, and later the US, as a key ally of the rulers of Saudi Arabia. In the latter case, the US is considered to be "invading" the very center of Islam by occupying the land of their most holy shrines (Mecca and Medina) with "crusaders". Islamic extremists also decry American subversion of Islamic values by godless materialism. Unlike the Palestinian-based terrorists, al Qaeda struck early on against the homeland of their great enemy in the 1993 World Trade Center bombing. Eight years later they finished the job.

By removing the troops from Saudi Arabia and ending the Iraq embargo, the Bush administration could reduce the source of anti-American feeling in the Mideast back to just the Israeli-Palestinian conflict, which already follows a pattern that does not include large scale attacks against the American homeland. Unilateral withdrawal from Saudi Arabia and termination of the Iraq embargo would likely reduce the probability of further terrorist attacks within the US from al Qaeda or like-minded terrorist groups. Just as Soviet withdrawal from Afghanistan ended the jihad against Russia, so would American withdrawal end the jihad against the United States. But this would essentially amount to American surrender to the terrorists. This would be diplomatically unwise as well as a political disaster for the Bush administration. The only acceptable way to accomplish the twin goals of withdrawal from Saudi Arabia and ending the Iraqi embargo would be if the *cause* of both these policies were to go way. This cause was the intransigent Iraqi regime. The obvious solution was regime change.

Regime change requires that the Hussein government be replaced by something else. The political unacceptability of replacing one dictator with another meant that regime change would have to be accompanied by a program of nation building. And this is what has happened. One can rightly point out that the US presence in Iraq is far more glaring than its presence in Saudi Arabia ever was, and so constitutes a greater provocation for more terrorism. It does. But the US presence in Iraq, unlike that in Saudi Arabia, was not at the request of the indigenous government. The US forces are an army of occupation left by a conqueror. One does not need to be a terrorist criminal to strike at Americans in Iraq, as one had to be to do the same in Saudi Arabia. Hence American forces in Iraq can serve as a "lightening rod", drawing Arab nationalist anger to Iraq (and away from the American homeland). Better the terrorists attempt to engage the heavily-armed US forces in Iraq, who have the authorization and means to fight back, than the US civilian population.

Seen from this perspective, nation building and the war on terror are natural consequences of the first Iraq war. The first Iraq war occurred because of the breakdown of the old Cold War international system. Prior to this breakdown, a third world would-be Napoleon like Saddam Hussein would have to obtain the blessing of either the US or the USSR before embarking on a war of conquest. Saddam Hussein had received tacit approval from the US for his war against Iran, a nation that spurned both the US and the USSR. When Hussein contemplated the invasion of Kuwait, which was not an enemy of the US like Iran, there was no functional USSR with which to consult, and the US failed to clearly communicate the proper message to the Iraqi dictator about wars with countries other than Iran.

Thus, the war on terrorism and both Iraq wars stem directly from the end of the Cold War. That is, they are a consequence of the US entry into the world power phase of the leadership cycle. There are other cyclical aspects of the troubles in the Mideast. Mideast oil producers were able to humble the US in 1973, during Kondratiev summer (a time of naturally rising commodity prices), by quadrupling the price of oil and mounting an oil embargo. When Kondratiev summer turned to Kondratiev fall after 1981, the "oil weapon" became neutered and Arab oil producers were forced to adopt a much more submissive stance with respect to the US.

Rank-and-file Arabs did not understand how cycles of international finance and commodity prices could dramatically reverse the bargaining position of Third World commodity producers with respect to First World commodity consumers. They saw what appeared to be "co-opting" of their leaders by the West. The House of Saud (rulers of Saudi Arabia) had become decadent and weak, unworthy of stewardship over the very center of Islam. Proof of their decadence was their acceptance of "Crusaders" on holy soil. What had happened was that the Kondratiev upwave (favoring producers) had turned to downwave (favoring consumers). The House of Saud was paralyzed by the Kondratiev downwave, powerless to use their once potent "oil weapon" to further Arab causes after the 1970's. A good deal of the animus of Islamic nations against the US finds its origins in the Kondratiev wave and in the Kondratiev-linked leadership cycle.

The origins of the war are not the only cycle-influenced aspect of the Iraq war. The prosecution of the war is also aided by our current position in the leadership and Kondratiev cycles. The former ensures that no other power will have the strength or desire to check US freedom of action. The latter makes the economies of much of the developed and developing world dependent on the US economy. To keep their economies afloat other nations must sell to the US, which creates a huge US trade deficit. Ordinarily a deficit would lead to a fall in the value of the dollar relative to other currencies, which would eventually largely correct the trade imbalance. This would have the effect of reducing foreign exports to the US, which is undesirable. Hence, foreign nations must loan the dollars they receive from their trade surplus with the US back to the US. The vast source of credit made available to the US government means it can run large federal deficits without affecting interest rates. As a result, President Bush can have his war and tax cuts too. This ability to shift the financial burden for the war away from US taxpayers greatly softens conservative opposition to an expensive, idealistic, essentially liberal war.

Despite these cyclical advantages, the Iraq war could become a serious political liability. The key problem is that Iraqi nation building has no natural support among Bush's conservative core supporters. Conservatives support the war now because they support Bush, not because they like the idea of nation building. The natural supporters for this sort of policy are progressives, who largely are hostile to the Bush administration. A lengthy occupation will create a large population of entitlement-seeking veterans, who will require expensive programs to deal with problems stemming from the war. To deal with them, the Bush administration will likely steer to the left on some issues, while trying to hold a rightward course on others. A good example of this today is the passage of a Medicare prescription drug benefit coupled with right wing judicial appointments. The future, assuming Bush wins re-election, could see more welfare spending, especially for veterans, with conservative social policy to try to balance it out.

The Iraq war well illustrates how the various socioeconomic cycles combine to create an environment in which it is almost impossible to steer a completely conservative course in policy. This, of course, is what makes the present period a liberal era.

# Chapter Eight

# Issues for the current liberal era

In this chapter I discuss the effect of a new political era on a number of important issues. For each I will present the issue, its causes, what can be done about it and what a liberal era says about how the problem will actually be addressed.

## The Social Security Crisis

Everybody is aware that a crisis in the Social Security system is looming. The enormous baby boom generation will bankrupt the Social Security system simply because there are so many of them relative to younger generations, who will be paying into the system. This is a real problem. Social Security is structured as a pay-as-you-go program. Taxes paid by workers below retirement age are received by retirees. Over the long run the two must balance as described by equation 8.1.

8.1       retirement income = (number of workers/retiree) x (tax rate) x
          (worker's income)

I will focus on an average worker who makes the median wage for this discussion. The retiree is also an average worker, who when he worked also earned
the median wage. Let $\rho$ be the revenue raised by Social Security per retiree,
which, over the long run, is the amount that can be paid out to beneficiaries in
a pay-as-you-go system like social security. Equation 8.1 can be written in terms
of $\rho$ as follows:

8.2       $\rho = (N_W/N_R) \cdot T \cdot I(t) = R\,T\,I(t)$

Here I(t) is the median worker real income at the present time (time t) and T
is the social security tax rate, which is currently 10.6% for the pension fraction
of the total payroll tax. $N_W$ and $N_R$ are the number of workers and retirees,
respectively. The ratio between them, R, is the number of workers who support
one retiree. Define Tr as the average time since retirement and I(t - Tr) as median worker real income Tr years ago, when today's average retiree retired. Dividing
equation 8.2 by I(t - Tr) gives:

8.3       $\rho/I(t\text{-}Tr) = R\,T\,I(t)/I(t\text{-}Tr) = R\,T\,(1+r)^{Tr}$

Here r is the average annual growth rate in median real income. The term on
the left side of the equation is the potential retirement income for a social security beneficiary expressed as a fraction of that retiree's income while working.
This ratio I will denote as P, the retirement payout ratio. With this definition,
equation 8.3 becomes

8.4       $P = R\,T\,(1+r)^{Tr}$

When social security was established, the median wage was rising in real
terms. For the fifty years before 1973, real wages grew at an average rate of 2.6%.
What this means is the income received by the average retiree when he was still
working was less that that earned by the average worker in the present, reflecting
the growth of real wages over the period of time the average retiree has been
retired. For example, assuming a retirement age of 65 and life expectancy at age
65 of 83, I estimated that the average age of a recipient of the Social Security old
age pension would be about 76. That is, she has been retired for about 11 years
(Tr = 11). With r = 2.6% and Tr = 11, equation 8.4 becomes:

## 8.5    P = 1.32 R T

The fraction of working income the retiree can receive (P) depends directly on the number of workers paying into the system relative to the number retired (R), the rate at which they are taxed (T), and their income relative to what average workers earned when the average retiree retired (1.32). If variable birth rates are ignored, a crude value for R can be obtained from the ratio of years worked to years retired. Life expectancy at age 65 is 83, so the typical retiree spends 18 years retired. If we assume 42 years worked and 18 years retired, on average, this gives a value for R of 42/18 = 2.3. The current social security tax rate is 12.4%, but 1.8% goes to disability insurance, leaving 10.6% for retirement pensions. If T = 10.6% and R = 2.3 are plugged into equation 8.5, a value of 0.32 is obtained for P. According to the social security administration the current ratio of median benefits to median income is 0.30, which is lower than the 0.32 figure. That is, the current tax rate of 10.6% should be sufficient to handle the pension problem even in a "steady state population", in which birth rate is relatively fixed over time.

But there is a problem. It is the assumption that wages rise by 32% during the time the average retiree has been retired. This was true before 1973, but not since. Today's median-wage workers do not earn any more than those of decades previously. As a result, the 1.32 in equation 8.5 becomes 1.0 and P becomes 0.24, which is too little.

Here we come to the key issue. Social security was created at a time when wages and the standard of living they buy grew continuously. The income and standard of living of retirees is "frozen" at a level related to what they had experienced when they were working. In an economy with rapidly rising real wages, the pension received by a retiree after a couple of decades of retirement is small compared to what workers are earning now. It is *not* small compared to the *expectations* of the retiree, which were formed when he/she was still working, when real wages were much lower. As a result of wage growth, up until the 1970's typical retirees were poor by the standards of younger working people. Yet by the standards of the 1950's, when 1970's retirees were working people, these retirees were *not* poor. This growth in real wages makes the burden of providing for retirement easier for workers since they make more money than the retirees did while they were working,

Today's retirees are no different than previous generations. Their retirement income and standard of living are marked to the income they received while working. But, the lack of wage growth since 1973 means that the incomes and standard of living of today's working people are no higher than those of retirees.

That is, today's workers make no more than did today's retirees when they were working. As a result, the burden upon workers is higher than it was when today's retirees were working. The only way to maintain a pay-as-you-go system today is for a sufficient number of working people to pay into the system (larger R) or for each worker to pay more (higher T). Because the birth cohorts from before the 1950's are smaller than those afterward, there still exists a relatively large number of working people relative to the number of pensioners. That is, R is high.

Figure 8.1 shows a plot of a crude estimate for the number of retirees relative to workers (R). I simply calculated the average birth rate for people born 60-75 years ago and that for those born 20-60 years ago and calculated the ratio of the two. I multiplied this ratio by the 2.3 figure estimated earlier for the ratio of years worked to years retired. This crude measure gives R of 3.3 for today compared to the actual value of 3.4 and projects a value of 2.1 for 30 years from now, compared to 2.1 from official estimates. It seems to do a pretty good job of capturing this key factor for funding retirement programs. Also shown is the social security tax rate since 1965, the fraction of average income that can be paid out to retirees (P in equation 8.4) and the current ratio of benefits to income obtained from the Social Security website (dotted line).

Figure 8.1 Estimate worker/retiree ratio, tax rate and payout (P) since 1965

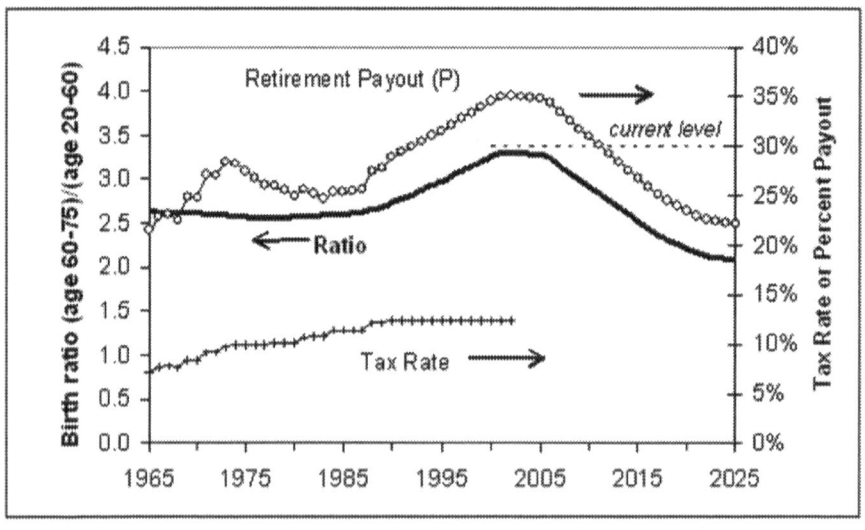

The figure shows P falling after the mid-1970's, which was caused by the end of rising real wages in 1973. This gave rise to the social security crisis in the early 1980's, which was addressed by increases in the tax rate. After the mid 1980's, as the huge late 1950's and early 1960's birth cohorts moved into the workforce, the ratio of workers to retirees began to rise and P rose with it. Today, potential retirement payout (P) is greater that the actual amount paid out. Social security revenues exceed expenditures today, and the excess is loaned to the government. The social security system is accumulating a surplus, referred to as the social security trust fund, which is in the form of government debt. That is, the social security trust fund holds the same sort of assets as government bond mutual funds hold.

Towards the end of this decade, P will start to fall and in 2018 retirement payments will exceed revenues, requiring gradual liquidation of the trust fund. The date projected from the crude model is 2012, six years earlier than the official projection, suggesting that the crude model presented here is conservative in its projections. By 2018, substantial increases in Federal income taxes will be necessary to repay the government debt held in the social security trust fund. This need for increased Federal revenue coupled with a tax-adverse electorate has the makings for a serious political crisis over social security. This crisis has demographics as its immediate cause; the retirement of the baby boomers threatens to overwhelm the system. In a larger sense, we can also place blame on the lack of real wage growth since 1973. Figure 8.2 shows the effect on P of resumption of real wage growth at its pre-1973 rate in 2006 and afterward. Were this to happen, it would largely solve the coming social security crisis. Basically, the negative effect of demographics would be offset by rising real wages. The pre-1973 situation would arise, albeit with a higher tax rate to compensate for the lower value of R.

Figure 8.2. Projected retirement payout (P) if pre-1973 wage growth began in 2006

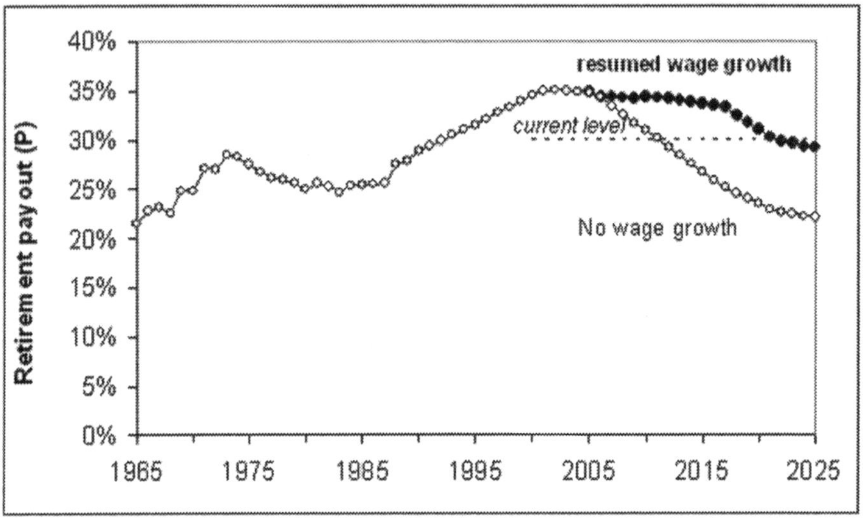

Hence, a critical issue in the social security crisis is this problem of stagnant wage growth. The cycle explanation for stagnant wage growth was the peaking of the mass-market economy in 1973 with no new economy to pick up the slack. The mass-market economy peaked in 1973 (Table 5.1), 56 years after the preceding railroad/industrial economy did. That is, the mass-market peak followed the standard Kondratiev cycle timing with economic peaks spaced 50-60 years apart. The growth boom of the new information economy began in 1980, 7 years after the peak of the last economy. In contrast, the growth boom for the mass-market economy began in 1907 (Table 5.1), ten years *before* the peak of the previous economy. Relative to the old economy, the information economy arrived 17 years late. The cause of the delay was Kondratiev cycle lengthening produced by the entrainment of the K-cycle into the saeculum and political cycle. The result of this delay was that the old economy was forced to soldier on after 1973 with no relief from the new economy. Saturation of the markets for the products of the mass production economy forced business increasingly to seek revenue growth through price increases rather than output expansion, which helped reinforce the inflationary nature of the Kondratiev summer period.

After the Federal Reserve sent interest rates skyward in a successful attempt to break the back of inflation, the Federal Government kept the economy on life support by massive deficit spending. Only after the 1990 recession, by which time the 17-year lag period had passed, could strong, low-inflation growth begin, which was powered by innovation rather than pricing power.

The 1990's resemble the 1920's, the noontide of the last growth boom. The "new era" bull markets of both decades were powered by public fascination with the life-transforming aspects of startling new technologies. In the 1920's it had been the automobile and radio; seven decades later it was the PC and the internet. Both periods were conservative eras and Unraveling turnings. Both saw an edgy youth culture expressed by a Reactive generation, and defined by a distinctive sexually-charged musical style: jazz in the 1920's and rap in the 1990's. These similarities reflect the operation of a growth boom in mid-growth phase. Growth booms put a premium on individuality, risk-taking and self-reliance that gave rise to the social and political characteristics of both decades.

Figure 8.3. Real wage growth during selected periods

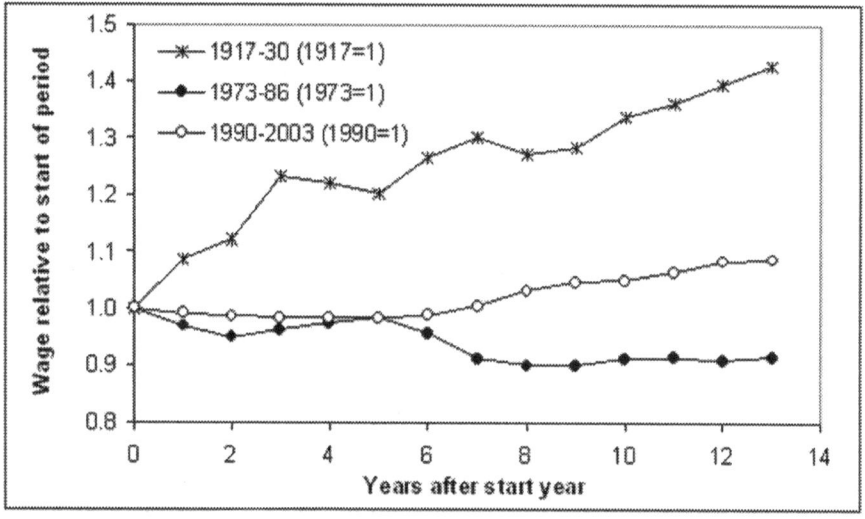

Figure 8.3 compares the 1917-1930 period with the 1973-1986 and 1990-2003 periods in terms of real wage growth. The comparison with 1973-1986 is based on position with respect to the old economy; both periods are the 13 years following economic peaks in 1917 and 1973. The comparison to 1990-2003 is with respect to the new economy; both periods are 10-23 years into the growth

boom. The first comparison shows a huge difference in wage growth. Wages after the 1917 peak of the railroad/industrial economy grew strongly, while those after the 1973 peak actually fell. This difference reflects the presence of a growth boom in its middle years during the 1917-1930 period and the absence of a growth boom during the bulk of the 1973-1986 period. The growth boom for the information economy was only getting underway at the end of this period. The second comparison shows growth in real wages for both periods, as should be expected for the middle years of a growth boom. Wage growth was greater in the 1917-1930 period, however, which shows the effect of the larger size of the mass production economy as compared to the information economy as was described in chapter five.

The end of real wage growth after 1973 reflects two factors. One is cycle lengthening, which created a 17-year gap while the old economy was in decline and the new economy was either not yet underway or too small to provide much growth on its own. The second is the shortage of sizable leading sectors in the information economy, which has muted what wage growth did occur after the information economy growth boom really got going.

A solution to the leading sector shortage would likely produce the sort of growth in real wages seen during the last growth boom. One way to do this would be by restructuring the way health care is administered in a way that would encourage its development as a leading sector. Another would be an energy policy designed to promote the development of a leading sector in alternative energy. This growth would head off the social security crisis. That is, solving the problems of healthcare that prevent it from becoming a leading sector would not only solve the crisis in healthcare, but also help solve the crisis in social security at the same time. Similarly, development of a replacement for oil will likely have a similar impact. The leading sector shortage is a major cause of the problems the nation will face with social security. Government action to promote the development of new leading sectors can be thought of as a "liberal" solution to the social security crisis. Assuming the hypothesis of a liberal era is in place, a solution along these lines could occur in the next 15 years or so. It will not happen if it turns out that the Reagan conservative era has continued on throughout this decade. A conservative solution, consistent with extension of the Reagan era, is private savings accounts, also called social security privatization, which is described in the next section. If the hypothesis that we entered a liberal era in 2001 is wrong, then privatization will probably be tried and its flaws revealed, helping to pave the way for the transition to a liberal era at a later date.

# Social security investment accounts: a non-solution

Suppose no solution to the leading sector issue emerges? In this case, keeping social security solvent would require tax increases, cuts in benefits, or both. Conservatives argue that private savings is the preferred way to provide old age insurance. Their argument is the pay-as-you-go nature of social security lacks the investment aspects of retirement programs based on private savings. In pensions or 401(k)s, retirement savings are used to produce an investment return that funds retirement instead of relying on future payers into the system. If individuals invested their social security contributions, they would get much more retirement income than they do under social security as presently structured.

To present this argument more explicitly, I will start by considering the problem of a worker making the median wage saving for retirement. I will put everything in real (constant dollar) terms to avoid having to deal with inflation. Since real wages have not risen in the last 30 years, I will assume that the real income of the worker saving for retirement is constant over the saving period. The question becomes: how much must one save and for how long, in order to provide a given retirement income until death? This question can be formalized a follows. Assume a worker invests S constant dollars per year for T1 years at a real return of 1% and expects to live T2 years after retirement. What retirement income (P) can he expect?

A solution to this problem is given in Figure 8.4. Here it is assumed that saving starts at age 40 and retirement assets are planned to last until age 90. In this case, T1 is the period from age 40 to the retirement age and T2 is the period from retirement to age 90. Thus, selecting retirement age fixes both T1 and T2. Retirement payments (P) are directly proportional to the amount saved (S). Thus, what one needs to know is the ratio P/S, which appears on the vertical axis of Figure 8.4. Retirement age is on the horizontal axis. The only parameter left is the investment return (I%) which is expressed as a series of curves for 2% through 10% real returns.

As an example, consider a worker who expects to retire at age 65 and invests his money in safe government bonds paying a real return of 2%. Moving along the 2% line in Figure 8.4 gives P/S of 1.6 for retirement at age 65. Let us assume the worker plans to use his savings to provide income equal to 50% of his working income after saving (this is the income he currently uses to live on and pay his taxes). Any additional income will have to come from part-time employment. If he saves 24% of his current income (S=24%), he will obtain a retirement income of 38% (P=1.6 x 24%) of his income. This 38% is one-half of his after-savings income of 76% (=100%-24%). Thus, the solution to the problem of how much to save to meet this 50% income requirement in 25 years starting at age 40, is to save 24% of one's income. This assumes a 2% real return on savings.

Figure 8.4. Pension as function of rate of return and retirement age (saving starts at 40)

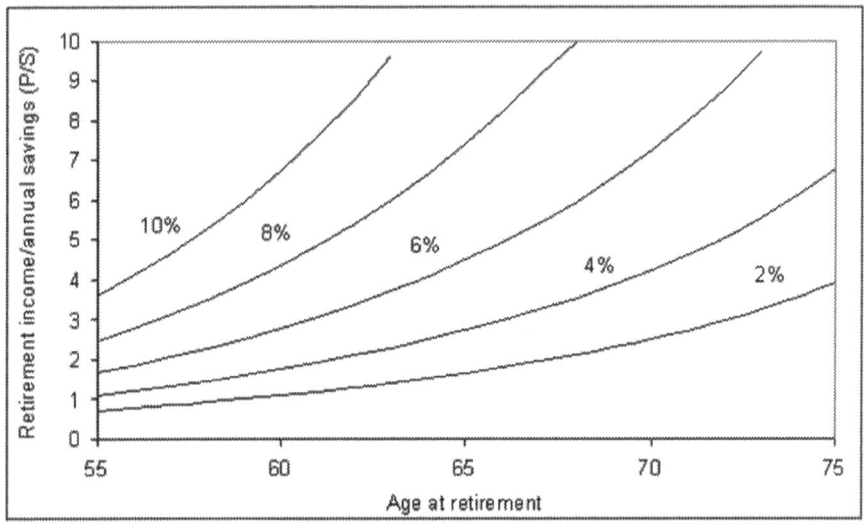

Most workers would balk at the possibility of saving 24% of their income. This is, after all, nearly twice their and their employer's contribution to social security. One way to reduce the savings requirement would be to retire later. If a retirement age of 70 is chosen, P/S becomes 2.5. In this case, he would have to save only 17% of his income. This is better, but still not very attractive.

Another thing he can do is start saving earlier. Figure 8.5 shows the same type of graph except saving is assumed to begin at age 25. In this case, retirement at age 65 would require a savings rate of 14%, while retiring at 70 would require only 10%. Another way to reduce savings requirements would be for the worker to pay into a retirement fund with an insurance feature that paid an inflation-adjusted income upon retirement until death based on fixed contributions while working. In this case, he need only save enough to cover retirement until the *average* age of death (the insurance feature protects him if he happens to live longer than the average). On the other hand, if he dies early, his heirs receive none of his savings, these go to pay the benefits of those who do live longer than average. Life expectancy at age 65 is about 83. Using 83 as the age of death, 25 as the age when contributions begin, and assuming a fee of 0.5% from the insurance company to run the program, retirement at age 65 would require a 12.5% savings rate, about the same as the 12.4% for social security. In order to do better than social security one must invest in something having a higher rate of return.

Stocks provide the best historical return, close to 7% in real terms since 1802 (Siegel, 1998). Using 6% as a more conservative estimate for expected real return from stock investments, Figure 8.4 shows a P/S ratio of 4.5 for starting saving at 40 and retiring at 65. With this ratio, a savings rate of only 10% would be required. This result is clearly superior to the deal one gets from social security and serves as the basis for comparisons between private savings and social security.

Figure 8.5. Pension as function of rate of return and retirement age (saving starts at 25)

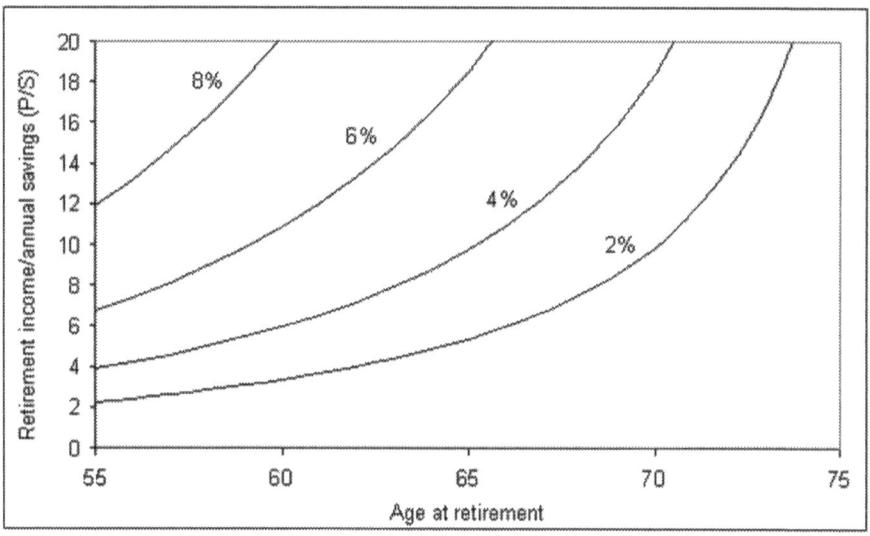

Stocks are risky and do not produce a 6% real return over all time periods. One can deal with risk by employing a balanced portfolio consisting of both stocks and bonds. A 50% mix of each would produce an expected return of about 3.5%. The same 10% savings, if begun at age 28, would provide the same benefit as the all-stock strategy. So it seems that private savings soundly beat the public pension program and that the conservatives are right. Social security should be scrapped in favor of individual savings accounts invested in a broad-based stock index and a diversified mix of bonds.

There is a problem with this analysis. Although perfectly valid for an individual, it is not valid for the entire population. If the entire population attempted to save for retirement in this way, the investment return of stock and bonds would fail to deliver much above a 2% real return. In other words, any broad-based program of mandatory individual savings accounts to fund retirement would create a situation much like the first example of a worker using government bonds as an investment vehicle. That is, a social security return is a realistic return for a universal retirement program.

## *Why an investment-based universal retirement system cannot work*

The reason for this counterintuitive result is subtle. To show this I will construct a hypothetical investment-based retirement system for the entire population. Using this example I will gradually consider all the elements that would be needed in such a system and then show how this system provides an inferior result to the current system.

The first thing to realize is that investment is not the same thing as savings. Savings refers to the accumulation of income not spent. Savings are accumulated in the form of highly liquid vehicles such as bank accounts and money market funds. These types of assets have shown a real return of about 1% in real terms over the course of the twentieth century (Dimson *et al.*, 2002). This return is even lower than the 2% return from social security and so are completely unsuitable as an investment vehicle for retirement.

In order to obtain a higher return, the retirement saver must purchase investment products. This investment product can be a variety of things: stocks, bonds, real estate, commodities, collectibles, etc. Investment products provide return in two ways. Some pay an income directly to their owner. Examples include most bonds, some stocks, and rental property. Investment products can also produce a capital gains (loss) return through increases (decreases) in the price of the investment between purchase and sale.

A universal retirement system employing personal savings would feature two populations: workers and retirees. Workers accumulate investment products. They are net buyers of investment products; both through their own savings and by reinvesting their investment income. Retirees spend their investment income and are net sellers of investment products (for the capital gains).

The income received by retirees comes from capital gains and investment income. Capital gains income comes from the sale of an investment product. The *net* retirement income obtained through capital gains for retirees as a group comes from the *net* purchase of the associated investment products by workers as a group. For example, suppose a retiree had purchased rare coins during his working life. He now sells them to provide income for retirement. Every dollar he obtains from sale of his coins comes from the buyer of the coins. The amount of money he and other sellers of coins can obtain from sale of their coins depends on the ability of the buyers to pay for them.

It is not difficult to see that retirement income produced via the capital gains mechanism represents a net transfer of income from workers to retirees. If there are many workers looking to accumulate assets (coins) for retirement relative to the number of retirees selling them, the price of the asset (coin) will be high and the retiree will get a large income from his sales. If there are few workers per retiree, the assets will fetch a low price and the retiree will obtain a small income from his sales.

Using capital gains to finance retirement involves a transaction similar to that of social security. Retirement income is provided directly from worker incomes. To the extent that retirees are relying on capital gains returns, *they are relying on a pay as you go system*. The big difference is that under social security, workers are required to pay into the system. Under a saving system, workers can chose not to buy the investment products retirees are selling at the price the retirees need to obtain to get a decent capital gains return. This makes relying on capital gains more risky than social security.

Over the long run, the amount of return that can be achieved via capital gains will be limited by the increase in the ability of the buyers to afford assets. As the population gets richer, as measured by growth in real GDP per person, the price of assets should rise in tandem. Indeed, the average capital gains return from stocks over the last 200 years has been a bit under 2% in real terms, about the same as the growth rate in GDP per person (Alexander, 2000).

Pay-as-you-go social insurance programs generate this same return by the growth of taxable income over time (which increases contributions per worker) and by investing surpluses in government bonds (which relies on future increases in GDP that will yield increased tax revenues in the future). Both social security and capital gains returns assume that future contributors (buyers) will be richer and so able to pay more in taxes or more for assets.

Table 8.1 Sources of personal income for year ending September 30, 2003

| Type of income | Billions of dollars |
|---|---|
| Employee Compensation (less social insurance) | 5361 |
| Social Insurance | 770 |
| Interest Income | 1082 |
| Self-employed | 834 |
| Government Transfer Payments | 577 |
| Dividend Income | 466 |
| Rental Income | 121 |
| Business Transfer Payments | 37 |
| **Personal Income** | **9249** |

But the private savings mechanism also makes use of investment income. Unlike capital gains income, investment income is paid regularly; it does not depend on the willingness of workers to buy assets. Table 8.1 shows a breakdown of personal income by source. Three income sources in Table 8.1 correspond to investment income: interest, dividend and rental. In total, they amount to 1.67 trillion dollars. The income received by working people is roughly the sum of employee compensation, social insurance and self-employed, which totals to $6.97 trillion. Investment income is then equal to 24% of working income. If we assume that retirees only require 70% of the income of working people, existing investment income is sufficient to support a retired population equal to 34% of the working population, or about three working people per retiree (less than today's ratio of 3.4 but more than the 2.1 expected in several decades).

To this investment income, I now add capital gains income. Significant capital gains income would be realized from the gradual sale of retiree investment products to workers. An important point needs to be made here. In the example I am developing here, it is assumed that the retirement assets of a particular retiree are not "owned" by that retiree. That is, his heirs do not inherit upon the death of the retiree. Upon the death of a retiree, his retirement assets would go to his spouse or if he has no living spouse, to the retirement trust. That is, retirement assets would be analogous to social security benefits, which can go to a spouse after death of the primary earner, but not to his heirs. The way this would work is that upon retirement, a worker would be required to buy an annuity that would provide his and his spouses retirement income for the remainder of their lives. So the investment and capital gains income that I refer to as being received by the retiree would actually go to the annuity trust rather than the individual retirees. The general results I obtain form the subsequent arguments will still be the same. The trust is still conducting investment activities on the behalf of retirees and with their accumulated assets.

Since capital gains income is pay as you go, it would work (on average) much like the situation for social security as it is today, which was described by equation 8.3. Equation 8.5 presents a version of equation 8.3 that is applicable for capital gains income. In this equation, CGI is capital gain income, R is the ratio of workers to retirees, T is the tax or contribution rate and r is the average growth rate in real wages.

8.6     $CGI = R\,T\,(1+r)^{Tr}$

Assuming no growth in real wages (r = 0), R = 2.1, and the current tax rate (T) of 10.6%, capital gains income can be expected to provide about 22% of median income to the median retiree. Subtracting this from the 70% requirement gives 48% of median income to be provided from investment income. Investment income is then enough to provide the rest of the income for a population of retired people equal to 50% (=24%/48%) of the working population, that is a ratio of workers to retirees (R) of two. Thus, this investment program could work if it held all of the income-producing assets.

This analysis assumes that all investment income goes solely to the retiree's annuity trust. Strictly speaking, this is not be the case because a fraction of income-producing assets would necessarily be owned by workers still saving for retirement. However, since workers are accumulating assets, all investment income generated by their assets goes to purchase additional assets from retirees, who are net sellers of retirement assets. That is, all investment income produced by worker's assets provides additional capital gains income to retirees beyond that accounted for by equation 8.6. The net effect is that all investment income goes to retirees.

What I have ignored so far is that investment products already have owners. In order to use this investment income to fund a universal retirement system, it is necessary for workers to initially purchase all of the investment products from the current owners so that they end up in the annuity assets when the workers retire. This means that additional funds will have to be raised through general taxation to provide retirement income to existing retirees while this new investment-based system is being implemented. Let us assume that the necessary taxes are raised and used to provide this income until retirees who have participated in the investment-based system during their working years now fill most of the ranks of the retired. Will this sort of investment-based global pension program work?

The answer is no. To see this we must consider the impact of an investment-based global retirement program on the price level of investment products. The price of investment income (which is what workers are buying for their retirement) is simply the inverse of the associated product's yield. For stocks, the relevant yield is the dividend yield, which has averaged 4.4% since 1900. For bonds the yield is the interest rate, which has averaged about 5.3% since 1900 for a mix of corporate and government bonds. This means that the average price for the dividend income in Table 7.1 would be 10.6 trillion dollars, while that for the interest income would be $20.4 trillion. Assuming a yield from rental property similar to that for bonds, an estimate of $2.3 trillion for rental income is obtained. In total, assuming investment products sold at their historically average price, the price of all the investment products underlying the $1.67 trillion of investment income is about $33 trillion. Our hypothetical retirement system would have to buy all of these assets. The current outlay of $770 billion for social security is enough to buy 1/43rd of these assets at their average prices every year.

As the economy grows the amount of investment income it generates will rise and so will the value of investments behind the income. The outlay for social security will grow in tandem, however, and should continue to be about 1/43rd of the total value of investment products at their average historical price.

So it would seem that after an initial 43 year period, during which time general tax revenues would be used to provide retirement income to those grandfathered in under the old system, the same social security contributions presently provided by workers would buy the investment assets needed start up this hypothetical investment-based retirement approach. Afterward, sufficient investment returns would then be generated in our economy to fund retirement for everyone using this investment-based system.

There is still a problem. Although 43 years of public savings are sufficient to purchase all the investment assets (at its historic average price) needed for the system to work, in practice, if any trust fund attempted to do this, they would find that they could not buy the needed assets. The reason is that these investments have current owners who would receive the $770 billion of worker contributions each year through sale of their assets. As the majority of investment products are owned by wealthy people, they would not spend the proceeds of the sale, but instead re-invest them. As a result, most of the $33 trillion of private wealth currently in investment products would stay in investment products. An additional $33 trillion from workers would go into investment products as well, with the result that after 43 years of contributions, the trust fund will own about half of the investment products, and will receive about half of the investment income. There will be twice as much money tied up in investments, meaning that their average price will have doubled. What has happened is simply that a new player (workers retirement savings) has entered into the markets for investment products, driving up demand for investment income. The price simply rises in response.

So in reality, the requirement to buy the investment products means that the global retirement program I am discussing here will end up with roughly half the investment products that it set out to purchase. It will obtain half of the capital gains income as well. This would be enough to fund retirement for a retired population less than 26% of the working population, that is, the ratio of workers to retirees (R) would be about 3.8, corresponding to a retirement age of at least 71 with current life expectancy. The present social security system would do a better job than this without the transition costs.

The key idea here is that an investment-based universal retirement system provides no benefit relative to pay-as-you-go, *as long as there is a requirement to buy the investment products*. Indeed, the result of such buying would be to drive up prices of investment products, reducing yield. This would create a highly stimulatory environment that would make formation of financial bubbles more frequent and possibly destabilize the financial system. We have *already* seen the effect of such a program on a small scale in the 1990's stock market. Contributions to 401(k) accounts invested primarily in stocks swelled stock valuations to lofty levels in 2000. As a result, stocks bought in 2000 will return less than money market funds for at least 20 years (Alexander, 2000). Should individual retirement accounts funded through social security contributions become reality, long-term stock returns will likely become permanently depressed (or at least as long as the program is in place).

The reason why private savings fails for a universal system of retirement, but succeeds for individuals, is this competition for assets. The existing social security system provides a significant fraction of all retirement income. It operates completely outside of the financial markets and so it does not distort market prices upwards. Of course, social security does not provide all retirement income. Many people receive pensions from their former employers and many others have private savings such as 401(k) accounts. These alternative retirement systems do compete for investment products. If the above analysis is correct, the growth of tax-favored individual retirement accounts in recent decades should have driven up the price of investment products, particularly stocks (the assets with the highest historical return). This would show up as reduced dividend yields, which indeed has been the case as shown in Table 8.2. In this table, dividend yields from 1871 to 2003 were broken into seven successive 19-year periods and the average for each period calculated. The yield from the most recent period clearly stands out as 3.3 standard deviations lower than the average value.

Table 8.2 Average dividend yield over successive 19-year period

| Period | Average dividend yield |
|--------|------------------------|
| 1871-1889 | 5.67% |
| 1890-1908 | 4.36% |
| 1909-1927 | 5.75% |
| 1928-1946 | 5.39% |
| 1947-1965 | 4.47% |
| 1966-1984 | 4.08% |
| 1985-2003 | 2.50% |

Advocates of investment-based retirement generally do not advocate a broad-based government-operated retirement program that makes use of investments. What is typically suggested is that individuals be allowed to place a portion of their social security contributions into self-directed individual investment accounts. The above analysis still holds for such a scheme. Diversion of social security funds into financial markets would still increase prices and reduce yields. The *average* result will be the same as that for a global system, inferior to the current approach. Already, the proliferation of 401(k)s has probably reduced future long-term real stock returns by about a third. As workers inject more and more funds into financial products, the lower their future returns (as a group) will fall. Some individuals will do well (above average) and retire early, requiring that others do very poorly (below average) and be forced to work until they die. It is hard to see any advantage of such a system.

The current system is not just better for those who currently rely on social security for the bulk of their retirement. It is also better for those (such as myself) who are using private savings for retirement. By keeping social security funds out of the markets, returns are higher than they would otherwise be, and it is possible for individuals willing to save to obtain good investment returns on average and so to retire earlier than those relying on social security. Social Security rewards thrift by providing attractive returns to those willing to forego current spending. Diverting social security funds into the markets would create a situation like that in Japan, where workers save a huge fraction of their incomes and investment returns are poor.

The key idea here is the economy can only produce so much investment income on a per worker basis. Table 8.1 suggests that about one fifth of the income deriving from the output of workers is available to investors; the other four-fifths goes to the workers. As the economy grows, investment income rises, but so does other income. And with this rising income come increased expectations for retirement income. Thus the pie is fixed and must be split between workers saving for retirement and private investors. Currently, the majority of workers do not save anywhere near the amount required for retirement, most will rely on social security to provide a substantial fraction of their retirement income. Social security, because of its pay-as-you go nature, does not and has never competed with private investors for investment products, which has resulted in the high average yields for investments cited earlier.

Should workers now be required to invest their social security payments in investment goods a new competitor for investment goods will enter the market, one with *substantial* buying power. The result will be rising prices (and falling yields) which will depress investment returns. Today, with social security out of the investment business, workers are told to expect 10% returns from stocks. Given a 3% inflation rate, there is a zero probability that stocks will produce a 10% return over the 2000-2020 period (Alexander, 2000). Even from today's (Dec 2003) lower market levels, such a return is almost certainly not going to happen. The reason for this is that stock prices rose (and yields fell) so much over the past couple of decades. Should social security funds start to be invested in stocks and bonds at any meaningful level, dismal investment returns will extend further into the future, possibly becoming permanent.

Should investment of social security funds begin, there will be winners. Existing owners of financial assets will see a one-time bonanza as the prices of their assets are bid up. Even bigger winners will be those, such as corporate executives, who can create new financial assets at will (e.g. incentive stock options) which can then be sold to workers trying to accumulate investment assets for retirement. This was seen on a moderate scale during the 1990's boom when vast quantities of shares were created by corporate insiders and sold for billions to a gullible public. With social security funds flowing into the financial markets an opportunity for much larger transfers of wealth from the public to insiders exists. Other winners would include those who sell investment products such as brokers, investment bankers and securities dealers. It is not surprising such a policy would have a number of strong advocates. Those who advocate for investment of social security funds into investment products often stand to gain.

Private social security accounts is an example of conservative rent-seeking that can discredit conservative ideology and reinforce a shift towards liberalism in accordance with the ideological dissatisfaction model. If the cycle timing proposed here is valid, individual social security accounts probably will not even be tried, but if they are, they should result in public disaffection with conservative proponents of the policy. Here the Stock Cycle will have a strong effect. During the secular bull market of the 1980's and 1990's, consistently high stock returns created the impression that everybody could save enough to retire and thus didn't need social security. This is normal for a conservative era, conservative rent-seeking is either tolerated or simply not seen for what it is. But the secular bull market ended in 2000, and as the secular bear market drags on, the nature of this type of rent-seeking will become increasingly clear to millions of working Americans as they come to find that their 401(k) accounts are not particularly effective retirement vehicles.

Government encouragement of the development of more leading sectors is one potential liberal approach to the social security problem. Obviously, this policy would involve liberal rent-seeking on the behalf of those new sectors. Another approach would be to expand the 12.4% social security tax to all income, including investment income. In this case it would not be just wages and salaries that are taxed (which have been flat since 1973) but national income. Since 1973, while wages have been flat, national income has grown at a 1.1% rate. With this rate, equation 8.5 would become

8.7     P = 1.13 R T

Social security receipts would be larger with no change in tax rate and no change in retirement age, but the increase would not be sufficient. A higher retirement age or reduced benefits would be required. This sort of an approach amounts to rent seeking on behalf of the poor and improvident against the rich and responsible. Nevertheless something like this can easily be imagined when the Social Security crisis comes to a head in the 2010's. It is hard to imagine, as some future politician is likely to frame it, millions of Americans volunteering to give up their Social Security benefits so that billionaires may be lightly taxed.

In summary, barring the development of new leading sectors, two general approaches to the social security crisis can be envisioned, individual savings account (conservative) and increasing social security taxes on the well-off (liberal). The first will not work in practice for the reasons just described. Furthermore the existence of a secular bear market (poor stock performance) and Kondratiev winter (low interest rates) will produce the kinds of poor returns that will establish this fact in the minds of voters. Thus the conservative solution will be rejected. The only solution left is the liberal one. The social security crisis shows how the present constellation of cycles forces a liberal approach to this issue, just as they have with the Iraq war. The only way out is if new leading sectors can be created, in which case everybody wins, rich and poor, liberal and conservative. The next two sections discuss how this might happen in two important economic sectors.

## *Energy Policy*

This section discusses the so-called "peak oil" crisis. The peak refers to the time when global oil production will reach a peak from which it will subsequently decline. This peak is sometimes called the Hubbert peak after M. King Hubbert, a geophysicist with Shell Oil Company, who predicted in 1956 that oil production in the United States would peak by 1970. Hubbert's formula was really pretty simple. He looked at all the geological reports that were available at that time and determined how much oil was available beneath the United States. He extrapolating the exponentially-rising oil production rate in the US forward and determined that half of this oil would be gone by 1970. After this point, U.S. production would have to begin to decline.

Figure 8.6 shows that Hubbert was right. Not only that, but the figure shows that shortly after this peak occurred, the price of oil began to rise. Until 1970 the US could act as the swing producer, producing additional oil whenever demand rose. Once the Hubbert peak was reached, the US no longer could do this. The swing producer now became Saudi Arabia, who demonstrated their new status in the 1973 oil embargo, which increased oil prices substantially. Saudi Arabia and other Gulf oil producers were nowhere near their own Hubbert peaks at this time. Their price increase was a political move not reflecting the fundamentals of the oil business. As a result, oil consumers adopted new fuel efficient technologies that reduced demand for oil (see Figure 8.6). Rising oil prices reinforced already powerful inflationary forces which led the Federal Reserve to hike interest rates to stop inflation in 1981.

Demand softened for oil and prices collapsed in the mid-1980's. The oil weapon had been neutralized and the Saudis now manage their oil much like the US did before 1970 when it was the swing producer. Just as the US production reached its Hubbert peak, world production will also peak (Figure 8.7). In aggregate the world is expected to reach its Hubbert peak around 2010 (ASPO). After this date, oil prices can be expected to rise more or less as they did in the 1970's. In a nutshell, this is the "peak oil" crisis.

Figure 8.6. US oil production & consumption and the price of West Texas Intermediate (WTI)

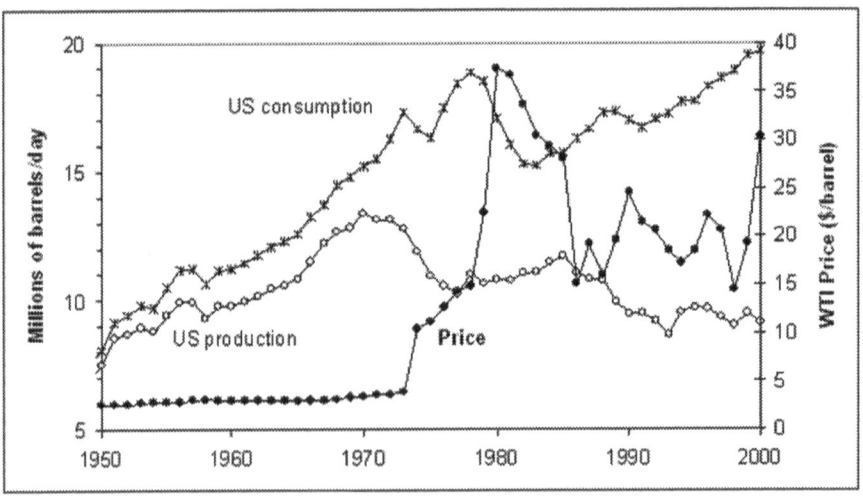

Figure 8.6 shows the effect the 1970's price rise had on US oil demand. Consumption fell in the recession after the 1973 embargo, but then rose above the 1973 consumption level in the subsequent expansion. Consumption peaked in 1978 and then fell below the 1973 level in 1980. It remained at or below this level for 14 years and began rising again in the 1990's. This example shows that the US was able to respond to the 1970's price increase in about seven years. But in the interim consumption rose despite soaring prices. In the event of the worldwide Hubbert peak, it will not be possible to increase production further after the price spike and so the adaptation might be even more severe than that in the 1970's. On the other hand, the oil market may well anticipate the peak by a few years and begin bidding up the price of oil before the actually peak comes so that adaptation can proceed more smoothly.

A liberal policy approach to the coming oil peak might be to acknowledge the inevitability of oil depletion and to anticipate the peak by raising the price gradually now, perhaps by a tariff on oil from terrorist-supporting nations such as Saudi Arabia and Iran. Such a tariff would encourage US oil companies to source their oil from elsewhere, bidding up the price of imported oil. This would increase the price of all oil in the United States, encouraging conservation and the development of alternate energy sources. It would also help the US to disengage from oil-producing nations hostile to America, which would likely advance the war on terrorism. As time goes on the tariff could be increased which would produce steadily-increasing oil prices in the US market, which would create a situation in which long-term investment in capital intensive energy sources like solar, nuclear and wind power would make sense.

Figure 8.7 World Oil production (source: ASPO)

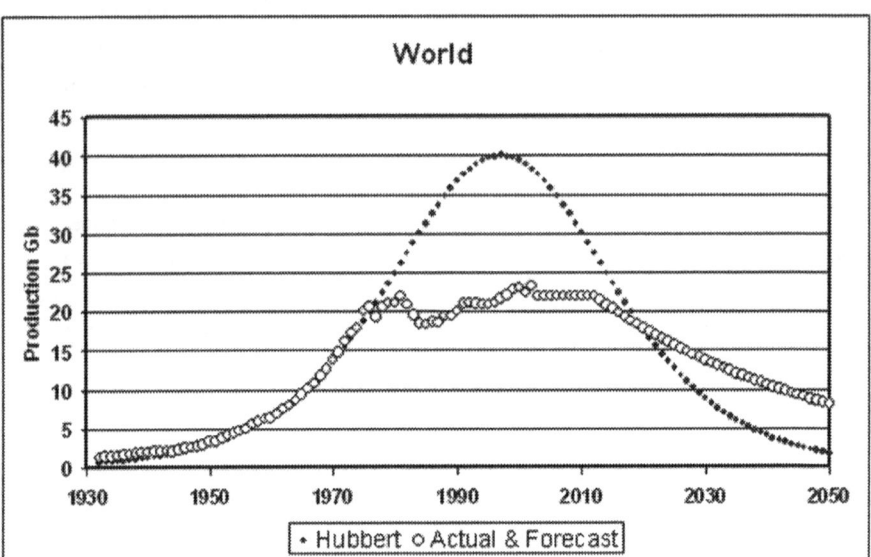

The extremely low interest rates on government bonds and high stock market multiples today show excess capital exists that is crying out for a place to go. Creating a new opportunity for profit in alternate energy by guaranteeing that oil prices will be high when long-term investments in alternate energy become operational would very likely ignite another massive bull market boom in alternate energy. It is possible that this boom would be so successful that US oil consumption would fall dramatically, delaying the Hubbert peak for quite some time and making the US completely independent of oil from terrorist-breeding regions of the Earth. Such a policy has much to recommend it, but so far it has not been proposed by any American political leader.

Conservatives question the peak oil concept. They quite rightly point to previous forecasts of imminent disaster due to resource depletion in the 1970's that did not come true, and suspect that peak oil enthusiasts are once again crying wolf. Conservatives also stress the adaptive properties of markets, which are well-suited to solving problems of resource allocation. They point out that government intervention into energy markets, whether through tariffs or government-sponsored research into alternate energy, can cause market distortions that can have unanticipated side effects that could worsen the problem. On the other hand, many conservatives have no problem with an aggressive US foreign policy designed to ensure the free flow of oil (at low prices) from the politically troubled Middle East. They fail to realize that this too is a form of market intervention and has unanticipated adverse side effects.

Countries typified by extremes of wealth and repressive governments in a democratizing world are *supposed* to be politically unstable. Resources extracted from such countries will tend to have high average market prices due to the action of speculators practicing arbitrage. Arbitrage refers to the purchase of excess commodity when the price is low for resale when the price is high, pocketing the difference. It is arbitrage that allows markets to act as regulators of the economy, providing a market to absorb excess supply when demand is low and making supply available when supplies are tight. The profits extracted by arbitrage produce a higher average price, which serves as a discount for the potential for disruptions in supply due to political instability. The greater the risk of interruption, the higher the discount and the more attractive alternate sources of energy become relative to energy from the politically unstable country.

Deliberate government policy to ensure stability in the Middle East eliminates this discount and makes Mideast oil artificially cheap, retarding the development of alternates and increasing the severity of the impact of the Hubbert peak when it does arrive. The vulnerability to peak oil created by decades of American support for authoritarian leaders in the Mideast is one of the side effects mentioned above. Another might be the al Qaeda jihad against the U.S.

Conservative foreign policy represents a form of rent seeking on the behalf of US oil producers and major consumers of oil, just as liberal tariffs and alternate energy programs constitute liberal rent-seeking on behalf of producers of alternate energy. The ideological dissatisfaction model and the sheer length the recent conservative era suggests that it will be the former rather than the latter that will be discredited. This suggests that the American people will become tired of the Iraqi operations much more quickly than they did in Vietnam, for example. Current plans to restore an Iraqi government in June 2004 suggest the administration is concerned about this as well.

## Health Care

The health care sector in the US economy is described by some as being in a state of crisis. As a percentage of GDP, healthcare expenditures are larger than those in countries with universal coverage, yet a large fraction of the population do not have insurance coverage. Health insurance premiums have been rising rapidly in recent years. Medicare is expected to run out of money before Social Security does.

In chapter five I suggested that were health care developed into a leading sector its growth could solve not only the problems of health care, but also many others. Such development would require that at least a portion of health care be conducted under a free market regime, for otherwise the necessary economic feedback needed to promote economic development along the lines of a leading sector cannot readily happen.

A market requires the interplay between supply and demand. Economic demand is the combination of need or want with the ability to pay. Health care is expensive; most people cannot afford medical treatment for serious illnesses. One might think there should be little economic demand for health care and it should be a small economic sector. It is not. Houses and automobiles are also expensive; most people cannot afford to buy them outright. Yet demand for these is strong and the building and auto industries are large economic sectors. Demand is strong for these products because people finance their purchases. That is, they borrow the money needed to purchase the item and then pay the loan back from future income.

If health care were financed like houses or autos, then a market system for health care might function. Although medical care is expensive, it typically is not more expensive than a house. A 25-year old patient who is treated (and cured) of a serious illness could finance his care with a loan that could be paid off over the next 30 years, much as he would pay off a mortgage. On the other hand, a 65-year old is not likely going to be able to pay off a 30-year loan and so would not be able to borrow funds to pay for needed treatment. Since the bulk of the need for healthcare arises late in life, use of finance is not an effective way to pay for it.

Suppose instead of waiting until one is ill to borrow the money, one borrowed enough to pay for possible future treatment while young so the loan could be paid back? The idea would be for a worker to borrow funds against future earnings and then invest them in a safe instrument. The investment would be held as collateral on the loan, and would only be available to the worker in case of illness. The worker would then make a regular mortgage type payment for the loan, but would gain a partial subsidy from the interest on the investment as long as he doesn't use it. Assuming he reaches old age without having gotten seriously ill, he would now have an asset that can be used to help pay for medical care when old.

For example, a 30-year loan at 7% interest with a $300 monthly payment would raise $45,000. Investing this at 5% in government securities would yield $188, making the effective cost of the $45,000 reserve against medical expenses $112 per month. After 30 years the loan would be paid off and the borrower would now have a $45,000 asset accruing interest at 5% to help pay for medical care in old age. Of course if the worker was unlucky and became ill while he was still repaying the loan, his asset would be depleted and he would have a greater burden to pay. There is also the risk of job loss or other financial mishap causing default on the loan. The risk of default after the savings have been exhausted constitutes the risk the investor makes in lending to the worker (and why the rate of interest on the loan is greater than the rate of interest in the investment).

This sort of financial deal provides a relatively small amount of money for potential medical costs at a fairly high cost. It is not really a good way to pay for larger, but unpredictable expenses like medical expenses. Insurance is the financial product that is designed to perform this very function. This is why health care is almost universally funded through health insurance.

Health insurance, especially that provided by a third party, was one of the impediments to the development of health care as a leading sector that I noted in chapter five. But, as we have just seen, paying for healthcare requires something like insurance; other ways of paying for healthcare will not work for most people. If no strategy for paying for health care for most people is available, then the size of the healthcare sector will be so small that it would fail to qualify as a leading sector even if it did function according to market economics. It would remain a luxury sector like the yacht industry and be a minor player in our economy. On the other hand, with employer-provided health insurance there is a disconnect between the recipient of the health care and the payer. As a consequence of this disconnect, the *value* of health care is not established. Based on what people actually pay out of pocket for health care, it would seem that it is a very low value service. Yet based on what is spent on health care, one would reach the opposite conclusion. Without a proper valuation there is no way for health care providers to receive the feedback necessary to improve their product. That is, there is no incentive to improve the value of the services provided since revenues are unrelated to quality of product. This lack of valuation is a sure sign of the lack of a properly functioning market in health care.

Here we come to the nexus of the problem with health care. Medical treatment is both very expensive and tends to occur late in life and so cannot be financed. Borrowing against future medical expenses is also not cost-effective and will not work. This leave insurance as the only practical option for paying for health care, which makes sense since this is the purpose of insurance. But insurance suffers from the asymmetry of information problem in which the tendency for healthy people do without insurance system makes insurance unaffordable for anyone who actually needs it. Group policies subsidized though employers eliminates this problem but creates the disconnect that causes the health care industry to fail to function according to market forces.

The government could require everybody who does not fall under Medicaid or Medicare to obtain health insurance, much as motorists are required to obtain auto insurance. To avoid the asymmetry of information problem, the government would negotiate with a consortium of health insurance companies to determine a single group rate for the entire population and people would be required to enroll in this group insurance plan. Such a plan would be have the consumers of health care held hostage by the suppliers. Since they would be forced to pay whatever premium the insurers required, there would be no market-based interplay between consumer and provider. Such a national health insurance system would guarantee that health care remained a low-productivity economic sector, a poor candidate for development as a leading sector.

The problem isn't really insurance *per se*, but the kind of insurance. Suppose *life* insurance was used to provide a pot of money to pay for medical procedures. The $300 per month used to purchase $45,000 in wealth available for paying future medical expenses in my earlier example might buy $300,000 in whole life insurance. This death benefit could be used to finance medical expenses of the insured while still living. The way this would work is the government would require all adults to obtain a certain amount of life insurance. Unlike heath insurance, there is no asymmetry of information problem with life insurance. People would be free to obtain their insurance from any company they choose. Like ordinary life insurance, there is no benefit payable to the insured; it goes to his beneficiaries. Life insurance obtained for the purpose of financing health care would have health care providers become one of the insured beneficiaries in exchange for provision of services. That is, health care providers would take a lump sum payable in the future (on the occasion of the patient's death) rather than cash up front. To prevent obvious conflicts of interest, the government would mandate that health care providers can only charge for successful treatment if they are accepting payment in this way. Providers of routine medical services that have little risk of causing harm would typically offer their services with two prices, one in terms of cash and the other in terms of an amount of the patients death benefit. Providers of procedures with low probability of success would only offer their services on a cash-only basis, as they could not charge for unsuccessful services using the death benefit payment method.

Young people would find that the cash price quoted to them for a service would be much less than the death benefit price, encouraging them to pay the cash price, raising the money through ordinary finance if necessary. The large difference in price from the two methods of payment reflects the long time the providers will likely have to wait to get paid. Old people would find the death-benefit price not too much greater than the cash price, because the providers are likely not to have to wait very long to get paid. They would tend to use their death benefit to pay for services.

Because healthy people who do not use up all of their death benefit would see the residual pass to their heirs, there is an incentive not to spend it all. Once the death benefit is exhausted there would be no more available to pay for health care. This would encourage people to minimize the use of this method of payment and to pay cash instead for whatever they can afford. In this way, each consumer of health care would be shopping with his or her own money, and with the death benefit everybody would have a significant amount to spend, especially when they become old and need it the most. That is, this sort of a scheme would create the market-based interaction necessary for development of health care as a leading sector.

This money is not free money; it represents forced savings by health care consumers to build personal wealth that cannot be spent on anything except for health care. Poor people are not going to be able to build personal wealth to pay for medical care under this sort of system due to inadequate income. Many individuals simply cannot afford to pay the amount needed to secure a $300,000 death benefit. Government would either have to subsidize the insurance payments for the poor, or provide a government health insurance plan along the lines of the existing Medicaid system for them. Similarly, children would be unable to pay into this sort of a system. Government would have to provide health insurance for all children whose parents are not wealthy. Since children are generally healthy, such insurance should not be exceptionally expensive.

I do not intend to suggest that a program like this will be implemented. It is simply one example of how health care could be restructured to be more market-orientated. There are many real problems with a scheme like this one. The program would require a substantial subsidy to low-income people; it necessarily contains a significant redistributive element. With levies for social security and this new life-insurance based health care payment, a large fraction of the population will be unable to pay much in regular income taxes. A program of this sort could provide a system in which the majority of the population participates in a market-based system that would create the highest possibility of igniting a leading sector in health care. But it carries a significant risk of backfiring unless it is carefully designed with backup facilities that would add to the cost and redistributive nature, which increases its political risk. In effect this program amounts to a type of national health insurance. As such, nothing like it could ever be implemented during a conservative era. If something like this were to even be seriously considered it would confirm that we have entered a liberal era.

Another option could be to break health care into two systems, one featuring free-market-based provision of high-quality health care to affluent and wealthy patients who can afford it, and the other featuring insurance-based provision of lower-quality services to those who cannot afford the market-based services. Since the poorest and sickest people would be in the insurance-based system, this system would run at an enormous deficit and would have to be government backed. The problem of this system is it would require direct taxes levied on the well-off (who are in the market-based system) to fund it. It is likely that affluent taxpayers would be unwilling to fund an expensive health care system for other people and such a two-tier system would collapse.

Something resembling a two-tier system might be produced by some tweaking of our existing health care system. For example, suppose the tax deduction for corporate provision of healthcare were modified so the deduction inversely scaled to employee income. For example, suppose a company could deduct health insurance cost multiplied by the factor $50,000/compensation. That is, a company providing insurance to an employee whose annual compensation was $25,000 could deduct twice the cost of such insurance, while they could deduct only half of the cost of an employee earning $100,000. This would encourage employees to cover their low-income workers, but not their high-income workers. High-income workers would either purchase their own insurance or finance major health care expenditures. That is, affluent workers would be encouraged to monitor their own expenditures and seek value for their money in health care, enforcing market discipline on health care providers.

Changes in tax law of this sort would not solve the problem of lack of insurance for low income people, although it would probably help some with this problem. What it would do is force millions of high-income people into the market for health care, in which they would perform the same calculations to optimize value from health care as they do for other economic transactions.

Modifications to the healthcare system do not have to be restricted to just the consumer (demand side). Modifications to the way health care is provided (supply-side) might also be effective. Roughly a third of health care costs is administration. Government investigation of administrative costs, with an implied threat of regulation, could reduce them. The government could provide free education to medical doctors and other high-salary health care workers in exchange for a period of service (at government salary levels) as employees in hospitals and clinics serving patients covered by government programs: veterans, Medicare recipients, Medicaid recipients etc. Government insurance programs typically pay less to providers than private patients. Government could make low-cost medical staff available to providers that take care of patients with public insurance, leaving other health care providers free to deny care to patients with government insurance. These other providers would then serve private pay patients, the rich and high-salary workers who lack company-provided health insurance. This group of providers and consumers would have free market characteristics and thus they could serve the function of developing health care into a leading sector.

Meanwhile, the poor, elderly and uninsured would be served by a second, essentially public health care system. Government would use its vast buying power to secure low cost drugs and medical equipment for sale at low cost to participating clinics and hospitals. In addition, the provision of high quality personnel at low cost would help reduce the costs of health care providers willing to serve poor patients and those with government insurance. The government would also have to restrict use of subsidies on private patients, as this would constitute unfair competition with private providers.

The government would provide education subsidies to produce a much larger number of trained medical personnel than are currently produced. The existence of large pool of personnel will also reduce costs in the private sector. In this way the government would provide lower cost medical professionals to private industry much as it does with scientific and engineering professionals through subsidizing their education. Training many more doctors is an investment as they will pay additional taxes after their government service is ended and they enter the private sector. These additional taxes could be considered as a return on the cost of educating them. Their public service in hospitals and clinics treating those at the bottom of the social scale will do much good as well.

A system like this would indirectly build a two-tier health care system without creating any new government health insurance programs. Additional spending would be in the categories of education and economic development policy. Large-scale purchase of drugs and medical equipment, even at a low price will allow drug and medical equipment manufacturers to recover their overhead costs and stimulate this economic sector. The manufacturers will be able to charge market rates to private health care providers and patients, which should help them to develop along the lines of a leading sector as well. This system would have government manipulating the health care economic sector in all sorts of unnatural ways and so would be a very unconservative proposition. Just about any action to produce a leading sector out of health care will be liberal politically. Conservative approaches amount to doing little or nothing.

## *Other Issues*

Several other issues facing our nation are fairly partisan in nature. A good example is environmental issues like global warming. Conservatives often deny that there are any issues at all and so there is no need for any policy. This is one reason why I have labeled environmental legislation as liberal events in Appendix A. If any legislative action in support of environmentalist issues is enacted in the coming years, it will serve as an indicator of a liberal era. Conversely, an absence of new environmental initiatives will help support the idea that the Reagan era continues. The hypothesis that a liberal era began in 2001 suggests that significant action on issues like global warming will occur over the next 15 years. Such action could reinforce energy policies. For example, a carbon tax is often proposed as a way to discourage carbon dioxide emissions that lead to greenhouse warning. Such a tax would increase the cost of oil relative to alternate energy sources and have much the same effect as the tariff I discussed in the energy section. Action on one issue (environmentalism) could thus "spill over" into another (development of alternate-energy leading sectors) and have impacts on yet a third (social security).

Another issue is deficit spending. The Bush administration is running large deficits because of tax cuts accompanied by large increases in Federal spending, both domestic and military. Deficits themselves may be neither liberal nor conservative today, but spending is liberal. Increasing spending is one of the reasons for my belief that a liberal era has already started. If tax-adverse conservatives remain in power, deficits will remain very large and government debt will grow tremendously in the coming years. This development will have serious consequences in how the social security and Medicare crises will work out.

I am not conversant with policy details in any of these issues. The purpose of this chapter has been to suggest some ideas on how a changed (or unchanged) political and economic terrain in the coming decade and a half will permit significant movement towards (or away from) solutions to many of the most pressing problems we face as a nation. In the case of the latter, we can expect a great deal of turmoil and unrest before the direction of movement is turned in the right direction. What this direction will be is unknown as are the nature of the solutions that will be adopted. The next decade or two should indeed be interesting times for us all.

# References

1. Alexander, Michael A. (2000a) *Stock cycles: Why Stocks Won't Beat Money Markets over the Next Twenty Years*, Writers Club Press, 2000.

2. Alexander, Michael A. (2000b) post dated August 21, 2000 in "The Kondratiev Wave and the Fourth Turning" on *The Fourth Turning* website (web.archive.org/web/20001205095600/http://www.fourthturning.com/c gi-local/netforum/thefuture/a.cgi/3—41).

3. Alexander, Michael A, *The Kondratiev Cycle: A Generational Interpretation,* Writers Club Press, 2002.

4. Alexander, Michael A, *Retiring Rich: The Ultimate IRA and 401(k) Investing Strategy,* Boca Raton FL: 21st Century Investors Publishing, 2003.

5. ASPO Statistical Review of Oil and Gas, Proceedings of the 1st International Workshop on Oil Depletion, Uppsala, Sweden, 23-25 May, 2002. Edited by K. Aleklett and C. Campbell, www.isv.uu.se/iwood2002.

6. Berry, Brian J., *Long-wave Rhythms in Economic Development and Political Behavior*, Baltimore: The Johns Hopkins University Press, 1991.

7. Braudel, Fernand, *The Wheels of Commerce*, Vol. II of *Civilization and Capitalism*, trans Sian Reynolds, New York: Harper Row, 1982.

8. Dehio, Ludwig, *The Precarious Balance: Four Centuries of the European Power Struggle*, 1948, reprint ed., New York: Vintage Books, 1962.

9. Dent, Harry S., *The Great Boom Ahead*, New York: Hyperion 1993.

10. Dent, Harry S., *The Roaring 2000's: Building the Wealth and Life Style you Desire in the Greatest Boom in History*, New York: Simon and Schuster, 1998.

11. Dimson, Elroy, Paul Marsh and Mike Stanton, *Triumph of the Optimists: 101 Years of Global Investment Returns*, Princeton NJ: Princeton University Press, 2002.

12. Elias, David, Dow 40,000: strategies for profiting from the greatest bull market in history, New York: McGraw-Hill, 1999

13. Ehrenreich, Barbara. *Nickel and Dimed: On (Not) Getting By in America*, New York, Owl Books, 2000.

14. Friedman, Milton and Anna Swartz, *The Monetary History of the United States 1867-1960*, Princeton, Princeton University Press, 1963.

15. Furfero, A. Joyce, *Macroeconomic Stabilization Policies: Goals, Institutions and Theories*, 8th ed. September 1, 2000. (www.drfurfero.com/books/231book/ch05j.html)

16. Garcia, René, and Pierre Perron (1995), "An Analysis of the Real Interest Rate Under Regime Shifts", *Scientific Series*, No. 95s-5, CIRANO—Centre Interuniversitaire de Recherché en Analyse des Organisations.

17. Glassman, James K. and Kevin A. Hassett, *Dow 36,000: The New Strategy for Profiting From the Coming Rise in the Stock Market*, Three Rivers Press, 2000.

18. Goertzel, Ted, "Generational Cycles in Mass Psychology: Implications for the George W. Bush Administration", International Psychohistorical Association's 24th Annual Convention, June 8, 2001 (www.crab.rutgers.edu/~goertzel/cycles.htm).

19. Goldstein, Joshua S. *Long Cycles*, New Haven: Yale University Press, 1988

20. Hamilton, James D., (1989), "A New Approach to the Economic Analysis of NonStationary Time Series and the Business Cycle", *Econometrica*, 57(2) 357-384.

21. Hoyt, Homer, "The Urban Real Estate Cycle—Performances and Prospects", Urban Land Institute Technical Bulletin No. 38, June 1960, in *According to Hoyt: 53 years of Homer Hoyt*, no publisher, 1970

22. Kadlec, Charles W., *Dow 100,000 Fact or Fiction*, New York: New York Institute of Finance, 1999.

23. Joseph Kitchin, "Cycles and trends in economic policy," *Review of Economic Statistics*, Jan. 1923.

24. Klingberg, Frank L., (1952) "The historical alternation of moods in American foreign policy", World Politics 4: 239-273.

25. Kolari, James W and Ariel M. Viale, "Nonlinear Co-Trending: The Fisher Effect and Back-to-the-Future Expectations", work in progress.

26. Krugman, Paul, *The Age of Diminished Expectations, Third Edition: U.S. Economic Policy in the 1990s*, MIT Press, 1994.

27. Lebergott, Stanley, *Manpower in Economic Growth, The American Experience Since 1800*, NewYork: McGraw-Hill 1964.

28. Levy, Jack S., *War in the Modern Great Power System, 1495-1975*, Lexington, Kentucky: University Press of Kentucky, 1983.

29. McGuinness, David M, unpublished manuscript., 2001

30. Mensch, Gerhard, *Stalemate in Technology*, Cambridge MA: 1979.

31. Modelski, George and William Thompson, *Leading Sectors and World Powers: The Coevolution of Global Politics and Economics*, University of South Carolina Press, 1996.

32. Mitchell, B. P. *International Historical Statistics: The Americas 1750-1993*, New York: Stockton Press, 1998.

33. Phillips, Kevin, *The Politics of Rich and Poor: Wealth and the American Electorate in the Reagan Aftermath*, New York: Random House, 1990.

34. Phillips, Kevin, *Wealth and Democracy: A Political History of the American Rich*, New York: Broadway Book, 2002.

35. Prechter, Robert R., *Conquer the Crash: You Can Survive and Prosper in a Deflationary Depression*, New York: John Wiley & Sons, 2002.

36. Rasler, Karen A and William R Thompson, *Great Powers and Global Struggle 1490-1990*, Lexington KY: The University Press of Kentucky, 1994.

37 Sahl, Robert, Oregon State University (www.orst.edu/Dept/pol_sci/sahr/cpi96.htm)

38. Schlesinger, Arthur, *Paths to the Present*, New York: Macmillan Co., 1949.

39. Schlesinger, Arthur M, *The Cycles of American History*, Boston: Houghton Mifflin Company, 1986.

40. Schumpeter, Joseph A., *Business Cycles: A Theoretical, Historical and Statistical Analysis of the Capitalist Process.* London: McGraw-Hill, 1939.

41. Schwartz, Peter and Peter Leyden, "The long boom: a history of the future, 1980–2020", *Wired*, July 1997.

42. Schwartz, Stuart B., (1974) "The Economy and Society of Colonial Brazil: A Brief Overview.", *The James Ford Bell Lectures* **12**: 4.

43. Shuman, James B. and David Rosenau, *The Kondratieff Wave*, New York: World Publishers, 1972

44. Smith, Walter B. and Arthur H. Cole, *Fluctuations in American Business*, New York: Russell & Russell, 1935, p 173-184.

45. Siegel, Jeremy, *Stocks for the Long Run: The Definitive Guide to Financial Market Returns and Long-term Investment Strategies*, New York: McGraw-Hill, 1998

46. Smith, Walter B. and Arthur H. Cole, *Fluctuations in American Business*, New York: Russell & Russell, 1935, p 173-184.

47. Social Security Administration (www.ssa.gov/pressoffice/factsheets/women.htm).

48. Sorokin, Pitrim A., *Social and Cultural Dynamics*, Boston: Porter Sargent, 1957

49. Strauss, William and Neil Howe, *Generations: The History of America's Future 1584 to 2069*, New York: Quill William Morrow 1991.

50. Strauss, William and Neil Howe, *The Fourth Turning*, New York: Broadway Books, 1997.

51. Strauss, William and Neil Howe, (1997b) *The Fourth Turning*, 1997, website (www.fourthturning.com)

52. Toynbee, Arnold, *A Study of History*, Vol 9, London: Oxford University Press, 1954.

53. United States Department of Labor, Bureau of Labor Statistics (www.economagic.com).

54. Wright, Quincy, *A Study of War*, 1942; reprint ed. Chicago: University of Chicago Press, 1965 p 230.

# *Appendix A:*
# *Liberal and Conservative Events*

Schlesinger (1949) did not describe his methodology for determining his political cycle. In order to extend his cycle beyond the late 1940's, I needed a methodology that reproduces his cycle prior to 1949 and can be applied after 1949. This method must also agree with certain common sense ideas about recent political movements. For example, the "Reagan Revolution" of the 1980's ought to appear as a swing towards conservatism.

The approach I took is analogous to what I did for the saeculum in *The Kondratiev Cycle*. In that book I characterized religious cycles by compiling a timeline of religious events and calculating a running frequency of events over time to determine periods showing a high frequency of events. Such periods were considered candidates for spiritual awakenings. A similar analysis was done with unrest events such as riots, strikes, popular uprisings, etc. For the political cycle I compiled a timeline of American political events, which is shown in Table A.1. I labeled each event as either liberal or conservative and then summed up the number of liberal ($N_L$) and conservative ($N_C$) events over a running 15-year period. The ratio $N_C/(N_L + N_C)$ is plotted in Figure 2.1 to show the political cycle.

With simple frequency analysis, such as that used for the religious and unrest cycles, bias can enter only in the collection of events to analyze. This method can introduce bias in two ways, through the collection of events and in how they are labeled. As I described in the *Kondratiev Cycle*, collection bias can be minimized by using all the relevant events from timelines obtained from a variety of sources. A suitably "dense" timeline will contain enough coverage of history to give a pretty good idea if cycles actually exist. For the political cycle I obtained such a dense timeline, but there is no way to eliminate bias from the labeling of events as liberal and conservative. The best I can do is present my own bias by presenting a list of 14 rules used to label events as either liberal (L) or conservative (C). For each event the rule used to assign that event as L or C is given in Table A.1.

I start with the key ideas debated in the election of 1800. This election was about the scope of the new federal government established by the constitutional convention thirteen years earlier. One side of the debate, represented by Hamilton and Adams, favored a strong central government. This faction had been in control of the government since 1789 and was known as the Federalists. Since Schlesinger considers the 1787-1800 period conservative, this means the Federalists and their favored policies are defined to be conservative. Schlesinger further characterizes conservatives as authoritarian. Based on these observations the following policies are assumed to be conservative:

0. Political developments supported by or favoring the conservative party.

1. Favors regressive taxes, especially (protective) tariffs; opposes progressive taxes.

2. Favors strong military and its use when necessary—not pacifist. Supports an active foreign policy. Military power was one of the key attributes of government in the late 18$^{th}$ century. A strong government implied a strong military and the will to use it.

3. Favors central banking as means to finance government—not to regulate economy.

4. Favors sound money (e.g. gold standard) and prudent governmental finance (anti-deficit). A strong government is one run on sound financial principles. This view (and #3) was inherited from the English Whigs following the Glorious Revolution, after which the British government adopted a formal budget and central banking.

5. Favors restricted voting, civil and collective bargaining rights, anti-sedition measures, and law & order over criminal rights. This factors in Schlesinger's idea of conservatives as authoritarian and the Jeffersonian's embrace of "democracy" as a core value that differentiated them from Federalists.

6. Favors strong private property rights (pro-slavery, anti-business regulation). The political theory of the day held that the principal purpose of government was to secure rights to property, hence support for strong government implies support for strong property rights.

7. Favors internal improvements designed to promote industry and commerce.

8. Opposed to wealth redistribution by government. This includes Indian removal, homesteading, public education and modern social welfare programs. These ideas follow from 18th century political theory about natural law and property relations that formed one of the bases for constitutional government.

These rules handle just about all of the events up to the 20th century. About the only significant category of 19th century events not handed are those pertaining to civil service reform. I was unable to assign these as either C or L and they are labeled as N for neutral. After the start of the 20th century, an increasing number of events cannot be labeled using these rules. In addition, with the rise of the Progressive movement, which redefined liberalism and affected conservatism, some of the existing rules were modified. The following four additional rules were designed to handle new issues or new interpretations of old issues.

9. Policies that promote resource conservation or environmentalism are considered liberal.

10. Legislation or court rulings that support traditional morality (e.g. pro-life) is considered conservative; legislation or court rulings that support "new" morality (e.g. prohibition, affirmative action) is considered liberal.

11. Gun control: liberals for, conservatives against.

12. Internationalist foreign policy supporting international organizations like the League of Nations or UN is considered liberal

When liberalism began to change to accommodate new progressive concepts, its old libertarian precepts began to be picked up by conservatives. Conservatives began to become more in favor of small government and low taxes although their support of the protective tariff remained strong for a long time. Since WW II conservatives have come to adopt free trade ideology and become anti-tariff. Finally with the Reagan Revolution, conservatives have become anti-tax in principle, even at the cost of deficits. Thus, I have added these rules:

13. After WW II, free trade becomes a conservative issue.

14. After 1975, tax cutting/limitation is a conservative issue.

## Table A.1 List of Liberal (L) and Conservative (C) Events Used in the Figure 2.1

| Year | Event | Rule | Align |
|------|-------|------|-------|
| 1765 | Stamp Act Congress | 1 | L |
| 1773 | Boston Tea Party | 1 | L |
| 1776 | Virginia Declaration of Rights | 5 | L |
| 1776 | Declaration of Independence | 5 | L |
| 1777 | Articles of Confederation | 5 | L |
| 1787 | Constitution | 5 | C |
| 1788 | Bill of Rights | 5 | L |
| 1790 | Fed Government assumes state debts | 0 | C |
| 1791 | Taxes on Spirits | 1 | C |
| 1791 | Bank of US | 3 | C |
| 1793 | Proclamation of Neutrality | 2 | L |
| 1793 | Fugitive Slave Act | 6 | C |
| 1798 | Alien Act | 5 | C |
| 1798 | Sedition Act | 5 | C |
| 1800 | Revolution of 1800 | 0 | L |
| 1801 | Expiration of Sedition Act | 5 | L |
| 1801 | Repeal of excise taxes | 1 | L |
| 1801 | Louisiana Purchase | 2 | C |
| 1803 | Marbury v Madison | 0 | C |
| 1805 | Tripolitan War | 2 | C |
| 1807 | Neutrality Issues-Jefferson's embargo | 2 | L |
| 1807 | Slave trade Ends | 6 | L |
| 1811 | US Bank loses charter | 3 | L |
| 1816 | Second Bank of the US | 3 | C |
| 1816 | Protective tariff passed | 1 | C |
| 1817 | Erie Canal construction begins | 7 | C |
| 1819 | McCullough v Maryland (implied powers) | 5 | C |
| 1820 | Compromise of 1820 | 6 | C |
| 1820 | Choctaw Removal | 8 | L |
| 1823 | Monroe Doctrine | 2 | C |
| 1824 | American System | 0 | C |
| 1824 | Tariff Raised | 1 | C |
| 1825 | Creek Removal | 8 | L |
| 1827 | First State High School Law (Mass) | 8 | L |
| 1828 | Revolution of 1828 | 0 | L |
| 1828 | Tariff of Abominations | 1 | C |
| 1830 | Broader suffrage provided by revisions to some state constitutions | 5 | L |
| 1830 | Indian Removal Act | 8 | L |
| 1831 | Worchester v Georgia | 8 | C |
| 1832 | Tariff reduced | 1 | L |
| 1832 | Bill to recharter 2nd Bank of US vetoed | 3 | L |
| 1833 | Compromise Tariff (lowered) | 1 | L |
| 1833 | Jackson withdraws US funds from 2nd Bank of US | 3 | L |
| 1835 | Seminole War | 8 | L |
| 1836 | Sauk and Fox removal | 8 | L |
| 1836 | Creek forcibly evicted | 8 | L |
| 1836 | Specie circular issued by Jackson | 4 | C |
| 1836 | Gag rule in Congress on abolitionist petitions | 6 | C |
| 1837 | Chickasaw evicted | 8 | L |
| 1838 | Trail of Tears | 8 | L |
| 1839 | Slaves from Amistad freed by Supreme Court | 6 | L |
| 1840 | Independent Treasury Act | 3 | L |

|  |  | | |
|------|-------|---|---|
| 1841 | Independent Treasury Act Repealed | 3 | C |
| 1842 | Dorr's rebellion in RI liberalized voting requirements | 5 | L |
| 1842 | SC rules unconstitutional state laws prohibiting return of fugitive slaves | 6 | C |
| 1842 | Mass enacts 10-hr workday for children under 12 | 6 | L |
| 1846 | Mexican War | 2 | C |
| 1846 | Independent Treasury reinstated | 3 | L |
| 1846 | Wilmot proviso proposed and but never passed | 6 | C |
| 1853 | Gadsden Purchase | 2 | C |
| 1854 | Kansas-Nebraska Act | 6 | C |
| 1854 | Ostend Manifesto | 6 | C |
| 1854 | Convention of Kanagawa | 2 | C |
| 1856 | First of five U.S. interventions in Panama to protect the Atlantic-Pacific railroad | 2 | C |
| 1857 | Dred Scott Decision | 6 | C |
| 1860 | Lincoln Elected on Abolition platform | 6 | L |
| 1862 | Income tax | 1 | C |
| 1862 | Legal Tender Act | 4 | L |
| 1862 | Morril Act (land grant colleges) | 8 | L |
| 1862 | Homestead Act | 8 | L |
| 1862 | Pacific Railway Act | 7 | C |
| 1863 | Emancipation Proclamation | 6 | L |
| 1863 | National Banking Act | 4 | C |
| 1864 | Lincoln pocket-vetoes Wade-Davis Bill | 5 | C |
| 1865 | 13th Amendment | 6 | L |
| 1865 | Freedman's Bureau | 5 | L |
| 1866 | Civil Rights Act of 1866 | 5 | L |
| 1867 | Reconstruction starts | 5 | L |
| 1868 | 14th Amendment | 5 | L |
| 1869 | The first woman suffrage law in the U.S. is passed in the territory of Wyoming | 5 | L |
| 1869 | Redeemer Govts in Tenn. | 5 | C |
| 1869 | 15th Amendment | 5 | L |
| 1870 | Redeemer Govts in Georgia, NC and Virginia | 5 | C |
| 1870 | Sumner defeats annexation of Santo Domingo | 2 | L |
| 1870 | KKK Act | 5 | L |
| 1870 | First Black Senator | 5 | L |
| 1870 | Force Act | 5 | L |
| 1871 | Civil Service | -- | N |
| 1872 | Liberal Republican split | 0 | L |
| 1872 | Amnesty Act | 5 | C |
| 1872 | Tax eliminated | 1 | L |
| 1872 | Yellowstone national part created | 9 | L |
| 1873 | Silver demonetized | 4 | C |
| 1873 | Redeemer Govt. Texas | 5 | C |
| 1874 | Redeemer govt. Arkansas, Alabama | 5 | C |
| 1875 | Civil Service ended | -- | N |
| 1875 | Specie Resumption Act | 4 | C |
| 1875 | Supreme Court rules a state can prohibit a woman from voting | 5 | C |
| 1875 | Civil Rights Act | 5 | L |
| 1877 | Munn v. Illinois upholds Granger laws | 6 | L |
| 1877 | Executive Order prohibits Fed Employees from politicking | -- | N |
| 1877 | Reconstruction ends | 5 | C |
| 1878 | Bland-Allison Act | 4 | L |
| 1879 | US back on Gold Standard | 4 | C |
| 1881 | Tennessee first state to segregated railroad cars | 5 | C |

| 1882 | Chinese exclusion act | 5 | C |
|------|----------------------|---|---|
| 1883 | Pendleton Act (Civil Service) | -- | N |
| 1883 | Civil Rights Act of 1875 struck down | 5 | C |
| 1884 | Amendments to Chinese Exclusion Act | 5 | C |
| 1886 | Supreme Court: Corporations considered as persons under 14th Amend | 6 | C |
| 1886 | Interstate Commerce Commission | 6 | L |
| 1886 | Wabash v. Illinois overturns Munn v. Illinois | 6 | C |
| 1887 | First segregation in transportation laws | 5 | C |
| 1887 | Dawes Act | 5 | C |
| 1890 | Mississippi Plan to disenfranchise Blacks | 5 | C |
| 1890 | "Pitchfork Ben" Tillman elected on white supremacist platform | 5 | C |
| 1890 | Sherman Antitrust Act | 6 | L |
| 1890 | Sherman Silver Purchase Act | 4 | L |
| 1890 | McKinley tariff | 1 | C |
| 1893 | Supreme Court applies antitrust to Unions | 5 | C |
| 1894 | EC Knight case placed food production outside antitrust | 6 | C |
| 1894 | Wilson-Gorman tariff reduces rates slightly | 1 | L |
| 1895 | Supreme Court restrains Pullman strikers | 5 | C |
| 1895 | Supreme Court strikes down part of Wilson-Gorman Tariff | 1 | C |
| 1896 | William McKinley defeats populist William Jennings Bryan | 0 | C |
| 1896 | Plessey v Ferguson (Separate but equal) | 5 | C |
| 1897 | Dingley Tariff raised rates | 1 | C |
| 1898 | Spanish War | 2 | C |
| 1898 | Erdman Act | 5 | L |
| 1900 | Gold Standard Act | 4 | C |
| 1900 | "Fighting Bob" LaFollette becomes Wisconsin governor | 0 | L |
| 1901 | Last Black Congressmen for 28 years | 0 | C |
| 1901 | Northern Securities Suit (first trust-bust) | 6 | L |
| 1903 | Hay-Herran Treaty (Panama canal zone) | 2 | C |
| 1903 | Department of Labor | 5 | L |
| 1903 | Department of Commerce | 6 | C |
| 1903 | Elkins Act | 6 | L |
| 1904 | National Child Labor Committee | 5 | L |
| 1905 | NY Supreme Court finds max hr law for bakers unconstitutional | 6 | C |
| 1905 | Hepburn Act | 5 | L |
| 1905 | U.S. Marines help Mexican dictator Porfirio Díaz crush a strike in Sonora. | 2 | C |
| 1905 | U.S. troops land in Honduras for the first of 5 times in next 20 years. | 2 | C |
| 1906 | Pure Food & Drug Act | 6 | L |
| 1906 | Meat Inspection Act | 6 | L |
| 1906 | Employer's Liability Act | 6 | L |
| 1906 | Marines occupy Cuba for two years in order to prevent a civil war. | 2 | C |
| 1907 | Marines intervene in Honduras to settle a war with Nicaragua. | 2 | C |
| 1908 | U.S. Supreme Court upholds Oregon's 10-hour workday for women. | 5 | L |
| 1908 | Supreme Court finds hatters boycott antitrust violation | 5 | C |
| 1908 | Federal Court finds section of Erdman Act unconstitutional | 5 | C |
| 1908 | Employer's Liability Act struck down | 5 | C |
| 1908 | U.S. troops intervene in Panama for first of 4 times in next decade. | 2 | C |
| 1909 | Payne-Aldrich tariff reduced rates | 1 | L |
| 1910 | Mann Act | 5 | L |
| 1910 | U.S. Marines occupy Nicaragua to help support the Díaz regime. | 2 | C |
| 1911 | Supreme Court upholds injunction against AFL | 5 | C |
| 1911 | Hiram Johnson becomes CA Gov. | 0 | L |
| 1911 | Breakup of Standard Oil (peak of trust-busting) | 6 | L |

| 1912 | U.S. Marines intervene in Cuba to put down a rebellion of sugar workers. | 2 | C |
|------|--------------------------------------------------------------------------|---|---|
| 1912 | Nicaragua occupied again by the U.S., to shore up the inept Díaz government. | 2 | C |
| 1913 | Federal Segregation | 5 | C |
| 1913 | Progressive Income Tax passed | 1 | L |
| 1913 | Federal Reserve established | 3 | L |
| 1913 | Underwood act reduces tariff | 1 | L |
| 1914 | Federal Trade Commission | 6 | L |
| 1914 | Clayton Antitrust | 6 | L |
| 1914 | U.S. bombs, then occupies Vera Cruz, in a dispute with Mexico's new government | 2 | C |
| 1915 | Lafollette's Seaman's Act | 5 | L |
| 1915 | U.S. Marines occupy Haiti to restore order | 2 | C |
| 1916 | Federal Farm Loan Act | 8 | L |
| 1916 | Adamson Act (8 hr day RR workers) | 5 | L |
| 1916 | Keating-Owens Child Labor Act | 5 | L |
| 1916 | First women elected to Congress | 5 | L |
| 1916 | Marines occupy the Dominican Republic, staying till 1924. | 2 | C |
| 1917 | WW I begins | 2 | C |
| 1917 | Supreme Court struck down segregated neighborhood law | 5 | L |
| 1917 | Supreme Court upholds legality of yellow-dog contracts | 5 | C |
| 1917 | Marines intervene again in Cuba, to guarantee sugar exports during WWI. | 2 | C |
| 1918 | Keating-Owens Child Labor Act declared unconstitutional | 5 | C |
| 1918 | Sanger wins NY suit allowing doctors to advise their married patients about birth control | 10 | L |
| 1918 | Sedition Act | 5 | C |
| 1918 | Wilson's 14 points | 12 | L |
| 1918 | U.S. Marines occupy Panamanian province of Chiriqui for 2 yr to maintain public order. | 2 | C |
| 1919 | Palmer Raids | 5 | C |
| 1919 | Prohibition | 10 | L |
| 1919 | Senate rejects League of nations | 12 | C |
| 1920 | Women's Suffrage | 5 | L |
| 1920 | Harding wins on conservative "Return to Normalcy" Platform | 0 | C |
| 1920 | Sacho And Vanzetti arrested and convicted | 5 | C |
| 1921 | Supreme Court rules unions may be enjoined for restraint of trade | 5 | C |
| 1921 | US troops block W VA miners attempt to organize | 5 | C |
| 1922 | Anti-Lynching Law killed | 5 | C |
| 1922 | Cap gains tax reduced to 12.5% (stock boom begins) | 1 | C |
| 1923 | SC strikes down minimum-wage law for District of Columbia women | 6 | C |
| 1924 | Immigration Act | 5 | C |
| 1924 | KKK reaches height of influence in Indiana politics | 5 | C |
| 1925 | First female governor of a U.S. state elected | 5 | L |
| 1925 | American Indian suffrage granted by act of Congress | 5 | L |
| 1925 | Scopes Monkey Trial | 10 | C |
| 1925 | Top Tax rate reduced to 25% | 1 | C |
| 1925 | U.S. Army troops occupy Panama City to break a rent strike and keep order. | 2 | C |
| 1926 | Railway Labor Act | 5 | L |
| 1926 | Marines occupy the country to settle a volatile political situation. | 2 | C |
| 1929 | Joint Resolution of Congress lowers taxes | 1 | C |
| 1930 | Hawley-Smoot tariff | 1 | C |
| 1931 | Davis-Bacon Act | 5 | L |
| 1932 | Reconstruction Finance Corp | 6 | L |
| 1932 | Emergency Relief Act | 8 | L |
| 1932 | Federal Home Loan Bank Act | 6 | L |
| 1932 | Top tax rate to 63% | 1 | L |
| 1932 | Natl. Rec. Act forbids >1 govt. job / family; many women lose their jobs | 5 | C |

| 1933 | Civilian Conservation Corps | 8 | L |
|------|------|------|------|
| 1933 | Federal Emergency Relief Administration | 8 | L |
| 1933 | Glass-Steagull Act | 6 | L |
| 1933 | Plot to overthrow FDR and install Fascist Gov. | 0 | C |
| 1933 | Agriculture Adjustment Act (AAA) | 8 | L |
| 1933 | Federal Deposit Insurance Corp (FDIC) | 6 | L |
| 1933 | National Recovery Admin (NRA) | 6 | L |
| 1933 | Public Works Admin (PWA) | 8 | L |
| 1933 | Tennessee Valley Authority (TVA) | 8 | L |
| 1933 | US off gold standard | 4 | L |
| 1933 | Industrial Recovery Act | 6 | L |
| 1933 | Farm Credit Act | 6 | L |
| 1934 | SEC | 6 | L |
| 1934 | National Mediation Board | 5 | L |
| 1934 | National Firearms Act | 11 | L |
| 1934 | Federal Communications Commission (FCC) | 6 | L |
| 1935 | NRA declared unconstitutional | 6 | C |
| 1935 | Works Progress Administration | 8 | L |
| 1935 | National Youth Administration | 8 | L |
| 1935 | Social Security | 8 | L |
| 1935 | AFDC Begins | 8 | L |
| 1935 | National Labor Relations Board (NLRB) | 5 | L |
| 1935 | Banking Act | 6 | L |
| 1935 | Rural Electrification Administration | 8 | L |
| 1935 | SC rules contraceptives not obscene & can be imported | 10 | L |
| 1936 | AAA unconstitutional | 8 | C |
| 1936 | Top tax rate to 79% | 1 | L |
| 1936 | Soil Conservation and Domestic Allotment Plan | 8 | L |
| 1937 | FDR attempts to pack court--looses popularity | 0 | C |
| 1938 | Federal Firearms Act | 11 | L |
| 1938 | NLRB unconstitutional | 5 | C |
| 1938 | Fair Labor Standards Act (Min Wage & Max workweek) | 5 | L |
| 1938 | Agricultural Adjustment Act | 8 | L |
| 1939 | US v Miller (upholds right to bear arms) | 11 | C |
| 1939 | Relief Act (18 month limit on WPA) | 8 | C |
| 1940 | Selective Service Act | 5 | C |
| 1940 | Alien Registration Act of 1940 | 5 | C |
| 1941 | Lend-Lease Act | 12 | L |
| 1941 | Atlantic Charter | 12 | L |
| 1941 | WW II begins | 2 | C |
| 1942 | Office of Price Administration | 6 | L |
| 1944 | GI bill | 8 | L |
| 1945 | Atomic bombs dropped on Japan | 2 | C |
| 1945 | UN Charter signed | 12 | L |
| 1946 | Employment Act of 1946 | 8 | L |
| 1946 | Committee on Civil Rights | 5 | L |
| 1947 | Truman Doctrine | 2 | C |
| 1947 | Taft-Hartley Act | 5 | C |
| 1947 | U.S. Supreme Court says women are equally qualified with men to serve on juries | 5 | L |
| 1947 | National Security Act | 2 | C |
| 1948 | Marshall Plan | 12 | L |
| 1948 | Truman ends segregation in Military | 5 | L |
| 1948 | Alger Hiss charged with espionage | 5 | C |

| 1949 | Truman's "Fair Deal" largely rejected by Congress | 8 | C |
|------|---------------------------------------------------|---|---|
| 1949 | Housing Act of 1949 | 8 | L |
| 1950 | McCarthy's "I have a list speech" | 5 | C |
| 1950 | McCarren Act (monitor commies) | 5 | C |
| 1950 | NSC 68 rept calls for +Military & -Social spend for Cold War | 8 | C |
| 1950 | US backs French In Vietnam | 2 | C |
| 1950 | Korean War begins | 2 | C |
| 1951 | HUAC activities | 5 | C |
| 1952 | McCarren-Walter Act (ideology as basis for immigration) | 5 | C |
| 1953 | US backs coup in Iran | 2 | C |
| 1954 | Communist Party Outlawed | 5 | C |
| 1954 | Army-McCarthy Hearings--McCarthy discredited | 5 | L |
| 1954 | US backs coup in Guatemala | 2 | C |
| 1954 | Brown vs. Topeka | 5 | L |
| 1956 | Interstate Highway Act | 7 | C |
| 1957 | Little Rock HS desegregation | 5 | L |
| 1957 | Civil Rights Act of 1957 | 5 | L |
| 1958 | Eisenhower Doctrine | 2 | C |
| 1958 | National Defense Education Act | 8 | L |
| 1959 | Landrum-Griffin Act | 5 | C |
| 1960 | U2 incident | 2 | C |
| 1960 | CIA begins training anti-Castro guerillas | 2 | C |
| 1961 | SC upholds Florida rules making it less likely for women than men to be made jurors | 5 | C |
| 1961 | Peace Corps | 12 | L |
| 1961 | Kennedy initiates largest peacetime defense buildup in US history | 2 | C |
| 1961 | Bay of Pigs Invasion | 2 | C |
| 1961 | President signs $1.25 Minimum Wage Bill | 8 | L |
| 1962 | Fed Govt. enforces court order admitting James Meredith to U Miss | 5 | L |
| 1963 | President announces naval quarantine to halt Soviet missile buildup in Cuba | 2 | C |
| 1963 | President signs Nuclear Test Ban Treaty | 12 | L |
| 1963 | Top tax rate to 70% | 1 | C |
| 1963 | The Equal Pay Act | 5 | L |
| 1964 | Poll taxes outlawed | 5 | L |
| 1964 | Civil Rights Act | 5 | L |
| 1964 | Economic Opportunity Act (War on Pov) | 8 | L |
| 1965 | Johnson sends troops to Vietnam | 2 | C |
| 1965 | US invades Dominican Republic | 2 | C |
| 1965 | Voting Rights Act | 5 | L |
| 1965 | Higher Education Act | 8 | L |
| 1966 | Miranda v. Arizona | 5 | L |
| 1967 | "Guns and Butter" deficit fiscal policy begun | 4 | L |
| 1968 | Gun Control Act | 11 | L |
| 1968 | Sex discrimination by govt. contractors forbidden / affirmative action for women. | 10 | L |
| 1968 | Open Housing Act | 5 | L |
| 1969 | 7th Circuit Court rules women meeting the physical requirement can hold men's jobs | 5 | L |
| 1969 | Nixon wins presidency on anti-war platform, begins withdrawal | 2 | L |
| 1970 | Nixon extends Vietnam War into Laos and Cambodia | 2 | C |
| 1970 | US backs coup in Chile | 2 | C |
| 1970 | Philadelphia plan (Affirm Act) | 10 | L |
| 1970 | Clean Air Act | 9 | L |
| 1970 | First Earth Day | 9 | L |
| 1970 | EPA formed | 9 | L |
| 1970 | OSHA Act | 9 | L |

| 1971 | 26th amendment grants vote to 18-year olds | 5 | L |
|------|--------------------------------------------|---|---|
| 1971 | Full School Desegregation | 5 | L |
| 1972 | Bureau of Alcohol, Tobacco & Firearms established | 10 | L |
| 1972 | Title IX bans sex discrimination in education programs receiving Fed funds | 5 | L |
| 1972 | Supreme Court upholds right to contraceptive use by unmarried persons | 10 | L |
| 1972 | Equal Employment Act | 5 | L |
| 1973 | SC affirms the EEOC ruling against sex-segregated help wanted ads | 5 | L |
| 1973 | Endangered Species Act | 9 | L |
| 1973 | Roe v Wade | 10 | L |
| 1973 | SC affirms the EEOC ruling against sex-segregated help wanted ads | 5 | L |
| 1973 | War Powers Act | 2 | L |
| 1974 | Nixon resigns | 0 | L |
| 1974 | Housing discrimination and credit discrimination against women outlawed | 5 | L |
| 1974 | Ford pardons Nixon | 0 | C |
| 1976 | Hyde Amendment, eliminates federal funding for poor women's abortions | 10 | C |
| 1976 | Resource Conservation and Reclamation Act (RCRA) | 9 | L |
| 1977 | Moore v East Cleveland (upholds right to bear arms) | 11 | L |
| 1977 | Clean Water Act | 9 | L |
| 1977 | Supreme Court: govt. not required to fund abortion as part of welfare | 10 | C |
| 1978 | Pregnancy Discrimination Act | 10 | L |
| 1978 | Humphrey-Hawkins Act | 4 | L |
| 1978 | Bakke case (Racial Quota constitutional) | 10 | L |
| 1978 | The Pregnancy Discrimination Act | 5 | L |
| 1978 | Federal Food, Drug & Cosmetic Act | 6 | L |
| 1978 | Proposition 13 cuts CA property taxes | 14 | C |
| 1980 | Lewis v US Felons may be denied right to bear arms | 11 | L |
| 1980 | CERCLA (Superfund) | 9 | L |
| 1980 | Reagan Elected on a Conservative Platform | 0 | C |
| 1980 | Supreme Court: no constitutional right for publicly-finance abortion | 10 | C |
| 1981 | State laws giving husbands unilateral control of joint property struck down | 5 | L |
| 1981 | Top tax rate to 50% | 1 | C |
| 1981 | Fed pushed interest rates to all-time highs to combat inflation | 4 | C |
| 1981 | Striking air traffic controllers fired by Reagan | 5 | C |
| 1981 | H.L. v. Matheson, U.S. Supreme Court approves Utah parental notification law | 10 | C |
| 1981 | Supreme Court rules that excluding women from the draft is constitutional | 10 | C |
| 1982 | Ratification efforts for an Equal Rights Amendment fail | 5 | C |
| 1982 | Helms bill challenging Roe v. Wade blocked by pro-abortion filibuster | 10 | L |
| 1982 | Tax Equity & Fiscal Responsibility Act | 4 | C |
| 1982 | US troops to Lebanon | 2 | C |
| 1983 | SC strikes down right to know laws and waiting periods | 10 | L |
| 1983 | ATT Breakup | 6 | L |
| 1983 | American invasion of Grenada | 2 | C |
| 1983 | Pershing missiles deployed in Europe | 2 | C |
| 1983 | Star Wars initiative | 2 | C |
| 1984 | Sex discrimination in membership policies of organizations forbidden by Supreme Court | 5 | C |
| 1984 | "Mexico City Policy" denies funds to foreign orgs that promote abortion | 10 | C |
| 1985 | SC strikes down state laws mandating use of specific abortion methods | 10 | L |
| 1986 | SC declares sexual harassment form of illegal job discrimination | 5 | L |
| 1986 | Graham-Rudman Act | 4 | C |
| 1986 | Stiffens penalties for armed felons | 11 | C |
| 1986 | Firearms Owners Protection Act (eases restrictions on gun sales) | 11 | C |
| 1986 | Law Enforcement Officer Prot Act (ban "cop-killer" bullets) | 11 | L |
| 1986 | Reagan administration secretly aids Contras in Nicaragua | 2 | C |

| 1986 | Top Tax rate to 28% | 1 | C |
|---|---|---|---|
| 1986 | Conrail privatized | 6 | C |
| 1986 | US air attack on Libya | 2 | C |
| 1987 | SC rules it is permissible to take sex and race into account in employment decisions | 10 | L |
| 1987 | Intermediate-range Nuclear Forces Treaty | 12 | L |
| 1987 | FCC Fairness Doctrine Abolished | 6 | C |
| 1988 | FDA bans importation of abortifacient RU 486 for personal use | 10 | C |
| 1988 | Anti-Drug Abuse Act | 5 | C |
| 1988 | JOBS Act | 8 | C |
| 1989 | SC: Constitution does not require public facilities be available for abortions | 10 | C |
| 1989 | US invades Panama | 2 | C |
| 1989 | Heritage proposes tradable emissions | 6 | C |
| 1990 | Crime Control Act (create "gun-free school zones") | 11 | L |
| 1991 | US invades Iraq | 2 | C |
| 1992 | Democrats win control of government | 0 | L |
| 1993 | The Family Medical Leave Act | 6, 10 | L |
| 1993 | Clinton issues five executive orders reversing abortion restrictions | 10 | L |
| 1993 | Top Tax Rate to 39% | 1 | L |
| 1993 | Motor Voter Law | 5 | L |
| 1993 | Earned Income Credit expanded | 8 | L |
| 1994 | Violence Against Women Act | 10 | L |
| 1994 | Early Head Start program | 8 | L |
| 1994 | Crime bill (3 strikes law, and 100000 police officers) | 5 | C |
| 1994 | GATT ratified | 13 | C |
| 1994 | Brady Bill (background checks before buying a gun) | 11 | L |
| 1994 | Viol. Crime Control & Law Enforce. Act (bans "assault weapons") | 11 | L |
| 1994 | Contract with America | 0 | C |
| 1994 | NAFTA | 13 | C |
| 1995 | Loans to Mexico | 12 | C |
| 1995 | Executive Order Preventing Permanent Striker Replacement | 5 | L |
| 1995 | US v Lopez ("gun-free school zones" unconstitutional) | 11 | C |
| 1996 | Telecommunications Act | 6 | C |
| 1996 | Male-only policy of state-supported Virginia Milt. Inst. found to violate 14th Amendment | 10 | L |
| 1996 | Anti terrorism Law | 5 | C |
| 1996 | Megan's Law | 5 | C |
| 1996 | Minimum Wage increased | 8 | L |
| 1996 | Kennedy-Kassebaum Health Insurance Reform | 6 | L |
| 1996 | Personal Responsibility Act | 8 | C |
| 1997 | Banned Federal Research on Human Cloning | 10 | C |
| 1997 | SC rules college athletics must have roughly equal nos. of each sex to get Fed money. | 10 | C |
| 1997 | Children's Health Insurance Program Created | 8 | L |
| 1997 | FDA Reform | 6 | C |
| 1997 | NATO Expanded to Eastern Europe | 12 | C |
| 1997 | Printz v US ("Background checks unconstitutional) | 11 | C |
| 1997 | Top Cap Gains tax to 20% | 14 | C |
| 1998 | Air Attacks on Iraq | 2 | C |
| 1998 | Balanced budget achieved | 4 | C |
| 1999 | Bosnian Air War | 2 | C |
| 1999 | Clinton Impeached | 0 | C |
| 2000 | Republicans win presidential election, gaining control of the government | 0 | C |
| 2001 | Democrats gain control of Senate by defection of senator Jeffords | 0 | L |
| 2001 | Bush Tax Cut I | 14 | C |
| 2001 | Patriot Act | 5 | C |

| 2001 | Dept of Homeland Security | 5 | C |
|------|---------------------------|----|---|
| 2001 | No child left behind act | 8 | L |
| 2001 | American ouster of Taliban govt. in Afghanistan | 2 | C |
| 2001 | ABM treaty revoked | 12 | C |
| 2001 | Comprehensive Test Ban Treaty revoked | 12 | C |
| 2002 | Bush imposes Steel Tariff | 13 | L |
| 2002 | Campaign Finance Reform Bill | 0 | L |
| 2002 | Republicans Win control of government | 0 | C |
| 2002 | Deficit Finance restored by Bush administration | 4 | L |
| 2003 | Partial-Birth Abortion Ban Act | 10 | C |
| 2003 | SC downs sodomy law | 5 | L |
| 2003 | SC permits Affirmative Action | 10 | L |
| 2003 | Bush Tax Cut II | 14 | C |
| 2003 | Bush Prescription Drug Plan | 8 | L |
| 2003 | Invasion of Iraq | 2 | C |

# Appendix B:
# Data sources and comments on analysis

*Monetary Data and analysis*

Prices: The pre-1913 US producer and consumer price indices were obtained from Global Financial Data, Sahl, and Lebergott (1964). Post-1913 data was obtained from the Bureau of Labor Statistics.

Interest Rates: The interest rates shown in Figure 5.1 are AAA bond rates after 1913 and long-term government rates before 1913. Long-term US government interest rates before 1913 were obtained from Global Financial Data. U.S. corporate interest rates (Moody's AAA) from 1913-present were obtained from www.economagic.com. Depression-era short term rates shown in Figure 5.6 come from Smith and Cole (1935), recent ones from www.economagic.com.

Money Supply: U.S. Money supply used in the construction of the stimulation variable (S) was M3 from 1959 to present and M2 from 1869 to 1959. M2 and M3 had almost identical values in 1959 so the two series were simply concatenated. Before 1869 the change in bank deposits was used to adjust the 1869 money supply level back to 1834. Before 1834 total currency was used to adjust money supply back to 1800. M3 was obtained from the Federal Reserve Bank of St. Louis, and pre-1959 M2 was obtained from the OSU Fisher college of business website. Bank deposits and currency were obtained from Mitchell (1993).

Government debt: Historical U.S. and U.K government deficits were obtained from Mitchell (1998). Recent U.S. deficits were obtained from www.economagic.com. The methodology used to find K-cycles in monetary data was described in Alexander (2002).

### Leading Sector Data and Analysis
U.S. leading sector data sources and methodology were described in Alexander 2002.

### Stock cycle and P/R
Identification of the Stock Cycle and construction and use of P/R is described in Alexander, 2000a.

### Kuznets Cycle
Identification and characterization of the Kuznets or real estate cycle is described in Alexander, 2003.

### War Cycles
War death data in Figure 6.1 was obtained from Goldstein (1988) who got them from Levy (1983). Capital ship data in Figure 6.2 was obtained from a plot in Modelski and Thompson (1996). Army data in Figure 6.3 was obtained from Rasler and Thompson (1994)

### Wages
Wage data were obtained from Lebergott (1964) and from the Bureau of Labor Statistics.

### Political Data
Data was gathered from the internet. Examples of sources consulted are listed below.

Defense spending
www.bedfordstmartins.com/history/modules/mod32/frameset.htm

Party composition of Congress
permanent.access.gpo.gov/lps12426/www.senate.gov/learning/stat_13.html
clerkweb.house.gov/histHigh/Congressional_History/partyDiv.html

Presidential elections summaries
www.presidency.ucsb.edu/site/elections/elections.php?year=1956
hwww.u-s-history.com/pages/h130.html

Presidential biographies
http://www.whitehouse.gov/history/presidents/

**Political Events**
Events listed in Appendix A were obtained from internet sites. Some sites present broad historical timelines, others are political in theme and specific to particular eras. Some sites focus on a particular issue. Examples are listed below.

Abortion
www.nrlc.org/abortion/timeline.html

African-American history
http://lcweb2.loc.gov/ammem/aap/timeline.html

Central Banking
http://www.civil-liberties.com/cases/bank.html

Welfare
society.searchbeat.com/welfare9.htm

Women's Rights
http://www.legacy98.org/timeline.html

**Timelines**
Detailed Timeline (1700-present)
www.geocities.com/KCunard73/Timeline1800.html

1815-1840
www.pinzler.com/ushistory/timeline4.html
www.curie.cps.k12.il.us/Web%20Based%20Instruction/US%20History/topic-notes/4-3.htm

1840-1860
www.angelfire.com/ga2/theng/timeline.htm

Post Civil War
www.amatecon.com/gd/gdtimeline.html

Progressive Era
campus.northpark.edu/history/WebChron/USA/ProgressiveEra.html
www.curie.cps.k12.il.us/Web%20Based%20Instruction/US%20History/topic-notes/10-1.htm

Great Depression
www.huppi.com/kangaroo/Timeline.htm
en.wikipedia.org/wiki/Timeline_of_United_States_history_(1930-1949)

Cold War
artsandscience.concordia.ca/hist253x/lectures/lecture17_txt.html

Recent
www.reagan.utexas.edu/
clinton3.nara.gov/WH/Accomplishments/

0-595-32721-4

www.ingramcontent.com/pod-product-compliance
Lightning Source LLC
Chambersburg PA
CBHW061356280526
45784CB00001B/274